For Robyn
Love,

Dad
7-6-14

The Essential Sheehan

ALSO BY DR. GEORGE SHEEHAN

Dr. Sheehan on Running 1975

Running & Being 1978, 1998, 2013

Medical Advice for Runners 1978

This Running Life 1980

How to Feel Great 24 Hours a Day 1983
Published in paperback as *Dr. Sheehan on Fitness*

Personal Best 1989

Running to Win 1991

Going the Distance 1995

The Essential Sheehan

———◆———

A Lifetime of *Running Wisdom*
from the Legendary
Dr. George Sheehan

Edited by Andrew Sheehan

ILLUSTRATIONS BY MONICA SHEEHAN

RODALE

© 2013 by The George Sheehan Trust

Portions of this work have been previously published in *Runner's World* magazine, as well
as *Dr. Sheehan on Running* (1975), *Running & Being* (1978, 1998, 2013), *This Running Life*
(1980), *How to Feel Great 24 Hours a Day* (1983) (published in paperback as *Dr. Sheehan on
Fitness*), *Personal Best* (1989), *Running to Win* (1991), *Going the Distance* (1995).

Runner's World is a registered trademark of Rodale Inc.

Printed in the United States of America
Rodale Inc. makes every effort to use acid-free ⊗, recycled paper ♻.

Book design by Nora Sheehan
Illustrations by Monica Sheehan

Library of Congress Cataloging-in-Publication Data is on file with the publisher
ISBN-13: 978-1-60961-932-9 hardcover
Distributed to the trade by Macmillan
2   4   6   8   10   9   7   5   3   1   hardcover

We inspire and enable people to improve their lives and the world around them.
rodalebooks.com

To Mary Jane and our sons and daughters,
who waited with patience and love while I sought the light—
and finally found my way home.

DR. GEORGE SHEEHAN

Contents

Foreword by David Willey,
editor-in-chief of *Runner's World* • ix
Introduction by Michael and Tim Sheehan • xvii
1 / Transformation • 1
2 / Play • 21
3 / Taking Back Your Day . . . Your Life • 39
4 / Misguided Modern Medicine • 59
5 / Training • 83
6 / Racing • 121
7 / The Marathon • 149
8 / Challenge and the Pursuit of Excellence • 189
9 / The Spiritual • 209
10 / Dealing with Our Lesser Angels • 231
11 / Cancer • 251
12 / Final Revelations • 273
Afterword by Ann Sheehan • 291
Acknowledgments • 297
About the author • 299
Index • 301

Foreword

BY DAVID WILLEY, EDITOR-IN-CHIEF OF *RUNNER'S WORLD*

NE OF THE FIRST things I did when I became the editor-in-chief of *Runner's World* in 2003 was to hang a framed photo of Dr. George Sheehan on the wall of my office. George, who began writing a column for the magazine in 1970, was the magazine's most popular and beloved writer before his death from prostate cancer in 1993. He wrote about running not only as a sport but as a method for living a fuller life. This approach helped land several of his books on the bestseller list, and anytime I look at one of those lists today or browse the "self-help" shelves at a bookstore, I think of him. George was writing self-help books before there was such a category; one can easily imagine his 1983 book, *How to Feel Great 24 Hours a Day,* being published today and successfully marketed to millions of readers yearning to live healthier, happier, better lives.

But calling George Sheehan a writer is like calling Muhammad Ali a boxer. It's true but incomplete. He was a popular speaker who filled auditoriums at races, sports-medicine conferences, and corporate retreats. He was called a guru and a philosopher-poet, and he regularly quoted classical writers such as Ortega, Tiberius, and William James, which naturally led some to accuse him of being obsessive and overwrought. But it is inarguable that he was a visionary and a pioneer who deserves credit for helping to launch America's first running boom. No one has ever done more to explain, simply, eloquently and honestly, the how *and* the why of living a running life. At his best, George connected running to something larger than putting one foot in front of the other.

I don't remember exactly where I found that photo, but it was with stack of race posters from decades past, forgotten. In the photo, George is sitting in a wooden rocking chair on the deck of his house in Ocean Grove, New Jersey, overlooking the Sound. He's dressed in running clothes, and a towel is draped over the back of his chair, but it's unclear whether he has just returned from a run or is about to set out. What is clear is that George is writing—or, more specifically, hunting and pecking away at what looks to be an old Royal typewriter perched on his deck's wall, seemingly a few inches from falling into the drink. There isn't a shred of artifice or self-consciousness to be found anywhere. The photo is still on my wall today (and on this book's cover), even though we moved into a new building several years ago. Beneath it is my own Royal typewriter. The symbolism isn't subtle: There are things from the past—even forgotten, old-school things—that still matter today.

As a longtime *Runner's World* subscriber and the son of a *Runner's World* reader in the 1970s and '80s, I had read George's column religiously. I should say columns, plural, because his contributions to the magazine appeared under a range of titles that reflected his growing popularity and the magazine's broadening readership, which grew to embrace beginning runners as well as the highly dedicated (and mostly male) crew that ran nearly every day and cared immensely about races and PRs. First there was a simple column called "Medical Advice." George was a medical doctor by training, after all—a cardiologist—with plenty of advice for runners eager to treat and avoid common injuries. That morphed into "Dr. Sheehan on Running" (also the title of one of his books), in which he spread his wings a bit more, followed by the insider-y "From Sheehan" and the slightly more forthcoming "From George Sheehan." Until his death, he wrote under "George Sheehan's Viewpoint," which sounds drier than it was, I assure you. Runners often say that running helped them "find themselves." For many of them, George held a lantern. In a 1988 profile of George for *Runner's World*, John Brant put it perfectly, describing his first encounters with "the proselytizing distance runner" at a newsstand during some luckless post-college years: "During the few minutes it took to read the column you forgot about your confusions and footlessness. When you were finished you put the magazine back on the rack. You rubbed your hands up and down the legs of your jeans. Then you broke out of the store and back to your rented room. You changed as fast as you could and took off running. You were no longer lost. Sheehan had reminded you that your life was pinned to something. He had granted you solace and permission."

In my first few months as editor-in-chief, I immersed myself in these columns again. Sure enough, they made me want to run and push myself to be better. More important, now that I was a bit older and married and had a family and priorities larger than my own health and fitness, they reminded me to continually try to live a heroic life. George strongly believed that all of us are here to do exactly that. "Our highest human need is to be a hero," he wrote.

"When we cease to be heroic, we no longer truly exist." That may sound a bit over the top to some, but George saw heroism as being within anyone's grasp, writing that "through ordinary experiences, the ordinary person can become extraordinary."

It's key to understand how George framed heroism: with a lower-case "h," not focused on public glory or on vanquishing opponents. Our only real rivals, he believed, are our youthful selves, and our most urgent struggles are against inertia and indifference. They need to be met every day, but "it doesn't matter if no one else is aware of this struggle—the hero needs no recognition. The deed is done, and the audience of one is satisfied." Can an early-morning run or 25 miles per week really carry such significance? Yes.

George's work also had an effect on me professionally. It thrilled me to discover anew how he expressed the idea that running and writing have something in common. Something approximating soul. Something I wanted to bring into our pages in a new way. I even stumbled upon a column that apparently had never been published, a very short piece called "Why Do I Run?" It was the last essay on running he ever wrote, in June 1993. We published it in the magazine with a bit of fanfare. But in a stroke of irony George would've probably enjoyed, it turned out that the piece had, in fact, been published in an obscure anthology we hadn't been aware of. Yet my hopes of publishing the work of the man *Sports Illustrated* called "perhaps our most important philosopher of sport" didn't subside, even if they went dormant for a few years. Eventually, I struck up a conversation with Andy Sheehan, the eighth of George's twelve children, about how to do it, and those discussions grew to include Andy's brothers Michael and Tim.

This book—the definitive survey of Dr. George Sheehan's life work—is a result of those conversations. Andy has collected the very best from a career's worth of magazine columns (George wrote 140 of them for *Runner's World*, as well as many others that were syndicated to newspapers) and books (he published eight of them, most notably *Running & Being*, all of which were based largely on his *Runner's World* work). The essays and excerpts are arranged into thematic chapters, echoing a technique George used in some of his own books, so the reader can dip in and out, quickly finding advice and inspiration about, say, training or racing or the marathon or what may have been George's favorite theme: play. But the book can also be read and enjoyed from start to finish. The work collected here spans the years 1975 to 1995 (George's book *Going the Distance* was published posthumously, two years after his death). Despite working with such varied material, Andy has deftly shaped hundred of puzzle pieces into a narrative arc, which begins with George taking up running at age 45 and moves with energy and purpose toward the final two chapters, entitled "Cancer" and "Final Revelations." No one could be better suited to the task than Andy. A lifelong runner and an investigative journalist, he has the technical chops the job requires. But more important are the intangibles. In 2001 Andy published a wonderful memoir called *Chasing the Hawk*, a searingly honest look at his own life struggles and his efforts to get to know his famous but often distant father. This book is informed by everything he learned while writing that one, and *The Essential Sheehan* would not have been nearly as essential, or as insightful, without his skill and understanding.

Similarly, throughout the book, running luminaries such as Alberto Salazar, Frank Shorter, Jeff Galloway, and Amby Burfoot share how George and his writing influenced them, and guided their running lives and careers. These contributions, along with the introduction written by Michael and Tim Sheehan, and the afterword written by their sister, Ann, make *The Essential Sheehan* more than just an anthology of a legend's most memorable writing. It's also a mini-biography of the legend, a self-described loner who later in life turned to those who had been there all along and the community of runners he had helped to form.

We—*Runner's World*, the Sheehan family, and Rodale, *Runner's World*'s parent company—embarked on this project to introduce Dr. George Sheehan to a new generation of reader-runners. After all, the sport has continued to boom since his death, and many of the runners fueling this growth—young women in particular—are likely unfamiliar with George's work or its formative importance on the running and fitness culture we now take for granted. We also believe that what George had to say about running—and about living an active, honorable, fulfilling, authentic life—is more timely than ever. In our over-digitized and under-exercised culture, George's writing may be more urgently needed now than when it was originally published. As a country, we are fatter and less healthy than we've ever been, and less connected to each other (I'm not counting Twitter or Facebook) or to the natural world.

But enough from me about why George's work is worth immersing yourself in, either anew or for the first time. His words always stood on their own:

> Running made me free. It rid me of concern for the opinion of others. Dispensed me from rules and regulations imposed from outside. Running let me start from scratch. It stripped off those layers of programmed activity and thinking. Developed new priorities about eating and sleeping and what to do with leisure time. Running changed my attitude about work and play. About whom I really liked and who really liked me. Running let me see my twenty-hour-hour day in a new light and my life style from a different point of view, from the inside instead of out.

Earlier this year, we reissued *Running & Being*, which spent months on *The New York Times* bestseller list when it was originally published in 1978 but had been out of print for decades. Both that book—a 35th anniversary edition with a jacket designed by George's daughter Nora and a new foreword from Kenny Moore, one of George's equals in running-writing excellence—and this one exist for a simple reason. As Joe Henderson, a longtime editor at *Runner's World* who collaborated with George on all of his columns, writes in these pages, "As long as his work is read, a part of George Sheehan lives on."

Indeed. I hope this book inspires people the way George did when he was alive, hunting and pecking a heroic way forward.

Introduction

BY MICHAEL & TIM SHEEHAN

W HEN GEORGE SHEEHAN ran for Manhattan College's powerhouse track teams of the late 1930s, his gaze was ever on crosstown rival Leslie MacMitchell, the premier miler of the day. Under the disciplined guidance of legendary coach Pete Waters, the young Sheehan rose through the ranks until there was no one between him and MacMitchell. In his last race for the intercollegiate championship, Sheehan once again took silver to MacMitchell's gold. He hung up his spikes and moved on to medical school the next year while MacMitchell went on to tie the world record. Sheehan never caught him—but he never lost the desire to be the best.

Twenty-five years later, when middle-age Sheehan faced the prospect of a settled life with no hills to climb, he would direct that drive for excellence toward a road that would take him and thousands of readers to new heights of physical, spiritual, and mental well-being.

Born the oldest of 14 children to a Brooklyn cardiologist and his wife, Sheehan received a Jesuit education and dutifully followed his father's path into medicine. World War II, marriage, and twins immediately followed. Sent to the Pacific as a doctor on a destroyer, Sheehan and his ship survived kamikaze attacks, and he landed in Nagasaki just days after its nuclear destruction. It was an experience he never discussed. After service, he returned to the most prized catch of the Jersey Shore, Mary Jane Fleming, establishing a successful medical practice in Red Bank, New Jersey, and producing 12 children of his own. Surprisingly for someone with strong introverted, loner tendencies, Sheehan filled his days with responsibility for his patients and for his ever-growing family.

In the early 1960s, after founding Christian Brothers Academy, an all-boys high school in nearby Lincroft, for his oldest sons to attend, he began to feel the urge to return to running and competition. He was now 45 years old, dissatisfied with his generation's equation for success, and in need of a change of course. Returning to the favored sport of his youth seemed the right choice, but in those days, running along your local streets would have been cause for a visit from police or your parish priest. To avoid the local gossip chain, he agreed to run in the privacy of his backyard, pounding out a dirt loop that he calculated to be 10 laps to a mile. His sweat, spit, guttural groans, curses, and body odor spilled into the house. After about a year, he was given the go-ahead by his wife to take it to the streets. In breaking free from the gate, he would find himself on the cutting edge of what was to become the great running boom of the 1970s.

His lunchtime became hour-long runs along a river road. Sunday mornings became road trips to any race he could find within a 2-hour drive. Running was his escape into a world of play and competition. It was also, more importantly, his road to self-discovery. After a few years of penning a weekly column about his newfound life in our local paper, he joined the staff of *Runner's World* magazine and quickly became the voice of the running movement. He was a medical expert, a record-setting masters runner, a student of the great thinkers of life, and, as the sportscaster Bill Mazer called him, a mensch to the world of fitness. He brought a depth and a willingness to write about his experiences that had never been matched. Over the next 25 years, he put out tremendous effort on the roads, in races, and at the typewriter, sharing all he had uncovered. Some might have thought it a bit too much information, but he felt as long as he was writing his truth, he didn't care what he shared.

His efforts earned him the respect of runners and nonrunners alike. His motivation was not to profit, but rather to open up new ways of thinking about sport and play, health and fitness, and the idea of making the best of who you are meant to be. As a writer, he was determined to teach his readers the various benefits of the athletic lifestyle. As a runner, he was determined to prove himself every time he entered a race.

When someone once charged him with being a legend in his own mind, he agreed—and added that everyone else should be, too. He saw sport as his theater for challenging himself, for challenging the world. When he saw the growing number of women discovering "this whole world the other side of sweat," he accurately assessed, "When I see women running, I see a new world coming." And when the only local race was a women's event, he would crash the party and race along.

In his fitness talks, he often used a quote from Irenaeus—"The glory of God is man fully functioning"—and by this he stressed body, mind, and soul. He would ask his audience, "If today could be a fair sampling of eternity, are you ready to go back to your Creator in your current condition?" He urged people to listen to their bodies. The rules of fitness were simple and the benefits enormous if you had the willingness to apply them. From the ancient Greeks to today, not much has changed in the idea of developing the whole self—not a self as compared to others, but you at your best. Running was his gateway to this greater goal.

Like any ego striving to be the best, he enjoyed the fame that came his way. But while he appreciated the recognition, the other trappings of fame became a burden, and soon it required more effort and stress to produce new material. It was during that time, in 1986, that he learned he had inoperable prostate cancer. He was 67 years old, and this sudden nearness of his mortality shifted his stride to a new focus. He acknowledged that while he helped create new rules of living an athletic life, when it came to completing his whole being some old rules could not be ignored: You can't do it alone. His goals up until then had been directed inward, focused only on his performance. While he always liked to be around people, he rarely reached out. He viewed a handshake as an aggressive act. He thus began a new approach to life, with a child's desire to have his friends, his family, and his Creator in his reach at all times. This final change allowed him the chance to achieve the perfect maturity that St. Paul once wrote about.

As he approached his date with death, he examined this new journey with hope of uncovering some wisdom to share. He and the cancer would battle each other until the end, but he was determined to make the most of his time in order to make his best offering to his God. Through it all he never stopped striving. Whether it was running in a local 5-K or in the 70-and-over 800-meter World Championships, he gave his all, often collapsing at the finish line. For it was through this effort that he found his peace.

His thirst for new experiences and new topics kept his writing fresh up until his final days. He was driven by a sense that he had fallen short of his best, like those second-place finishes he suffered in college. He was humble enough to believe that despite his efforts, he could always give more. But he did in fact give his all, and the arc of his life experiences indeed produced the classic book he had hoped to write. Looking over his body of work, one can only be amazed by its size, its depth, and its quality.

With these selections from his essays, we hope to present to you his classic message of going back to the body in order to enjoy the benefits of health, the joy in play, and the rewards of self-discovery. If you find some of your own thoughts in our father's words, then you have found a great friend to carry along on your quest to achieve your personal best.

The Essential Sheehan

1/ *Transformation*

*L*ightning may strike when you are 21 or not until you are 70. Today may be your day to leave the herd.

THIS RUNNING LIFE, 1980

AT THE AGE OF reason, I was placed on a train, the shades drawn, my life's course and destination already determined.

At the age of 45, I pulled the emergency cord and ran out into the world. It was a decision that meant no less than a new life, a new course, a new destination. I was born again in my 45th year.

The previous "me" was not me. It was a self-image I had thrust upon myself. It was the person I had accepted myself to be, but I had been playing a role.

"It took me a long time to discover that the key to acting is honesty," an actor told anthropologist Edmund Carpenter. "Once you know how to fake that, you've got it made."

In time, we fool even ourselves. Sooner or later, however, we come to question the trip planned for us, the goals we are given, our itinerary to death. Sooner or later, the self-image becomes not worth preserving. The person we are presumed to be seems unsatisfactory and inadequate. Sooner or later, it becomes important that we feel important and have the feeling that what we are doing is important.

When I stepped off that train, I had lost my sense of purpose, my faith in what I was doing, my caring for creation and its creatures. And when I stepped from that train, I found I was not alone. Millions of Americans who had been told Sunday after Sunday to be born again were now going through the shattering experience of rebirth. Only the experts don't call it that. They call it "middle-aged melancholia," or a "new cultural phenomenon of the fourth and fifth decade," or more simply "change of life."

The authorities agree that we come upon this stage of our lives unprepared for the reality of advancing years and receding rewards. White-collar worker, blue-collar worker, housewife and career woman, no one seems immune to the crisis that sets in after the forties get under way. Each of us in his own way comes to this revelation and faces the problem of living according to the person we really are.

This is not only inevitable, it is desirable. "He who does not really feel himself lost," wrote Ortega, "is lost beyond remission. He never finds himself, never comes up against his own reality."

Finding one's reality does not come without plan or effort. Being born again is no easy task. Technique and training and much hard work are needed. And we are always faced with the knowledge that it is an undertaking that will never be completed. Every day will be a fresh start.

Most experts suggest we make a new start in a new career, develop new interests. I say begin at the beginning. Begin with the body. The body mirrors the soul and the mind, and is much more accessible than either. Become proficient at listening to your body and you will eventually hear from your totality—the complex, unique person you are.

I did it that way. I stepped off that train and began to run. And in that hour a day of perfecting my body, I began to find out who I was. I discovered that my body was a marvelous thing, and learned that any ordinary human can move in ways that have excited painters and sculptors since time began. I didn't need the scientists to tell me that man is a microcosm of the universe, that he contains the 92 elements of the cosmos in his body. In the creative action of running, I became convinced of my own importance, certain that my life had significance.

Fitness may have something to do with this. The physiologists have shown us that those who remain the perpetual athlete are two and even three decades younger physically than their contemporaries. And with this comes an awareness, a physical intelligence, a sensual connection with everything around you that enlarges your existence.

If decreases in the body's functions are due to non-use and not to aging, is it unreasonable to suggest that our mental and psychological and spiritual capabilities deteriorate the same way?

If so, our rebirth will be a long and difficult task. It will begin with the creative use of the body, in the course of which we must explore pain and exhaustion as closely as pleasure and satisfaction. It will end only when we have stretched our minds and souls just as far.

But there is an alternative. You can always get back on the train.

—*DR. SHEEHAN ON RUNNING,* 1978

I AM A RUNNER. Years ago that statement would have meant little more to me than an accidental choice of sport. A leisure-time activity selected for reasons as superficial as the activity itself. Now I know better. The runner does not run because he is too slight for football or hasn't the ability to put a ball through a hoop or can't hit a curveball. He runs because he has to. Because in being a runner, in moving through pain and fatigue and suffering, in imposing stress upon stress, in eliminating all but the necessities of life, he is fulfilling himself and becoming the person he is. I have given up many things in this becoming process. None was a sacrifice. When something clearly became nonessential, there was no problem in doing without. And when something clearly became essential, there was no problem accepting it and whatever went with it.

From the outside, this runner's world looks unnatural. The body punished, the appetites denied, the satisfactions delayed, the motivations that drive most men ignored. The truth is that the runner is not made for the things and people and institutions that surround him. To use Aldous Huxley's expression, his small guts and feeble muscles do not permit him to eat or fight his way through the ordinary rough-and-tumble. That he is not made for the workaday world, that his essential nature and the law of his being are different from the ordinary and usual is difficult for everyone, including the runner, to comprehend.

But once it is understood, the runner can surrender to his self, this law. And become, in the Puritan sense, the "free man," the man who is attached only to the good. In this surrender, the runner does not deny his body. He accepts it. He does not subdue it, or subjugate it, or mortify it. He perfects it, maximizes it, magnifies it. He does not suppress his instincts; he heeds them. And goes beyond this animal in him toward what Ortega called his veracity, his own truth.

The finished product is therefore a lifetime work. This giving up, this letting go, the detachment from attachments, is an uneven process. You should give up only what no longer has any attraction to you, or interferes with something greatly desired. That was Gandhi's rule. He advised people to keep doing whatever gave them inner help and comfort. I have learned that also. Whatever I give up, whatever innocent indulgences, ordinary pleasures or extraordinary vices, I do so from inner compulsion, not in a mood of self-sacrifice or from a sense of duty. I am simply doing what comes naturally. For the runner, less is better. The life that is his work of art is understated. His needs and wants are few, he can be captured in a few strokes. One friend, a few clothes, a meal now and then, some change in his pockets, and, for enjoyment, his thoughts and the elements. And though he's on the run, he's in no hurry. Concerned at times with tenths of a second, he actually responds to the season, moving through cycle and cycle, toward less and less until body and mind and soul fuse, and all is one.

I see this simplicity as my perfection. In the eyes of observers, however, it appears completely different. My success in removing myself from things and people, from ordinary ambition and desires, is seen as lack of caring, proof of uninvolvement, and failure to contribute. So be it. A larger view of the world might include the possibility that such people are necessary. That the runner who is burning with a tiny flame on some lonely road does somehow contribute. And while a world composed solely of runners would be unworkable, a world without them would be unlivable.

—RUNNING & BEING, 1978

EACH OF US IS born with a 70-year warranty, but few of us read the instructions. We blindly go through life without consulting a manual for the operation of the human machine. The maintenance and preservation of our bodies doesn't concern us. We believe that longevity and freedom from malfunction have been built in by the Creator.

And they have. But we can live long and stay healthy only if we take care of our bodies as we would our automobiles. We have to follow certain rules to get maximum performance and maximum longevity out of what we were born with. We have to apply the biological wisdom gained over the centuries to our day-to-day living.

Make no mistake about it: Nature does not allow for error, and she is not reluctant to inflict capital punishment. Deviations from the correct regimen can certainly diminish one's daily well-being and eventually one's life span. True, aging is inexorable. And death is inevitable. But neither should occur before its appointed time.

Individual behavior determines individual health. It is up to us to avoid unnecessary illness and premature death. It is our own decision to be active or sedentary. To age fast or age slowly. To die at our time or before it.

But even if we are committed to following the rules, we may have to search to find them. Our disregard for the past puts us in the position of relearning truths that have been known for centuries. We should not ignore the conclusions of previous civilizations and cultures that have gone through the process of establishing rules for the optimum function of the human body.

What we need to know was already known by generations that have gone before us: Cro-Magnon men, the Greeks, the Romans, the

Victorians, and, in contemporary life, people in Alameda County, California—a group researchers have found to be extraordinarily long lived, happy, and productive. Back in 1972, the average American thought all you had to do to assure health was eat a balanced diet, get a good night's sleep, and visit the doctor regularly—clearly an incomplete program for getting the most out of our bodies. But that year, we learned from these Californians rules that we can profit from following.

These rules, which have come to be known as the Alameda Seven, are as follows:

1. Exercise regularly.

2. Eat a good breakfast.

3. Don't eat between meals.

4. Maintain weight.

5. Don't smoke.

6. Drink moderately.

7. Get a good night's sleep.

These observances have stood the test of subsequent scientific investigation. They work. People who follow six of those rules live significantly longer than those who follow one or two. And not only do they live longer, they're less likely to be hospitalized, and they're more energetic and productive as well.

After all, our aim is not only a long life but one free of incapacitating disease. We want to get sick as little as possible, and if we do, we want to recover quickly. We would like to live a fully functioning life until the last possible moment. And the Alameda Seven will apparently ensure that as well. A study done in 1984 showed that those observing the rules had aged successfully—that is, they remained independent and healthy, free of debilitating disease.

How best to live long and live well? Following the Alameda Seven is a good start—and has good precedent. For past generations, lifestyle was their pharmacopoeia. They had no antibiotics, no cures for infectious disease. So the caveman had to be fit to survive.

Now we have grown soft, freed for the most part of the scourges of pneumonia and tuberculosis and other life-shortening diseases. Our longevity may be increasing, but so are the diseases having to do with the way we live. We die of the affluence and the sedentary life that prosperity has given to us. If we are indeed to prosper, we must look to the rules of the generations that preceded us and that had to struggle for existence—the people who read the warranty and followed it.

—RUNNING TO WIN, 1992

◆

WHEN I BEGAN RUNNING in 1963, the fitness experts and the sports medicine specialists had yet to arrive on the scene. Dr. Kenneth Cooper's book on aerobics was still five years off. Becoming fit, therefore, was something I had to do on my own—my body became my instructor. It gave me the answers to those initial questions: How far? How fast? And how often? In a very short time, I learned the first and greatest commandment in fitness: Listen to your body.

Although I didn't know it at the time, I was rediscovering an ancient law, a tradition that went back to the Greeks. The Greeks explored their physical limits much the same as we do now. Their Olympic Games were based on the same philosophy as ours. Their attempts to go higher and faster and farther foreshadowed present-day competition. And they did all this using the body simultaneously as teacher and pupil.

In those days, people were expected to read their body like a book, learning what enabled them to perform well and what would interfere with performance. According to Tiberius, by the age of 20, an individual should take responsibility for his own health, knowing what was harmful or beneficial, and be able to take care of himself without medical aid.

Socrates was of the same mind. He felt that an intelligent man who was careful about his diet, exercise, and drinking habits should know better than a doctor what was good or bad for him. Centuries later, psychologist Abraham Maslow expressed the same idea, calling such people "self-actualizers." These people, wrote Maslow, become finely tuned to how best their bodies work and to those actions that harm them.

By the time we reach adulthood, we should be able to read the messages our body sends us. Technology is not only unnecessary; it is inadequate. The body has information that is technologically inaccessible. We are the sole recipients of this otherwise unavailable data. Why, then, should I need more than my own body to guide my program and record my improvement?

Back in 1963, that question was irrelevant. I had nothing to resort to other than my body. It had to give me all my answers. I didn't check with a physician before I began running. I didn't take a stress test. And I never checked my pulse. I simply went out and ran.

I quickly made my first and greatest discovery. Running is play. It is being a child again. I would go out on the roads and get lost in a child's world. I ran short and fast, I ran long and slow. I was having fun because my body was having fun. I was enjoying running because my body was enjoying running. And while this was happening, my body became better and better at running. Without consulting a book or an expert, I became fit. Even better, I became an athlete.

My experience has convinced me most of the testing and monitoring of fitness programs is unnecessary. We need little if any pretesting before getting into an activity. Nor do we need to check our pulse or do all those annoying and occasionally alarming computations involving heart rate. The only things that should prompt us to see a doctor are things that would ordinarily send us to a doctor for treatment—things such as excess cholesterol, overweight, diabetes, or high blood pressure.

My body, over the years, has given me the correct answers to all my questions on running. I have had no need for other experts. But even if there were other avenues of information, there is one question only the body can answer. And it is the question that holds the answer to every successful lifelong fitness program: "Are you having fun?"

—*RUNNING TO WIN,* 1992

◆

I WAS ON A radio show discussing exercise with a woman who did not exercise. "The spirit is willing," she told me, "but the flesh is weak."

I had, of course, heard the excuse many times before. But for the first time, it occurred to me that the opposite was true. The flesh is willing; it is the spirit that is most often weak. Our bodies are capable of the most astounding feats. But the horizons of our spirits do not reach beyond the TV, the stereo, and the car in the garage.

The flesh is not only willing; it is eager for action. The flesh is filled with everything our spirit lacks: strength and energy, endurance and stamina. We come from a breed that crossed continents on foot and trekked from pole to pole. Even now, we see housewives running marathons, stockbrokers in Outward Bound, retired executives climbing Everest.

We are of a flesh that asks for more and more challenges, that seeks one frontier after another. What is missing is not physical energy. The fuel is there, waiting to be ignited. We need some spark to light the fires, something to get us into action.

From the moment we wake up in the morning, we cop the plea that the spirit is willing but the flesh is weak. We lie abed as the alarm clock, the radio, and the family take turns trying to get us up. Still we remain immobile until the last possible minute. Yet how many calories does it take to overcome inertia and get out of bed? Whose bodies are so exhausted that they can't get their feet on the floor? I can plead that I'm in a semi-coma, not yet ready for coordinated action, but similar scenarios recur throughout the day. The body is ready, willing, and able, but the spirit is becalmed. Where there is no emotion, there is no motion either.

What is missing is the spiritual energy called enthusiasm. It is from lack of enthusiasm that the failures of the spirit multiply during the day. When we are enthusiastic, we develop a determination to equal the endurance of our muscles, a fortitude to match the courage of our hearts, and a passion to join with the animal strengths of our bodies.

To succeed at anything, you need passion. You have to be a bit of a fanatic. If you would move anyone to action, you must first be moved yourself. To instigate, said Emerson, you must first be instigated. I am aware of this every time I lecture. For an hour before the talk, I can be seen walking alone, muttering to myself, gradually building myself to a fever pitch so I will find it completely natural to end a talk standing on a table with nothing on but my Levi's—and with the pants legs rolled to my knees.

But the spirit has more to offer than just this excitement. It gives us the motivation when the excitement is missing. The spirit is what gets us through when everything else fails. As Oxford professor Ralph Johnson points out in his paper "Factors in Human Endurance," a person's ability to survive often depends on the qualities of his personality.

The mind-body relationship is particularly striking in the historical accounts of explorers and mountain climbers, people in extreme situations and stretched to their limits and beyond. The explorer Captain Scott, writing of one of his men, commented, "Browers came through the best. Never was there such a sturdy, active, undefeated man." Of Scott himself, one of his companions wrote, "Scott was the strongest combination of strong man in a strong body that I have ever known—and this because he was weak. He conquered his weaker self and became the strong leader we went to follow and came to love."

Behind the enthusiasm, behind the inspiration, behind the passion, there must be the will. We can choose. We can decide. We can will to do it our own way. When we do, nothing can prevail against us.

Otherwise, we are merely wishing, idle dreamers in the world of the flaccid spirit. We must want something and want it badly—want it with the zeal and passion and enthusiasm of a Don Quixote or a missionary. Then, we will suddenly find ourselves in motion, with a clear focus on our goal. Once moved, the spirit and the flesh are like a matched team of horses, each asking more of the other. Fused by the will for that brief and wonderful moment, the flesh and the spirit become one.

I am—just as you are—a unique, never-to-be-repeated event in this universe. Therefore, I have—just as you have—a unique, never-to-berepeated role in this world. Mine is a personal drama for which I am at once author, actor, and director.

Unfortunately, this perception comes late in life. It was something I knew as a child—not clearly, of course, but nevertheless with certainty. My life as a child was my own. It was filled with the play and invention, the energy and intensity, the humor and intelligence that becoming the person you are demands.

But all too soon, we become members of the herd. We learn herd rules, herd regulations, herd morality, herd ethics. We become part of society. Society must be preserved, so we accept the obligations it imposes.

Others have raised questions about this necessity. "Are we sent here," asked Thoreau, "to do chores and hold horses?" The answer, says society, is yes. Work has to be done. And if work is not available, then make-work has to be devised. We must be kept busy. The idle mind begins to think, the idle body begins to play, and that is dangerous for the herd.

In such moments, those childlike moments, we may see ourselves as we are and recognize the life we should live. Some happy few have these revelations early. But most of us submit to the herd, with little resistance. We behave docilely until we have fulfilled our obligation to procreate, until we have used our productive years in support of the institutions that keep society on an even keel.

But then what? The forties have arrived. The herd no longer needs us, nature no longer protects us, the race no longer cares. We are on our own. We have served our purpose.

What then are the prospects? Wonderful! Perhaps even better than wonderful. We can now return to the play and invention, the energy and intensity, the humor and intelligence we knew as children. The pressures that made us supportive of the herd are dying out. Each of us is feeling the urges that make us different rather than the same. Each of us is sensing the infinite varieties of body and mind, of values and temperament that make us unique.

And with that comes the knowledge that the chores are over. There are no more horses to be held. We know now about the herd. We need no longer be bound by those rules, need no longer act out those roles. Somehow, we will find the strength and the courage and the insight to make our own rules, to act out our own drama.

That is the paradox. In what others consider the twilight years, we will be more than we ever were before. At a time when we are supposed to take to the easy chair and be content with serenity and a large book, we are transformed with energy. We have a vigor and a toughness youth cannot match, and for the first time since our childhood we know how to play.

Why must this all wait until we are 40? It need not, I suppose. It just happened that way in my case, but I am a slow learner and a creature of habit. For you, it might be different. Lightning may strike when you are 21 or not until you are 70. Today may be your day to leave the herd.

—THIS RUNNING LIFE, 1980

———◆———

I WAS BORN A coward, and by any normal standards still am one.

Function follows structure, says the rule of biology, and I don't have the structure to fulfill the function of the red-blooded American male. We all know what that function is: to face up to bullies, look your enemies in the eye, and never retreat. Americans are supposed to work 30 hours a day, 8 days a week; know what teamwork means; and rise from office boy to president. The United States of America expects you to be a hero, to stand up and be counted, to show the stuff you are made of.

I know the stuff I am made of: pipe-stem bones, an overbite, and a long, tender nose. I have poor teeth and one slightly crossed eye, am tone deaf, and have a pain threshold at the level of a firm hand-shake. I am constructed 180 degrees out of phase with the pioneer spirit, the derring-do, the raw courage, and the adventurousness that made America great.

Since man is a totality, a physical psychological whole, I have other drawbacks. I jump at loud noises, and when younger perspired if a girl entered the room, and was known to vomit if sent to the principal's office. I found early on that standing up to bullies meant either a blow to the nose, sending me into a black pit of indescribable pain, or a shot to the mouth, leaving my upper lip full of teeth.

We are built, wrote physiologist Walter Cannon, for fight or flight. I was built for flight, and nature never intended me to do anything else. I fulfill the function of my particular structure by taking to my heels when trouble brews.

But what American boy would accept that, or what American parent? Is it possible that someone can find contact sports painful to the point of nausea, get faint at the prospect of tackling a runner in the open field and still be all any American can be—a hero to himself? The answer is yes.

Take my operation, for instance. A gallbladder operation is an elective, clean, soft-tissue operation involving only minor trauma. Mr. Average American with his high pain threshold usually can breeze through the hospitalization part of gallbladder surgery—the part I don't want to talk about or even remember. The pain of those few days was beyond my imagination. I never knew such agonies existed. While others were grumbling about being kept in the hospital, I was still struggling to get out of bed.

Where I finally triumphed was during my post-operative recovery.

That's where being thin and bony came to mean something. That's where I outdistanced those muscular heroes who were packing their bags 3 days after leaving the operating room. That's where I found that physical cowards can handle pain—as long as it is self-inflicted. We can suffer and endure as long as the enemy is ourselves.

Ten days after my surgery, I started jogging. Less than 3 weeks after the surgery, I ran 35:01 in a 5-mile race over very tough hills at Van Cortlandt Park [in New York City]. Within another month, I had brought that 7-minute-a-mile average down to 6:30 in a 9-mile face on the same course, my best time in 3 years.

Each race was as painful as any I can remember. The hills were almost unbearable. There were miles and miles of groans and gasps, interspersed with appeals to the Almighty. But that is something that happens almost every weekend in a runner's life. It is the kind of pain he can handle—and others can't.

Some muscular surgeons called my post-operative recovery "fantastic," but it was no odd or wonderful thing. It was just an ordinary accomplishment for thousands of distance runners who are constructed like I am. We would rather run 26 miles into a near-coma than be hit on the nose or even have someone threaten to hit us on the nose.

For runners, as for others, the first rule is to know that you are normal. To find this normal, you can use some rules suggested 30 years ago by anthropologist Earnest Hooten.

"The body," wrote Hooten, "will guide us most rapidly and unerringly to the mind and personality. Body structure affords the safest and most accessible takeoff for the exploration of individual personality."

Translated, this means that if you have a weak little body fit for running from fights and altercations, you should do so. Your body tells you who and what you are. If you listen well, you can be a success, perhaps a hero, even though no one else may be aware of it.

Just remember, function follows structure—and so does fulfillment.

—*THIS RUNNING LIFE,* 1980

———————◆———————

"KNOW YOURSELF."

What was written on the temple of Apollo, we must now write in even larger letters where we can see it every day. Know yourself, so you may live that life peculiar to you, the one and only life you were born to live. Know yourself, that you may perfect your body and find your play. Know yourself, that you are not only the patient but also the therapist. Know yourself, that you may accept that knowledge.

For the Greeks, the time for this discovery was leisure—a time that also included activities like health, self-expression, character formation, personality, and self-adjustment. Included, of course, were play and the training of the body. We are, wrote Plato, playthings of the gods and life must be lived as play. The body, in Plato's opinion, was the source of all energy and initiative.

Therefore, we must know our bodies, their strengths, their weaknesses, their likes, their dislikes. Socrates stated that a sensible man should know what is good or bad for him better than any physician. And later, Tiberius said that anyone who had lived for 20 years should be able to take care of himself without a doctor.

We are, then, to become experts in ourselves. I should learn not from books or from others, but from my own experience. I should understand myself by self-study rather than by consulting the professional. The body is here to be seen. Visible, measurable, it delivers its message.

Stripped down before a mirror, it reveals to me who I am. Similarly, I can know my own temperament—that level of my personality where I express my desires and motivation and interact with other people. Here again, I am as circumscribed as I am in my body. I have a particular mixture of traits which I can change only in a very narrow range. Like me or not, I am what I am.

—THIS RUNNING LIFE, 1980

What Dr. Sheehan Means To Me

BY SARAH ADAMS, DAUGHTER

BEING ONE OF 12 children, I never had a lot of one-on-one time with my father. But that all changed when I started high school in September 1967. Every morning he would drive me to my school in Red Bank, New Jersey, 20 minutes from home. The mornings were hectic, and he would always hurry out of the house with his coffee mug in hand. These were the days before there were cup holders in cars, and it would spill everywhere during the trip.

I was going through my adolescent changes, but I could see that he was changing, too. He had started running and writing as well. He had a weekly column, "The Innocent Bystander," in the *Red Bank Register,* and he was always searching for inspiration and material for his next piece.

When he began running, it created a minor scandal in our town, and there were times I felt embarrassed by comments like "Why does your father run around in his underwear?" But in high school, we formed a bond when I went out for the track team. While I worked out with the girls, he would run with the boys' team, and I was no longer embarrassed by his running. He took me to Van Cortlandt Park in New York City for cross-country meets and to the Penn Relays. I loved it.

As he and I were evolving, the world was changing too. The car radio bleated updates on the Vietnam War, the civil rights movement, protests, and politics. So much to talk about. Then he'd change the station to sports. We loved to talk about the 1969 Mets, the Knicks, and the Jets. It was an exciting time, and it was exciting to be his copilot.

One beautiful April morning, Dad had just returned from the Boston Marathon, his favorite race. We were both in a good mood, and the world seemed full of promise. He uncharacteristically changed the radio channel to a rock station. It was playing the Young Rascals, singing "A Beautiful Morning." He smiled as he drove down the road. "Let's listen to this today," he said.

2/ Play

*I*n stickball, no matter what your ability, there was an occasional
Miracle when broom met "Spaldeen," and the ball would go high and far up the block
for an unbelievable distance. It would be a memory never quite erased by past
or subsequent failures . . .

RUNNING & BEING, 1978

SOME CHRISTMASES AGO, THE school where my daughter taught
kindergarten had an open house. I visited her classroom. The entire
room was covered with drawings of angels, but angels only a child
could see and no theologian had ever imagined. They were of every
shape and size, every color of the spectrum, uniformly joyous.

I thought, "Please, don't let them grow up."

An impossible plea, of course. We all grow up. We lose the wonder and imagination and trust that come with childhood, and then
pass as childhood passes and are lost forever.

Or so I thought, until in France I went to see the Matisse chapel in Vence. Entering that chapel was like re-entering that kindergarten—only better. Here was the final, glorious manifestation of those childhood visions. Here was the work of, as Blake wrote, "a child grown wise." Here was all that joy, all that certainty and trust done by a master's hand. Matisse had transformed a room not much larger than my daughter's kindergarten into a world of flowers and light.

When Matisse wrote about the chapel, he said it was the fruit of a huge, sincere, and difficult striving—not a labor he had chosen, but rather something for which he had been chosen. He had succeeded because he had learned the secret of aging. It is to become once more a child.

Later, when I visited the Musée Matisse, I was struck by this same progression in his work. The museum is on the outskirts of Nice, a villa in a small park. Immediately in front of it is a children's playground with brightly striped booths, a May Pole, and a small platform for games and dancing. I could sense already what I was to meet inside.

In the first rooms, I saw Matisse becoming that accomplished artist. There were the usual nudes, the still lifes, and the landscapes done impeccably well. Then, gradually, I could see the bold line taking over, the reduction to essentials, childlike drawings done by a genius. The master expressed the uninhibited energy, passion, and perception of the child. The complete control of his art allowed him to play, capturing everything in a single line and the simplest of colors.

This, surely, is what Picasso meant when he said it takes a long time to become young. The advantage of age is that you can become that child again, and better—for now you are a child who has the tools, a child who has been twice home, who has seen the worst in the world and yet who, like Matisse, is able to go beyond to the real world.

The young-old see the miracle that each day represents. True aging occurs not in retirement but in rebirth, in a new kindergarten, a new making of angels, a new chapel to a new and understanding God.

—THIS RUNNING LIFE, 1980

◆───────

To PLAY OR NOT to play? That is the real question. Shakespeare was wrong. Anyone with a sense of humor can see that life is a joke, not a tragedy. It is a riddle and like all riddles has an obvious answer: play, not suicide.

Think about it for a minute. Is there a better way to handle "the slings of and arrows of outrageous fortune" or take up arms against "a sea of troubles" than play? You take these things seriously and you end up with Hamlet or the gang who came back from World War II, wrote Wilfred Sheed, "talking about dollars the way others talked of God and sex."

Neither of these ways works. Neither will bring us what we are supposed to be looking for, "the peace the world cannot give." That is also part of the riddle. You can have peace without the world if you opt for death, or the world without peace if you decide for doing and having and achieving. Only in play can you have both.

In play you realize simultaneously the supreme importance and the utter insignificance of what you are doing. You accept the paradox of pursuing what is at once essential and inconsequential. In play you can totally commit yourself to a goal that minutes later is completely forgotten.

Play, then, is the answer to the puzzle of our existence, the stage for our excesses and exuberances. Violence and dissent are part of its joy. Territory is defended with every ounce of our strength and determination, and moments later we are embracing our opponents and delighting in the game that took place.

Play is where life lives, where the game is the game. At its borders, we slip into heresy, become serious, lose our sense of humor, fail to see the incongruities of everything we hold to be important. Right and wrong become problematical. Money, power, position become ends. The game becomes winning. And we lose the good life and the good things that play provides.

If the common man has erred in this century, it is in his failure to realize the importance of play. The aristocracy never made that mistake. Aristocrats know that work is a luxury and play is a necessity of life. When money and position give the freedom to pursue the good life, work is seen to be a diversion, a distraction from the most basic and the most—to use Maslow's word—actualizing human activity, play.

We are slowly awakening to this truth. Teachers now see the ideal learning environment is the environment of children at play. Physical education is being revived by bringing play back into its curriculum. Health and fitness, every medical journal is telling us, comes only to those who play hard and often.

And finally, the theologians, always the last to learn, are starting to ask themselves if play might not be the primary activity of man. Theologian Gabriel Moran has called play "one of the most intriguing and potentially fruitful interests of contemporary theology." Certainly, a case can be made that the true object of life is play.

Plato spoke of man as "God's plaything" and urged everyone to "make the noblest games the real content of their lives." And in Proverbs we read, "His delight was in playing with the children of men."

We have missed the point of all this because we have not understood play. It is not, as we believed, simply a method of relieving tension and providing relaxation. Nor is it a service activity preparing us for the more serious and important everyday world, the real world.

Play, as the true player knows, is the most real thing that he does. Indeed, one must play with a passionate involvement, play as if his life depended on it, if play is to mean anything at all.

One man's play can, of course, be another man's boredom. Anyone reading the Lawrence Shainberg article on Frank Shorter in the *New York Times Magazine* would realize that. Shorter's idea of play is running 22 miles a day at a 6-minutes-per-mile clip, occasionally interspersing these tortures with a series of agonizing interval quarter-mile runs. And the whole joyful routine ends in a marathon where he has to "redline" (maintain as long as possible the fastest pace one's body can bear) and "go it on mind alone" (the task that confronts a runner when he has superseded the normal limits of his body).

Yet there can be no doubt this mixture of pain and pleasure is play. It exists of and by itself and serves no utilitarian purpose. Why does he do it? "There's always the feeling of getting stronger," Shorter told Shainberg. "I think that's what keeps me going."

That explanation may be inadequate for some, but for me it contains enough theological implications for a doctoral thesis. Strong is Anglo-Saxon for what the Romans called *virtus,* and from this Latin root comes man and virtue. The growing strength that Shorter feels is obviously as spiritual and intellectual as it is physical.

Shorter belongs to that group of people that William James said resent confusion and must have purity, consistency, and simplicity. The marathoner is by most standards a peculiar guy. He has found freedom through the acceptance of rules, has cured his loneliness with solitude, and has discovered the peace inside of pain. He is a blood brother to another peculiar guy, Henry David Thoreau, who spoke of his play (walking) in this way:

"If you are ready to leave father and mother, and brother and sister, and wife and children and friends, and never see them again—if you have paid your debts and made your will and settled all your affairs and are a free man, then you are ready for a walk."

Even for the free man, life is a dangerous and difficult game. Man, the player, must train long and hard before he can move through life with the simple, certain, leisurely grace of the expert. Still, it is the only game in town.

—DR. SHEEHAN ON RUNNING, 1975

———◆———

WHEN EXERCISE BECOMES PLAY, it becomes a self-renewing compulsion. It becomes part of each day, part of your life. The fitness that ensues is simply a bonus. In fact, if fitness remains the primary purpose and the play is never discovered, in all likelihood the fitness program will fail. Only people with the proverbial gun in their ribs will persist. Only those under doctor's orders—because of a prior heart attack or some disease requiring exercise—will persevere in an activity that they find boring, mindless, and time-consuming.

Play, of course, is quite the opposite. It occupies us totally, and time passes without our noticing it. Play is one of those peak experiences described by Abraham Maslow. It is the priceless ingredient in exercise. We should be like children at play.

Suppose you accept this thesis, acknowledge the need to play and the benefits of the exercise that comes with it. How would you find your play?

First, you must discover what you do best, which means analyzing your body structure. Function follows structure, so the body usually reveals how it functions best.

Having done that, you must analyze your temperament to see how you like to play. Are you built for flight, fight, or negotiation? Is your tendency under stress to withdraw, to socialize, or to become aggressive? Is your nature predisposed to detachment, dependence, or dominance?

All of us have a little of each tendency in us, but one force is dominant and usually decides whether we prefer to play sports as a loner or part of a highly social activity, or want to go head-to-head physically with an opponent. Fortunately, our structure usually goes along with these choices.

The solitary individual usually is thin-boned, stringy-muscled, and equipped for endurance sports. He finds running an intensely satisfying exercise—play which indeed can become part of his lifestyle.

The socializers may not be natural athletes. If their bodies possess neither strength nor endurance, they can still enjoy sports like golf, doubles tennis, cycling, skiing, skating, and running. They are particularly good at aquatic sports. But the primary and engrossing part of their play-exercise is other people.

The hitters, on the other hand, need other people not as companions but as opponents. They play the big game in tennis, tend to increase the suspense in golf by betting, and often become engaged in activities such as the martial arts, weight lifting, and hitting the heavy bag.

Having begun with the question, "Why exercise?" we find that the answer is to be found in yet another question: "Why play?"

When we begin an exercise program, it is almost always for the wrong reasons. We seek physical fitness because we believe we have our bodies and want to do something to them, not because we are our bodies and wish to find out who we are.

It is an understandable error. Historically, society—the church, the school, the corporation—has taught us an abnormal view of the body. The preachers have warned us against the excesses of the flesh; that the body is an instrument of the devil, something to be disciplined and denied. The intellectuals have taught us that the body is a mere conveyance, a mundane vessel for the triumphs of the mind. Keep the body in repair and it won't bother our essential function, which is thinking. And what of businessmen? They have perceived the body as a machine, a tool. Fitness makes us better workers, improves our output.

The body, then, has been treated as a second-class citizen. Anyone who would think otherwise must develop his own rules, come to a different view of the universe. He must question what he hears from the pulpit, wonder how his childhood teachers could miss the point, and look on the laws of supply and demand as necessary only for the preservation of the herd. He must somehow discover that his body is equal with his soul.

Oddly enough, this unity occurs most readily in play and sports, and in those exercise programs where the magical and the mystical have taken over from the practical and the pragmatic. We should know, as Ortega said, that life demands two different kinds of effort—

one stemming from sheer delight, originality, creativity, vitality, spontaneity; the other effort ruled by compulsion, obligation, utility. The former is sport, the most important part of life. The latter, work or labor, ranks second.

Ortega concludes, "Life . . . resides in the first alone; the rest is relatively mechanical and functioning."

The millions who get into exercise programs will succeed or fail, therefore, inasmuch as they move beyond the details of fitness—beyond tables and charts and schedules—and into the vital, creative area of play. Beyond fitness itself, everyone is a child—a child at play but also a child, as Blake said, grown wise.

The truth is that play is where we live. In running and climbing and swimming, in hunting and fishing, in riding horses and playing games we become ourselves and open ourselves to experience. There, we find an inward calm and peace. There, thinking and feeling have a clarity that occurs almost nowhere else. And there, we discover a wholeness, a completion, and an integrity that make us want to celebrate our being. Away from daily life, away from politics and religion, from economics and science; we see the universe and ourselves as being much more than logic and reason have taught us.

Exercise to lose weight. Run to lower your blood pressure. Bicycle to reduce your cholesterol. Swim to increase your cardiac function. Play tennis to help your breathing. Golf so you'll sell more clients. Do calisthenics to clear your brain. All those things are good. But beyond all this fitness is the discovery of who you are.

—THIS RUNNING LIFE, 1980

"I THINK, THEREFORE I am" is the philosophy of the incomplete man.

"We are happy," writes David Cole Gordon, "when, however briefly, we become one with ourselves, others, and the world of nature." Sport certainly provides such moments. The fact that they mostly defy description may cause outsiders and observers to doubt their existence. But all athletes know the truth of "I play, therefore I am."

Some of the good things in play are physical grace, psychological ease, and personal integrity. The best are the peak experiences, when you have a sense of oneness with yourself and nature. These are truly times of peace the world cannot give. It may be that the hereafter will have them in constant supply. I hope so. But while we are in the here and now, play is the place to find them—the place where we are constantly being and becoming ourselves.

Philosophers have hinted at this over the centuries. Now theologians are taking a hard look at the thought that we must become as little children to enter the Kingdom. If so, there is nothing more characteristic about children than their love of play. No one comes into this world a Puritan. If there is anything children care less about, it is work and money and power and what we call achievement. They live in love and security and acceptance. Nowhere in their world is the need to prove their right to exist, the necessity to be a success.

What happened to our play on our way to becoming adults? Downgraded by the intellectuals, dismissed by the economists, put aside by the psychologists, it was left to the teachers to deliver the coup de grâce. Physical education was born and turned what was joy into boredom, what was fun into drudgery, what was pleasure into work. What might have led us into Eden led us into a blind alley instead.

Play, of course, says otherwise. You may already have found that out. If you are doing something you would do for nothing, then you are on your way to salvation. And if while you are doing it you are transported into another existence, there is no need for you to worry about the future.

I suspect that, more often than not, politics, religion, money, and the law are the real sanctuaries from reality, whereas sport is an immediate, engrossing human experience which involves man in his wholeness, completely realized in all his aspects.

Take the long distance runner. Here is the object of a phrase "the loneliness of the long distance runner," which in many ways encapsulates all our false notions about sports. The lonely long distance runner stands for "my husband, the nut," or "my roommate, the character," or "my brother, the misfit." He raises an image of some oddball who has confused his priorities and has settled into a permanent semi-adolescent state of isolation, unable to rise above the level of play and games.

Try again. Smith, the runner in that novel by Alan Sillitoe, was lonely only when he wasn't running. "Sometimes," he said, "I think I've never been as free as during that couple of hours when I'm trotting up the path." There is no hint, you see, that his loneliness was part of his distance running. It may well, if we read his words correctly, have been the cure.

Thoreau had already spoken to us of the cure to be found in solitude. Thoreau was not lonely. He described himself when he described the sparrow hawk. "It appeared to have no companion in the universe and to need none but the morning. It was not lonely but it made all the world lonely beneath it."

Like the soaring hawk, Smith finds his freedom—his escape from the loneliness of the reform school—in his running. Only when his running becomes a source of prestige and gratification to the superintendent, when he realizes he is being manipulated, when his sport is being used in the "real" world, does his loneliness again intrude on him. Not the running but society thrusts him back into the lonely shell he had occupied.

Society, if we can believe sociologist Philip Slater, is presently engaged in thrusting all of us into a state of loneliness. Only Slater in his brilliant, bitter, and often despairing book, *The Pursuit of Loneliness,* says we go there willingly and knowingly, carried along by our belief in the scarcity principle—the assumption that the world does not contain enough wherewithal to satisfy the needs of its human inhabitants.

Hence, Americans seek competition instead of community, and involvement rather than engagement with social and interpersonal problems. The result, writes Slater, is that the returning traveler re-entering the United States is struck by the fanatical acquisitiveness of his compatriots. "It is difficult," he says, "to become reaccustomed to seeing people already weighed down with possessions acting as if every object they did not own were bread withheld from a hungry mouth." Another sociologist, Dr. Whitney Gordon, found something similar in a study of Muncie, Indiana. Muncie's predominant social values, he reported, were the importance of work, of enterprise, of upward mobility, of material rewards. "'Making it' for the worker after the two cars is the color TV, and if he has that, a camper is a status symbol," says Gordon. "'Making it' in the upper income groups is membership in the country club, travel abroad, or a Cadillac."

If that is reality, the long distance runner may indeed be seeking sanctuary from it. There is no scarcity principle in running. All can share without in any way diminishing the other. It is moreover a universal language understood by all men, an endeavor in which all men can relate and instantly be brothers. "Sports brings out," writes artist-photographer Robert Riger, "the classic greatness and dignity of man. In the struggle and in the race there is an almost divine accord of beauty and grace."

Can a plodder feel all this? Better, it's my guess, than any politician, cleric, businessman, or lawyer. What are *they* going to do when they grow up?

—DR. SHEEHAN ON RUNNING, 1975

---◆---

I REACHED MY PEAK in creativity when I was 5. I could draw and paint and sculpt. I could sing and dance and act. I possessed my body completely. And with it became completely absorbed in a life that was good and beautiful and joyful. I examined and tested and explored. I could not bear to watch. My every day was filled with the creativity that Rollo May defined: "the encounter of an intensely conscious human being with his world." I do not confuse creativity with talent. I never had talent. Few do. But I was aware and responded, and I responded totally. And I had what in older people is called purpose or dedication. At 5, I was creative and authentic. At 5, I did it my way. At five, I was like most 5-year-olds, a genius without talent. That genius came from energy and effort and taking risks. I would not know for years that Thoreau had commended arduous work for the artist. "Hard, steady, and engrossing labor," he said, "is invaluable to the literary man." And I would not read until even later that the Greeks had no word for art or artist. That they never separated, any more than I did, the useful from the beautiful. For them, either a thing was useful and therefore beautiful or it was sacred and therefore beautiful.

The 5-year-old does not yet know sin, but he may well know what is sacred. Poetry and painting and music are, according to Blake, "three powers in man of conversing with Paradise." The 5-year-old sees that Paradise correctly, not in technology but in the fairy story, in the great myths that control and guide our lives. And myth is meaning divined rather than defined, implicit rather than explicit.

At 5, I had the intuitive, instinctive faith that my cosmos, my family, and the world were good and true and beautiful. That somehow I had always been and always would be. And I knew in a way of a 5-year-old that I had worth and dignity and individuality. Later, when I read Nietzsche's statement that these are not given to us by nature but are tasks that we must somehow solve, I knew him to be wrong. We all had them once.

We lost them when we substituted watching for doing. When we saw the lack of perfection as a reason not to participate. When we became specialists and learned to ignore what was the province of other people.

For me, this meant no further interest in how things worked, in construction and making things, in crafts of any kind. I lost control of my life and in time became helpless in front of any malfunctioning machine. Now, if left to my own devices, I could not house or feed or clothe myself. Were I a castaway on a desert island, I would not know how to apply the efforts of all the scientists since the time of Archimedes. I would have to live as if they never existed. As if their talent and the products of their intense encounter with the world had never occurred.

And this all because my encounter, my absorption, my purpose, and my interest and intensity had never occurred. I had changed from a genius without talent into the worst of all possible beings, a consumer. The consumer is passivity objectified. Where the 5-year-old finds the day too short, the consumer finds the day too long. I had lost the absorption of the five-year-old and gained boredom. I had lost my self-respect and gained self-doubt. Being middle-class, I had neither the need to use myself physically to survive, which poverty imposes, nor the absolute freedom to complete myself physically that wealth allows the aristocrat.

The 5-year-old is just such an aristocrat. He seeks his own truth, his own perfection, his own excellence without care for the expense. He could well be a millionaire in his lack of concern for money and the family bank account.

But the 5-year-old is more than an aristocrat; he is the worker Thoreau commended. He is the artist the Greeks saw no need to define. He is the athlete we all wish to be. And the saint we will never be. Every 5-year-old is a success, just as every consumer is a failure.

The road back for a 59-year-old consumer is a long one. But there must be untapped resources of enthusiasm and energy and purpose deep in me somewhere. Somewhere I have the same creativity I had when I was 5. I suspect that it is hidden under my clean, neatly folded and seldom used soul.

If I were to suggest that creativity is a major requirement for playing this game of life successfully, I suspect most readers would feel the game was already lost. Creativity seems to most of us a rare commodity, a gift given only to exceptional people.

The truth is that each one of us has this creativity. It was more evident when we were children and playing, because creativity is playful and depends on a faith in ourselves and what we are doing. It is associated, therefore, with those adjectives we use to describe children's play—spontaneous, effortless, innocent, and easy.

"Almost any child," wrote Abraham Maslow, "can compose a song or a poem or a dance or a painting or a play or a game on the spur of the moment." So, I assure you, can we.

Creativity is a different way of looking at things, a different way of looking at ourselves. When we are creative, when we are at play, when we really believe in ourselves, we open ourselves to our own experiences. We discard preconceptions. We finally become aware. We begin to live.

Creativity, therefore, is a matter of seeing the ordinary as unusual, the commonplace as miraculous, the transient as eternal. It is seeing the new in the old, looking at things as if for the first time.

Not only the child and the saint, but also the athlete takes this creative view of what would strike us as routine. The spectacular things are the routine things done every day, consistently. Mainly, creativity takes the routine and makes it important, makes it worthwhile.

Joe DiMaggio, they say, never threw to the wrong base in his entire career. Was that merely reflex? Of course not. To accomplish that record, each individual throw had to be made with the intensity, fervor, and freshness of the very first throw. DiMaggio transformed an activity that could have become routine into a creative challenge.

Andrew Wyeth was another man who had a creative response to

familiar things. "I'm not much for the new thing or the new object," he said. "I like to go back again and again, because I think you can always find some new things. I'm actually bored by fresh things to paint. To make old things seem fresh is much more exciting to me."

If Wyeth can discover more in the everyday and the familiar, so can we. For myself, I now see that there are innumerable opportunities for creativity. All I need is the faith, the confidence, the ability to let go, and the attitude of play. Then, I can create—when I come together with my family or friends, when I write, when I run, or when I just sit on the beach and look at the sea. The most routine, the most simple act can be a creative event.

—RUNNING AND BEING, 1978

What Dr. Sheehan Means to Me

BY FRANK SHORTER

GEORGE SHEEHAN AND I shared the bond of having been mentored by the same man, Robert Giegengack. "Gieg," as he was known, was a young Phi Beta Kappa and classics graduate from Holy Cross when he coached George in high school, at the now-defunct Manhattan Prep. Years later, at the end of his career, he was my coach at Yale University.

We often talked about Gieg's training philosophy, style, and theory. We agreed that it was best described as Socratic, an ongoing encounter between teacher and student. I think it profoundly influenced both our running and George's evolution as a writer. From an early age we were taught to truly think about how and why we were out there moving down the road.

Every day at practice, we would warm up and then report to Gieg for instructions and for a stopwatch to carry with us. From experience we always knew in general terms whether it would be an easy or hard day, but the details were revealed only just before we set off. Often we would train out of sight and afterward report back for discussion. We would describe how it went, learning to visualize as we reported on our relative efforts; then Gieg would teach through interactive dialogue. Over time we learned how to do something very simple: coach ourselves.

This shared history allowed me to appreciate George's writing about the marathon in a very personal way. He could verbalize what I often felt on my long runs, preparing for an upcoming race, or what it was like to try to talk my way to the finish beyond 22 miles. Exploration is a word that comes to mind—that willingness to find out what the result of total effort might be, and in that way forget to be afraid of failure.

3/ *Taking Back* Your Day ...
Your Life

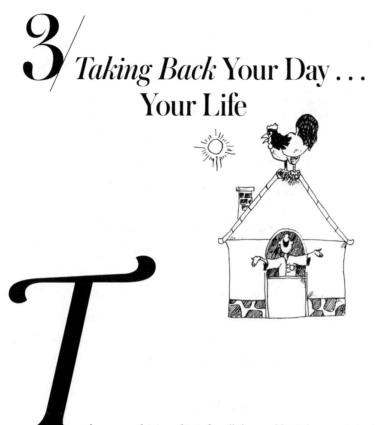

*T*he reason they say this is for all the marbles is because it is always
*for all the marbles. And the reason they say there is no tomorrow is because there is never,
at this very moment, a tomorrow. We are always at risk, always at hazard.*

RUNNING & BEING, 1978

GRADUATES OF DOWNSTATE MEDICAL School, families, friends,
and faculty:

Your dean said it was an honor to have me as a commencement
speaker. That you were about to hear from a distinguished cardiologist, philosopher, and an expert on fitness. That remains to be seen.
But those are not the reasons I am here. The real reasons are quite
simple. Your student body president, who extended the invitation,
said they were looking for an alumnus, someone who would keep

people from falling asleep, and they had no money. He hoped that would not matter. It didn't. At 57, I am willing to talk to anyone who will listen.

I will not deny I am a cardiologist. But I don't consider that important. Like most specialists, I am not intelligent enough to be a family practitioner. And of all the specialties, cardiology is the simplest and the safest for someone who is ambivalent and indecisive.

In common with most heart specialists, I am a Hamlet who is always wondering what to do. Fortunately, the patient improves or is even cured during the soliloquy. I also admit to being a self-taught philosopher. There is no other way for us physicians, for surely we must be the worst educated of professionals. We go through medical school in college to prove we can cope with medical school in medical school. We are never taught the humanities or their importance. Scientists, you see, need know nothing about yesterday. It is already incorporated in today's technology.

But to be human, to be a person, you must start with the Book of Genesis and work forward. You must always be on the alert to find the giants, the writers, the thinkers, the saints, the athletes who speak to you. Those who reflect your instincts, your temperament, your body, your mind, your tastes.

I do plead guilty to being fit. But only because at 44 I became bored with medicine. When I applied for the faculty at Rutgers Medical School citing that boredom was my only qualification, the application was rejected. I then turned to a higher ambition. To become a 44-year-old miler. And, in an absolute, unreasonable, single-minded dedication to that absurd project, discovered my body, my play, my vision, and, eventually, a new life. I found my truth.

I stand here now hoping to transmit some of that truth. But even more, I don't want to lie to you. "The old lie to the young," said Thornton Wilder. And never more than in commencement addresses. All over this land at this time of the year, there are speakers talking about hard work. Of the need for continuing study. Of the necessity of becoming men and women. They are urging graduates to succeed, to give service, to dedicate their lives to others.

I am here as an advocate for other values. I am here to speak not for work, but for play. Not for the mind, but the body. Not for becoming a man or a woman, but remaining a child. I am here to tell you that in your success will be the seeds of your failure. That in giving service, you will eventually do a disservice to yourself and your family and your patients. That in your dedication to others, you may die without actually have lived.

My experience has taught me that you must first and always seek the person you are. And this becoming unfolds through the intensity with which you use your body, through your absorption in play, and through the acceptance of the discipline needed to be an athlete.

At all times, you must protect your Self. Maintain a childlike wonder. Acquire if you can the ability to be careless, to disregard appearances, to relax and laugh at the world. If you are to succeed, you must always be on the alert. Establish priorities. Keep 1 hour a day inviolate. A full 60 minutes in which you retire from God, country, family, and practice. And there must be 1 day a week that is yours alone. Learn self-esteem, self-acceptance.

Know that you can be a hero.

It won't be easy. There are people out there waiting to kill you with their demands. They will want an 18-hour day. Then a 24-hour day. A 36-hour day if possible. The song tells you, "They will kill you if you let them. Don't let them. You have a friend."

But you have no friends. Those who call you by your first name are the worst. They will call you anytime, day or night, and especially on your day off. You are your only friend. The only protector of your body and its beauty. The only defender of your play and its delights. The only guardian of your childhood and its dreams. The only dramatist and actor in your unique, never-to-be-repeated living of your life.

Rise to that challenge. Live your own life. Success is not something that can be measured or worn on a watch or hung on the wall. It is not the esteem of colleagues, or the admiration of the community, or the appreciation of patients. Success is the certain knowledge that you have become yourself, the person you were meant to be from all time.

That should be reward enough. But best of all is the fun while you are doing it. And, at the very least, you will heal yourself.

—RUNNING & BEING, 1978

———◆———

IN 1910, ARNOLD BENNETT wrote a book on "the daily miracle," our supply of time. We wake in the morning, and our day is magically filled with 24 hours. No one can take it from you, and no one receives more or less than you receive. Genius is not rewarded with even an extra hour. Time cannot be bought. And no matter how much you waste it, the next day's supply will not be withheld from you. It is impossible to go into debt for time. Tomorrow is always there.

Out of the 24-hour day we have to spin a complex web of health, pleasure, contentment, respect, and the evolution of our immortal souls.

So our happiness depends upon how we use our time.

Yet how many of us put things off, living for a future when we will have more time? How many of us live on the allotted 24 hours a day? How many are waiting for a new day with more time?

"We shall never have any more time," Bennett writes. "We have and we always had all the time there is."

Let us review rapidly how we spend our day . . .

"Most of us," said Robert Louis Stevenson, "lead lives that 2 hours' reflection would lead us to disown."

At the least, we are haunted by a suppressed dissatisfaction with our daily lives. That is the way it is with me. I am one of that band of innumerable souls who are haunted by the feeling that the years are slipping by—and we have not yet been able to get our lives in working order.

Like so many, I find the day gone and nothing to show for it. Night falls, and I have not added a thing. I go to bed, and nothing has changed in my inner or outer world. I rise, earn the bread, and kill time. For that indeed is what I do, as surely as if I took a knife to an animal and let its lifeblood seep out.

Time passes hourly, daily, weekly, monthly, annually, with little or nothing to show for it. The questions hang in the air: "What have you done with your youth? What are you doing with your age?" Things do indeed go slip-sliding along. There is no end to the broken promises, most of them made to ourselves. Starting over is easy: I've done it thousands of times.

Bennett proposes that in one way or another we find 90 minutes a day for our own exclusive use. With this one and a half hours, he promises to help us approach each·day with zest. We will rise then, as Marcus Aurelius said, to the work of a human being, rid of the nagging knowledge that we are doing less than our best.

Amiel, the Swiss philosopher, wrote in his journal that "the morning air breathes a new and laughing energy into the veins and marrow. Every dawn is a new contract with existence." The dawn, Amiel said, is a time for projects, for resolution, for the birth of action.

"Early to bed, early to rise" is good advice whether you arrive home tired out or not. It is, for one thing, the classic physiology. It is the first choice of our bodies, the natural way to live. Were we to follow our body rhythms, those circadian cycles, it would be the normal way to spend our allotted, unchanging 24 hours. The gradual buildup in our physiological function and then the gradual decline, the flooding and ebbing of the tides in our bodies, are matched by our physical and mental activities. The closer we get to following the rhythm of the earth, the closer we get to our own internal rhythms.

Early rising puts us in harmony with those rhythms. It is truly a great beginning. Early rising followed by an early morning workout is an even better one.

There are those of us who are always about to live. We are waiting until things change, until there is more time, until we are less tired, until we get a promotion, until we settle down—until., until, until. It always seems as if there is some major event that must occur in our lives before we begin living.

Bennett rejects that excuse. He asks for minor adjustments, advises that we start modestly. He gives us simple, monosyllabic advice: Rise an hour earlier, bring your mind to heel, avoid the harsh word. Everything that he suggests requires little more than the will to do it.

The psychologist Abraham Maslow, in describing fully functioning people, said much the same thing: "People who are self-actualizers go about it in these little ways: They listen to their own voice; they are honest, and they work hard."

They find out who they are, said Maslow, not only in terms of their mission in life but in other ways: " . . . in terms of the way their feet hurt when they wear such and such shoes, and whether or not they like eggplant, or stay up all night if they drink too much beer." That is what the real self means, declared Maslow. These people find their own biological nature, their congenital nature, which is difficult to change or is irreversible.

We must become expert in ourselves; we must listen to our bodies, learn their strengths and weaknesses, yet all the while refuse to accept less than what we can do. There are great limits, and we do not know where they are until we get there.

The little ways we reach these great limits begin with knowing our bodies. This perception that things are right or wrong is much more sensitive than people give it credit for. Hans Selye, the expert on stress, once said that the thing that mystified him most was how people know they are sick. What moves a person to come to a doctor's office and announce that something is wrong—often when the most sophisticated medical testing is unable to find anything amiss. Science cannot make a diagnosis; yet the body knows that its homeostasis has been upset.

What we must do is perceive the static-free messages from inner space which tell us there is intelligent life there and it is attempting to communicate with us. For information to come through loud and clear, we must purify the body, must conform in every way to its proper workings. Research is always going on in the hope of helping us in this. But more often than not, the research simply proves what we already know. When we listen to our bodies, we need no textbook. When we are doing what our bodies tells us is best, we can be assured we are physiologically correct. There is not a single test that tells us as much as the body and what it perceives to be happening.

Maslow's self-actualizers discovered their own individual ways of fulfilling their potential. As Seurat's tiny dots eventually made a masterpiece, so the self-actualizers' minute attention to daily details made their lives works of art. They became specialists in the only subject that warrants being a specialist: the study of the self, the one science that makes you a successful practitioner in life.

This is not to say that success is assured, Bennett continually warned us. Always proceed with little steps, he advised. Never forget you are dealing with human nature. Always remember we want the easy way out. We want something for nothing. We blame others when things go wrong. We deny that we have control over our minds and bodies. We have become civilized animals and have lost the will to survive and the capability of doing so.

I once wondered why Maslow, when he places self-actualization as the highest need, put survival as the basic one. Now it is evident that we must learn to survive—becoming that wild, instinctive animal again, seeing plainly how destructive our lifestyle is.

We must live on the alert. Then we can get on with the business of becoming perfect.

—*HOW TO FEEL GREAT 24 HOURS A DAY,* 1983

———◆———

YOU WIN, THE EXPERTS agree, if the game is played in your rhythm. You lose if it isn't. Every basketball fan knows that. "We put on the press," a coach once told me, "not so much to create turnovers, but to upset our opponent's rhythm. To get them moving and not thinking." Most basketball fans know that, too.

But how many of us know that the same thing is happening in our lives every day? How many of us see that we are letting someone else set the rhythm of our lives, or that we face the equivalent of the Boston Celtics' full-court press when we get out of bed each morning?

The clock is where it all starts. This mechanical divider of time controls our action, imposes our workday, and tells us when to eat and sleep. The clock makes every hour just an hour. It makes no distinctions between morning and afternoon. Aided by electric daylight, it doles out apparently equal minutes and seconds until *The Late Show.* And then, Good night.

The artist, especially the poet, has always known this to be wrong. He knows that time shortens and lengthens, without regard to the minute hand. Knows that we have a beat foreign to this Greenwich metronome. Knows also there is an ebb and flow to the day that escapes the clock, but not us. And realizes that this rhythm, this tempo, is something peculiar to each individual, as personal and unchanging as his fingerprints.

The artists know this. The scientists have proved it. In *Biological Rhythms of Psychiatry and Medicine,* Bertram S. Brown writes, "Rhythm is as much a part of our structure as our flesh and bones.

Most of us are dimly aware that we fluctuate in energy, mood, well-being, and performance each day, and that there are longer, more subtle variations each week, each month, each season, each year."

There was a time when we could sit and listen to these rhythms, but now they can hardly be heard over the din of the mechanical clocks set up by school and business and society. Now we have commuting and TV, 3-day weekends and 12-hour workdays, March migraines and April ulcers, 21-year-old addicts and 45-year-old heart attacks.

Is anyone listening to his innards? But then, who listened to Socrates: "Know thyself"; or to Norbert Weiner: "To live effectively is to live with adequate information"; or to the Japanese philosopher Suzuki: "I am an artist at living, and my work of art is my life"? But that's what we must do to face that Celtics' press every morning.

Listen to what our bodies are trying to tell us. Know ourselves. Get adequate information. Become artists. Otherwise, someone else will control the pace, the game, and the score.

The Celtics are there and the press is on. They make us fit the job. Make us fit the hours. Make us fit the demands. Make us change to their tempo. March to their drummer. All the while, destroying our game plan. Our way of becoming all we are. Choking off what we do best.

They have made us prisoners of their artificial time, their mechanical clock. And all the while, they are planning the final irony: When we retire, they will give us a watch.

"Living the good life," wrote Nikolai Berdyaev, "is frequently dull and flat and commonplace." Our greatest problem, he claimed, is to make it fiery and creative and capable of spiritual struggle.

I agree. Life, except for a favored few, like poets and children and athletes and saints, is pretty much of a bore. Given the choice, most of us would give up the reality of today for the memory of yesterday or the fantasy of tomorrow. We desire to live anywhere but in the present.

I see that in myself. I start the day with an agenda of things to be done that makes me completely oblivious to what I'm doing. I arrive at work with no memory of breakfast and no idea of what kind of day it is. I am in perpetual concern or rumination about the future.

Numbers of people do the same thing in reverse. They avoid reality by living in the past. Nostalgia is their way of life. For them the good old days will never be equaled. Or emulated, for that matter, since these people rarely bestir themselves to any activity.

But for those active in mind and heart and body, the child and the poet, the saint and the athlete, the time is always now. They are eternally present. And present with intensity and participation and commitment. They have to be. When the athlete, for instance, turns his attention from the decision to be made this second and every second, he invites disaster. Should his concentration falter, should his mind wander to the next hole, the next set, the next inning, he will be undone. Only the now exists for him.

And the saint, for all his talk of heaven and the hereafter, knows that everywhere is right here, that all of time is right now, and that every man exists in the person in front of him. He knows that every instant he much choose and continue to choose among the infinite possibilities of acting—and being. He has no time to think on the future.

Nor has the poet. He must live on the alert. Always aware. Always observant. When he does this well, he teaches us how to live more fully. "The feeling of life is in every line of the poem," writes James Dickey of *The Odyssey* by Kazantzakis, "so that the reader realizes time after time how little he himself has been willing to settle for in living; how much there is on earth, how inexplicable, marvelous, and endless creating is." For such a man, Perfection Past is no temptation. Nor is it for the saint or the athlete. Their characteristic falls from grace are in the contemplation of future triumphs. Heaven, perhaps, or a masterpiece, or a world's record.

No athlete ever lived, or saint or poet for that matter, who was content with what he did yesterday, or would even bother thinking about it. Their pure concern is the present. Why should we common folk be different? Are we not all poets and saints and athletes to some degree? Yet we refuse to make the commitment. Refuse to accept our own reality and work with it. So we live in the might-have-been world of the past and the never-will-be world of the future.

What we need is an element of present danger, an intimation of tragedy, some feeling of powerful, implacable forces at our doorstep. We need a threat to the commonplace that will suddenly and for all time intensify its value.

Some years ago, that happened to me. I had run a personal best marathon in Oregon, and came home full of what I would accomplish at the Boston Marathon. Five days later, I came down with the flu, and everything of importance fell into place. I no longer cared what I ran at Boston, or indeed if I ran at Boston at all. What I cared about first was health, and then being able to run again. Just to run and feel the sweat and the breathing and the power in my legs. To feel again what it was like to toil up hills and to push through pain. Just that and perhaps that good tired feeling after a race. No past runs or future triumphs would comfort me. I was ready to repent and hear the Good News.

I know then what every poet and child, every athlete and saint knows. The reason they say this is for all the marbles is because it is always for all the marbles. And the reason they say there is no tomorrow is because there is never, at this very moment, a tomorrow. We are always at risk, always at hazard.

—*RUNNING & BEING,* 1978

WHEN I WAS PRACTICING medicine and running every day, writing weekly sports columns and racing almost every Sunday, people would ask me how I did it. The 24 hours did not seem long enough to allow for all those activities. How was I able to budget my time so effectively?

It was difficult at first. I found that running could not be simply added to my day. I would not get up early in the morning and do it, and running before bedtime was too much after my long day. Something had to go to afford running and writing full play.

And because both running and writing are play—play of the body and play of the mind—I was able to take my 24 hours and find a place for them. Once you find something that is playful and addictive and filled with satisfaction, your daily budget takes care of itself. New priorities are set. A new perspective, a new sense of proportion, takes over. Once I became a runner and then a writer, my expenditures of time were made only when they were compatible with those roles.

Over a period of time, I eliminated a number of activities from my usual day. Most of this surgery was painless. Lunch, I discovered, unnecessary. Eating a big breakfast left me with no need for midday food. All I missed was the idle chatter at the doctors' table at the hospital, and that noonday chatter became more inconsequential in its absence. Thoreau once said that we should not lunch with people unless we have a new idea to impart. On that basis, my luncheons could be reduced to monthly events.

Movies are no problem. Most are not worth seeing. A year's output in film is reduced to a handful that can stir me to tears or laughter or action. The others are no more than killers of time.

My rules for books are equally simple. I read the classics and pre-fer authors who are dead or older than I. If you are of another mind, pick up a bestseller list from 10 years ago, and you will get an idea how little of what is current will live on. A classic is a book that appeals from one generation to another. When people urge me to read a new book, I go home and read an old one. There are few good reasons to read novels. Robert Frost said he read no novels because he was too busy living his own life.

The passive role imposed by both the movies and novels puts me off. Like Frost, I want to be part of the action. I do not want to be a spectator. The trade-off for watching and reading is the stimulation of new ideas and the good quotes. For good quotes, books by the great thinkers are the best. Newspapers that contain the truth expressed by the common man come next. Movies are bad, TV the worst.

How many hours can you watch TV without hearing a remark clever and witty and insightful enough to repeat, much less treasure? How many months can you watch a late-night show and not learn one new thing that will change or illuminate your life?

My rules for budgeting my 24 hours are simple. No lunch, no nov-els, little TV. A rare movie, few magazines, a quick pass through the newspaper. Thus I reduce those hours in which I am a consumer and a spectator and increase the time when I am living my own life.

Do not underestimate the difficulty of turning over a new leaf. Be aware that even minor changes in our daily routines are resisted by forces as powerful as any commitment we can make.

We believe that change is a matter of willpower. Once we become determined enough, once a truly firm decision has been made, the new life will take place.

It doesn't work that way. It is true that we have to recognize the need for a change, true also that we must make the pledge to do it, true always that such a commitment follows observation and judgment. But no matter how long and proper the preparation, no matter how strong and enduring the motivation, we cannot add a new activity to our life without taking something else out.

Should I decide that I want to become fit and I am currently using up my allotted hours a day, then I must take something out of that day to make room for my new thing—in this case fitness.

Why not add it to the end of the day or the beginning? Because removing time from sleep ultimately fails. It does happen, particularly in the beginning of an athletic program, that less sleep is required because of less fatigue. But as activity increases, so does the need for sleep.

Nor is it easy to decide what is to be thrown away. We have to decide between good things, not good and bad. We have a surfeit of riches. Each has value, each is worth doing. But decide we must. Either we choose the status quo and our feeling of missing out, or we break the pattern and change course.

Whatever success you will have will begin with giving up something presently in your life for the new activity. Just how difficult this can be is seen from an analogy with government.

When Jerry Brown was running for governor of California, he campaigned on reduced government spending and elimination of unnecessary jobs. When he became governor, he suddenly discovered how difficult this was to do. Every job, regardless of its importance, had its constituency—people and groups ready to battle anyone who would change the status quo. Eventually Brown saw that the only way to decrease or eliminate a government job was to have a new one created in the private sector.

So too with human potential. You have to learn that everything you do every day has a deep-seated reason. It gratifies a need and offers psychological support. Therefore, begin where the rewards of the new activity can clearly outweigh what is being sacrificed.

—*RUNNER'S WORLD* MAGAZINE, OCTOBER 1982

———◆———

A FRIEND IN DALLAS gave me a watch. I had gone without one for more than a decade and had done nicely. I had handled my day without a watch and felt no need for one. I had, in fact, lost my watch while raking leaves one day and had not raked leaves or worn a watch since. I believe, you see, in signs.

Nevertheless, I took the new watch. He is a good friend and was quite insistent. He actually took it off his wrist and put it on mine. So I let it stay. Besides, it is a marvelous instrument—one of those modern-day wonders of miniaturization and circuitry. It not only tells time; it is a stopwatch that can give me lap times as well. Further, it has an alarm to warn me, for instance, when my time is up during a speech. It also gives the date.

When he gave me the watch, I told him I could see the value of all its functions except the date. When I run, I do not have a clock in my head. I usually have no idea what time I am doing, so a stopwatch can come in handy during a race or in training. And I do have a habit of speaking too long. It is not often a man my age with a large family gets a chance to speak for any length of time without interruption. Once I begin to interact with an audience, I forget time and need something or someone to bring me back to reality.

But the date—who needs that? Why all these additional elements in the watch just to tell me the date? The date, it seemed to me, was overkill. This Japanese watch had one capability too many, one function that was unnecessary.

"Irving," I said to my friend, "one thing I do know is the date." Now I don't know the date. The watch knows the date. I am a victim of what I have come to call the "Japanese Watch Syndrome." I have allowed technology to come between me and my perception of the world.

I can operate without knowing the date. It is, in fact, a desired state for anyone who wants to be a child, an athlete, or a saint. Knowing the date more often than not indicates a preoccupation with the past or future that is hostile to genuine living. Knowing the date is rarely accompanied by feelings of joy.

When I am concentrating on the date, the odds are that I am concentrating on nothing else that is important. Chances are, I am missing out on those experiences which occur only when I am in a timeless state where past and present and future come together.

I would like, however, when I finally come back to reality after those mystical moments, to have some idea of what day of the week it is and even what month without referring to that infernal watch. My aim in this life is to be as independent as possible. The watch continually reminds me of failure. I am, if anything, becoming more dependent and must fight this tendency every day.

If you look, you can see this dependency all around you. The machine (or the expert behind the machine) monitors our acts, replaces our instincts, substitutes for our intuitions, acts as judge for our insights. The machine tells us what to do. In the process, our instincts are no longer heard. The animal in us is caught and caged, and no longer has to live on the alert.

Our best course demands exactly the opposite. If I am to be a good animal, I must live on the alert. I must develop my instincts. I must be able to hear and interpret what goes on in my body. I cannot be a blind and deaf tenant of my body, I cannot relax and sit back without sacrificing yet another function and capability of my body to technology.

Technology must be seen for what it is—both good and bad. It frees us, certainly. It liberates us from work that is drudgery. It shortens the workweek. It transforms society and gives us leisure, which is simply, as the Greeks knew, a school for becoming oneself.

At the same time, technology has removed physical stress, atrophied our legs and bodies, and allowed us to gain weight as only affluent societies do. It has taken over the decision-making process in our day-to-day living. Computers now tell us what to eat, how to sleep, what shoes to wear, how hard and how long to exercise. We merely establish what we want done, and the experts can program us for it. No need to use, for instance, our inborn power to perceive exertion; they will do that for us with a treadmill. No need to trust the signals we are getting from our body; they will run a printout of 18 tests which will tell us exactly how we feel.

When this happens to me, I become no more than a guided missile, my life's trajectory already plotted out. I lose the chance to be me. I am now ruled by clocks, calendars, schedules, agendas; living in an environment that is self-correcting and almost void of physical stress.

Abraham Maslow spoke of "subjective biology" or "experiential biology" where we are aware of the inner signals in the body. He saw the great need to hear these "voices of the real self," to know what and whom one likes and dislikes, what is enjoyable and what is not, when to eat and when not to, when to sleep, when to urinate, when to rest.

My Japanese watch is a symbol. I may not have a real need to know the date, but there is no question that I no longer know it. Technology can do that. Our task is to use technology without being enslaved by it. It must help us become more human rather than less.

—THIS RUNNING LIFE, 1980

What Dr. Sheehan Means to Me

BY JEFF GALLOWAY

THERE WERE FEW DOCTORS in the mid-1960s who knew much about running injuries, and fewer still who wanted to help limping runners resume our addiction. My roommate at Wesleyan University, Amby Burfoot, connected with George and passed on his address when I was going through a rough patch. I remember clearly how comforting it was to hear from George that I would heal and run as well as I had before. It was obvious that he understood and respected our passion for running.

George connected because he had enjoyed his identity as a college athlete and felt what he described as "mild, lingering depression" as he moved into a successful career as a cardiologist. He was living the life of success with increasing demands, and became afflicted with the "hurry sickness" that separated him from the healthy lifestyle he suggested to his patients. But in his mid-forties he decided to practice what he was prescribing. He first became a "good animal," experiencing a regeneration of the body, mind, and spirit. Then he discovered the joy of writing about the journey. At the urging of Joe Henderson, George's column in *Runner's World* magazine first offered medical advice and then challenged us to find out who we really were, as we ran.

A decade after my Wesleyan injury consultation, George and I became friends through several projects, and had a continuing series of great conversations. We didn't agree on a number of issues, but each of us loved tearing apart the fibers of reasoning and sharing experiences.

He inspired us all, and not just through his writings. George was one of the most determined competitors, and loved every painful moment. Sensing that the health benefits of running were only the tip of the iceberg, he produced philosophical treasures that he felt were more significant, and that are included in this book. I learned so much from him. Moreover, I thank him for triggering in me the passion for helping others discover the unique vitality boost and empowerment of the spirit bestowed by running every day.

4/ *Misguided* Modern Medicine

*espite our multibillion-dollar "health services" bill,
the United States is the best place to be if you are sick—but one of
the last places to be if you wish to remain well.*

DR. SHEEHAN ON RUNNING, 1975

WHEN I BEGAN RUNNING in my mid-forties, I rewrote my life story. It has become a biography of pain. I have made a career out of suffering. I've discovered that the middle-aged person is the perfect laboratory animal for research in sports medicine. Whatever happens to an athlete will happen first to a middle-aged athlete.

Scientific progress was not my original intention. Fun was, and fitness, and perhaps achievement. I hoped to acquire the look and moves and self-confidence of the athlete—to be sleek, quick, and instinctive. There might even be a glorious reprise to a not-so-glorious collegiate record.

But I soon learned that injury was to be the dominant theme of my new vocation. "Running hurt" became commonplace. The fun was there, and so was the fitness, plus meditation and other values I had not suspected. But I was neither sleek nor quick nor instinctive. I was ragged and slow and uncoordinated, more often limping than not.

As time passed and my mileage grew, I developed every runner's injury in the books, and some that weren't. I went through a cram course in sports medicine. Instead of reading about diseases, I got them. I became a mobile medical museum.

Eventually, I took a biblical approach to these afflictions. The cause of man's infirmity is to be found in man himself. Germs and microbes were not the problem. No virus had produced these miseries. I was dealing with a loss of the body's integrity, its balance, its ability to remain in equilibrium with its environment, its capacity to cope.

My little disasters, my minor tragedies became opportunities to find that integrity, that balance, and the antidote to the stress of training. I began to ask questions and find some answers: answers to metatarsalgia and plantar fasciitis, to Achilles tendinitis and pseudo–Achilles tendinitis, to heel spurs and shin splints, to runner's knee and groin pulls, to stress fractures and sciatic neuritis.

Some lasted longer than others and gave me a better education. Four years of sciatica taught me how to sleep (on my good side with my bad leg drawn up), how to drive a car (only in bucket seats), how to sit (with the hips higher than the knees), how to have patience ("I had it for 2 years once," an older runner told me). I am a powerfully slow learner, but I began to learn.

Every painful mile I put on the roads adds more of this kind of information, but I still have trouble welcoming injury. When it arrives, I still go through that familiar sequence of every patient: disbelief, followed by fear, then rage, and finally depression.

I should, however, have a lot of time to work on that problem. After all, whatever happens to an athlete will happen first to an 80-year-old athlete.

—*RUNNING TO WIN,* 1991

◆

DESPITE OUR MULTIBILLION-DOLLAR "HEALTH services" bill, the United States is the best place to be if you are sick—but one of the last places to be if you wish to remain well. Recent statistics show that the overfed, under-exercised United States is 37th in life expectancy for men 40 years of age. (We were 11th two decades earlier.) Further, our women have a 6.8 years greater life expectancy than our men at that age, against 3.4 years in the leading countries.

People who planned to do something about this formed the National Jogging Association in the late 1960s. The NJA was the brainchild of Lt. Gen. R.L. Bohannon, MD, who boosted jogging as "the simplest, cheapest, least encumbered, most available, and most efficient way to build up the heart and lungs." Lt. Gen. Bohannon looked for little or no help from the medical profession, which he said had failed to recognize the current health gap—"the gap between absence of disease on the one hand and true *joie de vivre* with all its energy, vitality, and wellbeing on the other."

Bohannon then spelled out a program of an 8-minute calisthenics warm-up, 20 minutes of walking-jogging or jogging, followed by a cool-down of 5 minutes of walking—all of this to be done three times a week. "It is time," he said, "for every American to ascertain his proper program and get with it." However, the NJA has never had more than a few thousand members.

Another military man, Air Force doctor Kenneth Cooper, spread the jogging message in the late '60s, and the effect was almost revolutionary. Publication of his book *Aerobics* in 1968 set millions of people to jogging. But many, if not most, dropped out after a few days or weeks.

Dr. Cooper, a by-the-numbers researcher, did a prodigious amount of work on the effects of exercise. He documented its benefits to the heart, lungs, and muscles. He even systematized the relationship between muscular effort and future health. He said, "I'm practicing preventive medicine."

This methodical, scientific approach has given his book a solid foundation—solid enough to convince him that every American should follow his program. Obviously, not every American has followed it. Cooper, according to *Time* magazine, has enlisted eight million citizens in his program of graduated exercises (mostly jogging) designed to protect against [coronary artery] disease and prevent premature death. But these figures must include anyone caught on the street after curfew or noticed inquiring the way to the nearest YMCA.

I suspect that "aerobics" has not had more converts because Cooper seems to view fitness in a vacuum. Cooper's tables measure, as Bobby Kennedy once said of the gross national product (GNP), everything except what makes life worthwhile. The GNP, said Kennedy, can tell us everything except why we are proud to be Americans. Cooper's stats tell us everything except why people run and cycle and swim and enjoy using their bodies.

That, of course, is the key. And until Cooper and others interested in the preservation and perfection of the body spell this out, we will make little progress.

They are, you see, relying on individual conversions. And even Bucky Fuller, possibly the world's greatest optimist, has little faith in changing man. Change his environment, Fuller advises. It can be done without that, of course, but only by the way we are protected against smallpox and polio. By force. Shots for everyone will become athletics for everyone, and in doses recommended by medical authorities. Attention, America! Now run, jump, do anything to raise your pulse to 120 beats for 30 minutes a week.

But there is an alternative to the athletic-state or the exercise-your-heart-ailments-away argument of the aerobics plan. The answer is to consult your friendly neighborhood athlete, be he runner, tennis player, or average half-court basketball player. Why does he do it?

A composite of this latter-day athlete would show him to be little different from everyone else on the block. The future concerns him little. He is practically and philosophically a "today" person, a member of the "now" generation, whatever his age. Instant gratification is his mark.

This guy has discovered the truth of Brian Glanville's statement: "If you do not exercise the body, it corrupts—and the mind corrupts with it."

The neighborhood athlete is willing to let you in on the secret. Running pays off, and it pays off today. Exercise gives instant and exhilarating effects. There is a natural high to be obtained legally.

But to have this, we must tailor the addiction to the addict. Pick his sport according to his body build, his psychological needs, and the demands of his culture. The 5'6", 130-pound loner will find satisfaction where the corpulent, gregarious bon vivant would go nuts. The broad-shouldered, well-muscled extrovert is in a different category yet.

Some people need contests which are essentially a struggle with self, and others need games which are a classroom in interpersonal relationships. And those games may have to be games of chance or skill or strategy, depending on the individual. This complexity should not worry us, for it explains our failures and points the way to a rational plan for everyone to adopt.

Armed with this, Dr. Cooper could offer the athletic equivalent of the "Vermont Alternative" suggested by ex–New Yorker Bill Allen. "It offers," wrote Allen about Vermont, "an oasis of sanity and survival in a world full of suffering, cruelty, and chaos . . . and an answer to the question of the 1970s: 'Is there life after birth?' Not frenetic or freak-out life, but close to the heart's desire and a kind of grace beyond confusion."

Play and games and sport offer the same oasis. Only non-athletes will consider this an exaggeration.

—DR. SHEEHAN ON RUNNING, 1975

———————◆———————

WILL JOGGING BE ONLY a temporary insanity like Hula-Hoops, the twist, and psychoanalysis? Such an opinion was advanced not long ago in a "Talk of the Town" column of the *New Yorker.*

"Jogging is a pastime of overpowering ennui," according to this urbane commentator who sees only ultimate boredom for the jogger, followed by a return to a "short snooze, a martini, and the evening news."

To those of us who are mainline joggers and get withdrawal symptoms if we go more than 48 hours without running, such opinions seem incredible. And to compare our consuming avocation adversely with golf and tennis because we lack the "coordination and physical skills to pursue these difficult, interesting sports without embarrassment" is to miss entirely the total involvement of running.

This is not to say that there won't be dropouts, and many of them, from the jogging program. Chesterton wrote that you should never do anything "merely because it is good for you." Those who do will invariably be found out and will return to more palatable pursuits.

For those who endure, running will bring those values sought by all men: the habit of contemplation developed in solitary long runs; the art of conversation found again in running with a companion; the sense of community born in the communal anticipation, agony, and eventual relaxation of the competitive race; and, finally, the development of maximum physical capabilities which in turn help us to find our maximum spiritual and intellectual potential.

This is no small package. And if the *New Yorker* essayist sees only boredom on the faces of the joggers he observes, it is because he views the harried look of the average urban dweller as normal. What the jogger's face shows is not boredom but contemplation, which Thomas Aquinas described as man's highest activity save one—contemplation plus putting the fruits of that contemplation into action.

Be assured that true joggers will not be deterred by the *New Yorker* article any more than our forebears were discouraged a century ago by the editorial in *Scientific American* which accused oarsmen and long distance walkers of "pleading the old cant of promotion of health and all the rest of it," and warned that these activities would not be beneficial.

We do indeed plead the old cant of health, but are even more concerned about "all the rest of it"—i.e., the contemplation, conversation, and community that this activity offers.

Joggers May Be Running to an Early Grave

Faced with a headline like that, what do you do? Read the article, certainly. So now you know that some San Francisco researchers compiled reports on sudden deaths from coronary artery disease and found that more than half of them occurred during moderate to strenuous activity. Now what do you do? To jog or not to jog, that is the question.

Intellect, reason, intuition should go into that decision. How can I be the best possible me? What is the only possible life for me to lead? Can all this be accomplished without daily and vigorous exercise?

I doubt it. I also feel the dangers of strenuous exercise have been exaggerated, its value underrated. Any number of studies has shown that people who exercise regularly have fewer heart attacks than those who don't. Studies have also demonstrated that regular exercisers have a substantially better chance of surviving a heart attack should they have one.

In a 3-year Health Insurance Plan of New York study of 110,000 people, physically active men had only one-half the number of heart attacks of the inactive men, and in the most active men only one-eighth the number of deaths.

Such results have been repeated recently in a survey of 17,000 civil servants in England. There, in men reporting vigorous activity, the relative risk of developing coronary disease was about a third of that in men who did not exercise.

Further, the more active one is, the greater the protection. Dr. Thomas Bassler, editor of the American Medical Joggers Association bulletin, states that mileage is the best protection. He says he has yet to find a marathoner of any age having a fatal coronary attack.*

*EDITOR'S NOTE: Yes, my father could be a bit cavalier when it came to the dangers. Current wisdom says even seemingly healthy distance runners should have a stress test.

Dr. Richard Steiner, a pathologist-marathoner, says, "Long distance runs lower your blood pressure and slow your pulse." On top of that, the jogger-runner stops smoking, loses weight, and develops a relaxed, playful approach toward the absurdities of everyday existence. Distance running, the additive that cleans his arteries, also cleans his mind and soul.

Seen in this light, daily vigorous exercise is needed for the actual as well as the potential coronary victim. Heart disease is, if anything, more an indication for exercise than not. Still, exercise is not without danger. Neither is driving a car and crossing a street. You learn to exercise defensively just as you learn to drive defensively. You don't attack exercise with a stopwatch and measured miles.

"There is no evidence that speed protects," says Dr. Bassler, "but mileage does."

Pace, then, is paramount. Dr. Thomas Cureton has taken 12,000 people through his fitness course without a fatality. He simply uses common sense: a suitable warm-up (up to 20 minutes) to allow the body's physiology to accommodate to its function, and then a pace which the body can handle on a pay-as-you-go, aerobic basis.

The idea that pace is unique for each person goes back to Galen, the medical advisor to Marcus Aurelius. Writing about ball-playing, he said it was the best exercise for the body and lungs, and the most vigorous of all sports. He warned, however, that "the right degree must be found in practice. It cannot be expressed in writing."

Our present-day English translation of that rule is Bill Bowerman's "talk test." Jog or run, says Bowerman, at a pace at which you can converse with a companion. If a slow jog is still too fast for conversation, you have to start with a walk instead.

If you follow this advice, you will have come upon what Francis Bacon called for almost 4 centuries ago: "a safe, convenient, and civil way to prolong and renew life."

Most recreational directors, physical education instructors, and promoters of exercise-for-your-health programs feel much the same as the fellow who finds it difficult to give away five-dollar bills down Main Street. People just won't believe it's for real.

The programs they prescribe seem so sensible and so in keeping with our nature it is incredible that people don't accept them. But facts are facts, and there is no use railing against them. If the plane won't fly, there's no use appealing that the blueprints said it would. A bridge that insists on collapsing in defiance of all engineering theory will not respond to oaths and imprecations. Nor will our neighbors bestir themselves to physical activity unless we find the proper approach to the problem.

Threats fail. Horror stories of future heart attacks, diabetes, and strokes have predictably fallen on deaf ears. People are not inclined to do something just because it is good for them. Athletics in schools should be chosen on the basis of what the teachers would like to do themselves. This is the rule followed by James Herndon, author of *How to Survive in Your Native Land*. What you don't do the students won't do, was what Herndon found out.

"Why should we assume that the kids would want to do a lot of stuff that we didn't want to do, and wouldn't ever do of our own free will?" he asks. "Does the math teacher go home at night and do a few magic squares? Does the English teacher go home at night and diagram sentences?"

What about the physical education teacher? What about the other teachers? Can't they bring to the student the vitality of the drama, the aesthetics that they themselves get out of the sport? Can we find coaches who can make lifelong athletes out of their students?

We have forgotten that we are talking about play. We are dealing with one of the primary categories of life, one which resists all logical interpretation. Play has a deeper basis than utility. It exists of and for itself.

When we expose play to the function of promoting fitness and preventing heart attacks, we change its gold to dross. As countless fairy tales have told us, the choice of treasure over truth will always fail. What we need then is to conserve those mysterious and elusive elements of play which make it its own reward. We must remove anything that suggests practicality and usefulness. What we do must be fun and impractical and useless, or else we won't do it. If we become fit and impervious to heart attacks and all those other dread diseases, it will be because we don't care if we drop dead doing what we like to do.

We should be in sports not because they are practical but because they're not, not because we feel better but because we don't care how we feel, not because our fitness is increased but because we are so interested we don't even notice.

Play is the key. We all love to play. We like only the jobs that have a play element for us. Anything as practical as physical education or physical fitness is not going to get to first base with most of us.

—*DR. SHEEHAN ON RUNNING,* 1975

◆

TRIED AND TRUE RULES of the road for runners:

I. Keep a record of your morning pulse. Lie in bed for a few minutes after you awaken and then take your pulse. As your training progresses, it will gradually become slower, and after 3 months or so it will plateau. From then on, should you have a rate 10 or more beats higher than your morning norm, you have not recovered from your previous day's runs, races, or other stresses. Take a day or more off until the pulse returns to normal.

2. Weigh regularly. Initially, you will not lose much weight, and getting on and off the scales will seem a bore. Subsequent losses should be in the area of one-half to one pound a week. This equals 250 to 500 calories a day in output of energy over intake of food. What you lose in fat you will put on in muscle. Running consumes 100 calories a mile, and there are 3,500 calories to a pound, so you can see weight loss will be slow unless you do heavy mileage.

3. Do your exercises daily. The more you run, the more muscle imbalance occurs. The calf, hamstring (back thigh), and low-back muscles become short, tight, and inflexible. They have to be stretched. On the other hand, the shin, the quad (front thigh), and belly muscles become relatively weak. They must be strengthened. There are specific exercises geared to strengthening these muscles.

4. Eat to run. Eat a good, high-protein breakfast, then have a light lunch. Run at least 2, preferably 3 hours after your last meal. Save the carbohydrates for the meal after the run to replenish muscle sugar.*

5. Drink plenty of fluids. Take sugar-free drinks up to 15 minutes before running. Then, take 12 to 16 ounces of easily tolerated juices, half-strength "ades," tea with honey or sugar, defizzed Coke, etc., before setting out. In winter, that should be all you need. In summer, take an additional 10 ounces of fluid every 20 minutes during the run.

*EDITOR'S NOTE: Current wisdom is to fuel with a small dose of carbs right before running to give your body energy to burn instead of potentially burning your body's protein stores.

6. Run on an empty colon. Running causes increased peristalsis, cramps, and even diarrhea. Having a bowel movement before running and particularly before racing prevents these abdominal symptoms.

7. Wear the right clothes. In winter, this means a base of thermal underwear followed by several layers of cotton or wool shirts, at least one a turtleneck. Wear a ski mask and mittens. Use nylon, Gore-Tex, Lycra, or polypropylene if necessary to protect against wind and wet. In summer, the main enemy is radiant heat. Remember to wear white clothes and use some kind of head covering.

8. Find your shoes and stick to them. Heavy people do better in tennis shoes and basketball sneakers. High-arched feet do better with narrow heels. Morton's feet (short big toes, long second toes) may need arch supports in the shoes. If a shoe works, train in it, race in it, and wear it to work.

9. The fitness equation is 30 minutes at a comfortable pace four times a week. Your body should be able to tell you that "comfortable" pace. If in doubt, use the "talk test." Run at a speed at which you could carry on a conversation with a companion.

10. Run economically. Do not bounce or overstride. You should lengthen your stride by pushing off, not by reaching out. Do not let your foot get ahead of your knee. This means your knee will be slightly bent at footstrike. Run from the hips down with the upper body straight up and used only for balance. Relax.

11. Belly-breathe. This is not easy, and must be practiced and consciously done just prior to a run or a race. Take air into your belly and exhale against a slight resistance, either through pursed lips or by a grunt or a groan. This uses the diaphragm correctly and prevents the "stitch."

12. Wait for your second wind. It takes about 6 to 10 minutes and a one-degree rise in body temperature to shunt the blood to the working muscles. When that happens, you will experience a light, warm sweat and know what the "second wind" means. You must run quite slowly until this occurs. Then, you can dial yourself to "comfortable," put yourself on automatic pilot, and enjoy.

13. Run against traffic. Two heads are better than one in preventing an accident. Turn your back on a driver, and you are giving up control of your life. At night, wear some reflective material or carry a small flashlight.

14. Give dogs their territory. Cross to the other side of the road and pick up some object you can brandish at them. Never try to outrun a dog. Face the dog and keep talking until it appears safe to go on.

15. Learn to read your body. Be aware of signs of overtraining. If the second wind brings a cold, clammy sweat, head for home. Establish a [Distant Early Warning] line that alerts you to impending trouble. Loss of zest, high morning pulse, lightheadedness on standing, scratchy throat, swollen glands, insomnia, and palpitations are some of the frequent harbingers of trouble.

16. Do not run with a cold. A cold means you are overtrained. You have already run too much. Wait at least 3 days, preferably longer. Take a nap the hour you would usually spend running.

17. Do not cheat on your sleep. Add an extra hour when in heavy training. Also, arrange for at least one or two naps a week, and take a long one after your weekend run.

18. When injured, find a substitute activity to maintain fitness. Swim, cycle, or walk for the same time and at the same frequency you would normally run.

19. Most injuries result with a change in your training. A change in shoes, an increase in mileage (25 miles per week is the dividing line; at 50 miles per week the injury rate is doubled), hill or speed work, or a change in surface are all factors that can affect susceptibility to injury. Almost always there is some associated weakness of the foot, muscle strength/flexibility imbalance, or one leg shorter than the other.

20. Use of heel lifts, arch supports, modification of shoes, and corrective exercises may be necessary before you are able to return to pain-free running.

21. Training is a practical application of Hans Selye's General Adaptation Syndrome. Stress is applied, the organism reacts, a suitable time is given to re-establish equilibrium, then stress is applied again. Each of us can stand different loads and needs different amounts of time to adapt. You are an experiment of one. Establish your own schedule; do not follow anyone else's. Listen to your body. Train, don't strain.

—THIS RUNNING LIFE, 1980

I HAD COME TO Dallas to champion the cause of physical exercise for patients with lung disease. I was at the respiratory therapists' annual meeting to deliver the usual message: "Treat the whole patient." Specialists tend to forget this. They forget that disease is only part of the problem, and that they must treat the patient's illness and predicament as well.

Disease is a biological process. Illness is the impact that disease has on a patient's life. The predicament is the psychosocial situation in which the patient lives. There are instances where the disease may not be improved in any way, yet treating the illness and the patient's life situation can give almost miraculous results.

Specialists—and these respiratory therapists were specialists—know too much about disease and too little about health; too much about the limitations of the body and too little about its potential; too much about what goes on in their primary interest (in this case the lungs) and too little about what goes on in the rest of the body.

Just before my talk in Dallas I had taken a tour of the convention floor. One booth after another displayed machines and devices designed for new and better ways to diagnose and treat pulmonary disease. One instrument could take ordinary air in your house and change it into 95 percent oxygen. When I took a deep breath, another converted it into a computer printout with a half-dozen tests and graphs of my exhalation.

Now I was on the podium asking the therapists to turn their backs for a moment on all this shiny equipment. I wanted them to discard their specialist mentalities about the human body. For my allotted minutes, I wanted to be talking to generalists who saw that everything was connected to something else.

The lungs, I told them, do not exist in a vacuum. In real life they are connected to the heart, and the heart to the circulatory system, and the circulatory system to the muscles. Anatomy does not begin and end with the bronchopulmonary tree.

This holistic approach to the patient is extremely important in lung disease. Without it, the therapist may not understand the use of exercise in treatment. Exercise, you should know, has a bad name among the pulmonary specialists, because it does not improve pulmonary function. Study upon study has shown that.

"Breathing exercises and similar gymnastics performed under controlled conditions," reported one investigator, "have no substantial effect on ventilatory capacity and blood-gas tensions in groups of patients with obstructive pulmonary disease." This investigator went on to suggest that any improvement that occurs is psychological and due to the enthusiasm of the physician.

I looked out on the therapists and went immediately to the attack. I conceded that pulmonary-function tests don't change. Forget about these tests, I told them. Learn exercise physiology. Learn that the adaptation to exercise occurs mainly at the level of the heart, the circulatory system, and the muscles. The lungs deliver the oxygen, it's true, but the heart and muscles can learn to use it more efficiently.

The factors that influence our aerobic capacity are mostly circulatory and muscular, regardless of lung capacity. Indeed, even when the heart cannot improve, the changes at the muscular level can result in major improvements in aerobic capacity. Bengt Saltin, the Danish exercise physiologist, has made this point repeatedly.

"Increases in maximal aerobic power that accompany physical conditioning," he writes, "are predominantly due to increased muscle blood flow and muscle capillary density."

Get rid of your old ideas about the lungs, I told the therapists. They are not all-important. The lungs, I said, are no more than the gas tank. They take in the gas, which is oxygen. When you have a patient with lung disease, that gas tank is smaller. That makes things difficult but not impossible. The logical thing to do is to increase the efficiency of the car and engine so that you can get farther on that gas.

That is what exercise does. First it streamlines the body by lessening the percentage of body fat. Then it delivers more oxygen through an increase in blood volume and an increase in capillaries in the muscle tissue. The heart pump is improved, so all of this takes place more easily. And when this oxygen is sent to the muscle, more of it is taken up. Studies have shown that the difference between the oxygen going in to muscle and the oxygen in the veins coming out of the muscle is increased.

These are things none of the technology in the convention hall could do. What was needed was a solid understanding of exercise physiology. Then these specialists could treat patients with an air of confidence in an atmosphere filled with optimism. Enthusiasm always helps, but it also helps if you understand what you are doing. It is not enough to determine to treat the whole patient. You must first learn how that whole patient works.

—HOW TO FEEL GREAT 24 HOURS A DAY, 1983

———◆———

"HAVE YOU NOTICED," ASKED the man at the Boston airport, "that there is one place where there are never fitness programs?"

This man was an expert on fitness, a runner who had turned his avocation into a livelihood. He had run the marathon the previous day and was now returning to California, where he headed a firm that set up fitness programs for corporations.

I also am an expert on fitness—at times, it seems that all my time is occupied by fitness. I am continually in contact with people who are engaged in some way with fitness activities. But I had no ready reply to his question.

When I asked where this place with no fitness programs was, he answered, "The hospitals."

I knew he was right. Except for an occasional cardiac rehabilitation unit, most hospitals do not have fitness programs for either their personnel or their patients. Aerobic exercise is rarely used in a hospital setting. Seldom is a patient encouraged to make the effort to become fit.

Shortly after that conversation, I learned this truth firsthand. I injured a calf muscle and was unable to run, so I went to a hospital physiotherapy department to work out on the exercise bicycle while the muscle healed.

I had not been there in some time. For the past 2 years, my medical chores have been limited to reading EKGs and giving stress tests. I no longer manage the day-to-day care of patients, so I have no occasion to visit most of the hospital.

The physiotherapy department was twice as big as I remembered it and filled with a variety of new electrical machines. In almost every booth, there was a patient being treated passively on a table. In the midst of this impressive professional activity was the lone exercise bike, an ancient cast-iron monster called the "Everlast."

I mounted the bike and pedaled furiously for about 30 minutes. When I finished, a therapist came over to me. "Doc," he said, "you are the first one to use that bike in 2 years."

The one training machine in the department, the mainstay of any fitness program for the diseased or handicapped, had not been used in all that time.

"The last one to use it," he said, "was Felix."

I remembered Felix. He had been my patient. His chronic lung ailment made him short of breath at rest, and he could hardly make it from the bed to the bathroom. Felix was in and out of the hospital like a yo-yo. When I sent for his old records, I was told they might have to be brought in with a cart. Felix was a constant problem for himself and his doctors.

One day, it occurred to me that training might help him. Before I began running, I was out of breath after running 100 yards.

My improvement in endurance was not due to my lungs. My vital capacity, always high-normal, had never changed but my fitness had. Perhaps Felix could improve without changing his lung function.

"Felix," I told him, "you are going to PT tomorrow and pedal that exercise bike until you're exhausted. And you'll do that every day until you go home."

He did, and the change was remarkable. He still wheezed at rest, but his walking improved tremendously. Felix left feeling better than he had in years.

He came back to the hospital, of course. When he got home, he just sat around. You cannot put fitness in the bank; you have to earn it every day. So Felix returned for treatment—but at longer intervals than before, and he stayed for shorter times. During each subsequent admission, he rode the bike daily until he went home. Now, nobody rides the bike. No patient in this 600-bed hospital is training for endurance. No one is working for maximal physical function, no physician is employing physiology in the treatment of disease, no physician is treating the whole patient. Nor am I to be excused. When I left my practice, I forgot about Felix and the bike. It had been a one-time thing, and he had been the only patient I'd ever sent to use the bike. It did not occur to me then that there was a major role for fitness in the hospital.

It is quite understandable why there are no fitness programs in hospitals. The doctors know too much about disease and too little about exercise physiology. They rightly say there is no evidence that disease is in any way influenced by exercise. But they know so little about exercise that they are unaware of how much every patient will profit from training, regardless of the disease.

Improving physical work capacity will also improve the capacity to deal with any disease. Well-trained muscles can compensate for handicaps in other systems. Physicians have yet to elevate their consciousness about these capabilities in their patients and their own opportunities to develop them. Hospital patients follow orders. They can be sent to physiotherapy, told to pedal to exhaustion, made to become fit. Unfortunately, this unique opportunity for both physician and patient to use fitness is too often wasted.

—*RUNNER'S WORLD* MAGAZINE, OCTOBER, 1981

◆

UNLIKE MOTORCARS AND ALMOST every other mechanical device in this technological age, people do not come in new and improved models. Infants born this year will differ little from those born in the fifth century B.C. The rules for the sound body in which to house the sound mind are still the same. In health and fitness there is indeed nothing new under the sun.

Our science is, of course, much more complex. We have discovered more and more of the sophisticated mechanisms that make the body work. Yet all that we know can be reduced to one rule: "Use the benefits or lose them," and one admonition: "Use the benefits correctly."

The general rule has to be applied to a particular body. Each one of us must know what is best for us. By the time we are 21 the individualities should be ready to live our own personal versions of the good physical life, following Breslow's seven rules, based on the research of this famous husband-wife team of public health experts at UCLA.

EAT A GOOD BREAKFAST: Culture, experience, and tradition have made breakfast our principal meal. Wherever hard work is done, a big breakfast becomes the rule. When I travel the country I see the evidence of that still on the menus. In Arizona, the cowboy's breakfast; in Anaheim, the trucker's breakfast; in Minnesota, the farmer's breakfast.

DON'T EAT BETWEEN MEALS: This rule becomes easy to follow after a good breakfast. Otherwise we continue to follow the 90-minute feeding cycle of infancy. For the adult animal such behavior is inappropriate. We are responding to messages that are not there.

MAINTAIN YOUR WEIGHT: This must, however, be lean body weight. We should not gain in fat, and/or lose muscle. We should weigh what we did in our youth. If we do, we find that the rate of aging is so slow as to go almost unnoticed. Our weight and percentage of body fat are good indicators of how seriously we take our obligation to be fit.

DON'T SMOKE: Tobacco is simply an obvious example of any number of substances hazardous to our health. We should avoid all pollutants to whatever extent is possible.

DRINK MODERATELY: Unlike tobacco or other harmful agents, alcohol in small amounts seems to add to life rather than diminish it. High-mileage runners never smoke, but some have as many as three or four drinks a day. The evidence is mounting that two drinks a day may help an individual to live longer than one who drinks more or less. The reasons for this are not clear.

GET A GOOD NIGHT'S SLEEP: Sleep needs are clearly particular to each individual. It is essential to discover one's own sleep requirements. Incorporation of naps, now generally discredited, may bring us additional benefits.

EXERCISE REGULARLY: The fitness formula is a matter of mode, intensity, frequency, and duration. We must use large muscle groups as we do in walking, cycling, swimming, jogging, cross-country skiing, rowing, or any other similar activities. This exercise should be done at a comfortable pace (that middle ground between hard and easy) for 30 minutes, four times a week.

If you recognize these rules, it might not be because they go back to the Greeks and the Romans but because they go back to the Mets and the Knicks and the Rangers.

—HOW TO FEEL GREAT 24 HOURS A DAY, 1983

What Dr. Sheehan Means to Me

BY ALBERTO SALAZAR

AS YOU A YOUNG athlete, I remember trying to read as much as I could about how the world's best runners trained. Admittedly, I would pass right over Dr. George Sheehan's columns and essays, as my mind was solely focused on beating my competitors and running a personal best. At the time, I had little concern for the philosophical affairs of running and good health Dr. Sheehan wrote so eloquently about.

Although this attitude propelled me to a handful of victories and records, my unbreakable regimen of hard training and well-publicized death-defying racing wore me down. This likely cut my competitive athletic career short of its full promise. I didn't properly listen to my internal cues when my mind and body were telling me that I needed to take time for rest and recovery. I was, in Dr. Sheehan's words when describing a common misstep so many of us make, a "blind and deaf tenant" of my own body. Perhaps had I read a bit more of Dr. Sheehan as a youngster, I would have learned at an earlier age that taking the time to recharge my body, mind, and soul was just as important to my personal success as hard mile repeats on the track. Fortunately, it was a mistake that I wisely learned from, and I am now a much better coach for it.

As I now know, Dr. Sheehan's written words are not just for the nostalgic, quixotic, or philosophical reader. If you still have that competitive fire and you are willing and able to push yourself to achieve the goals you have set out for yourself, then read as much of Dr. Sheehan as you can get your hands on. All the keys to unlocking your potential and achieving your goals are right there in Dr. Sheehan's verses.

5/ Train*ing*

I just have to run at a comfortable level. Fast enough to dispel my worries about the world. Fast enough to enjoy the workings of my body. And slow enough to let me observe the world around me. Slow enough to escape into the world within.

—*RUNNER'S WORLD* MAGAZINE, DECEMBER 1988

MY PROGRAM GOES BACK almost 30 years, to my start in road racing. I took my cue from observing the old-timers in the game. Train 5 miles a day, 5 days a week, take a day off, and then race. Over the years, I modified this regimen, taking more and more days off, putting in one training day on the track doing interval quarters, but still racing every weekend.

At times, I've been astounded by how little training I need once I reach a peak. On occasion, I've limited my entire running program to one race a week, with no training in between. I followed such a schedule for as long as a month with no noticeable change in my racing times. I know of other runners who, for one reason or another, had to reduce their running to one race a week and had the same experience. One of my most formidable age-group competitors ran only on weekends, 20 miles on Saturday and a race on Sunday. I rarely beat him.

It now appears that other runners have also discovered that "less is more." The Bare Minimum Track Club in Columbia, South Carolina, has followed a program much like mine with considerable success. Members have done measurably better in both the 10-K and the marathon despite reducing their mileage to about 30 miles per week.

The Bare Minimum program centers on a long group run on weekends and a track workout every Wednesday night. Members claim that some of their success stems from other features of their program. "Bare Minimers" have learned to "reel out" other runners, widening their lead gradually rather than surging ahead, especially in the beginning of a race. They can also be distinguished from other competitors by a "brook trout" expression on their face—totally relaxed, mouth agape, a look that accompanies top performance achieved with minimum effort.

Research, however, would credit the success of the Bare Minimum program (and mine) to our high-intensity training. A report in the *Journal of Applied Physiology* on the relative importance of duration, frequency, and intensity in aerobic power and short-term and long-term endurance emphasized the paramount role of intensity. In this study, runners began by training 40 minutes a day, 6 days a week, running as fast as they could. Then in three separate trials, they reduced either frequency or duration or intensity. When intensity was maintained, reducing frequency by one-third (running 4 days a week instead of six) or duration by one-third (28 minutes instead of 40) had no effect. Further decreasing frequency by two-thirds (2 days a week) and duration by two-thirds (15 minutes instead of 40) had only minor effects over a 15-week period.

However, running less intensely while maintaining both frequency and duration caused significant decreases in oxygen uptake, heart function, and long- and short-term endurance (all measures of physical capacity). What's more, these dropoffs occurred rather rapidly—within 5 weeks of changing the training program. The·conclusions: Frequency has little effect on running ability, and duration is important only when reduced by two-thirds.

All this suggests that runners can cut their running programs significantly and still run as well (or even better) than usual. First, take off 3 days a week. On the remaining 4 days, run for a total of 3 hours. This may include a short distance race, a workout of interval quarters, and a couple of longish runs—45 minutes to 1 hour at an easy pace.

This is not to say that frequency and duration are unimportant. But it points out that high-intensity training—namely, interval training and races—is the key to getting the most out of one's ability with a minimum amount of time.

There are hazards, of course, to such programs. While high mileage can lead to injury, high intensity may lead to staleness. My difficulties have rarely been due to overtraining. More often, they've been due to over-racing. So from time to time and especially after setting a PR, I find it helpful to back off from interval workouts and to substitute leisurely runs to allow my body to recoup. There is a time, as the French farmers say, "when the land must sleep."

—RUNNING TO WIN, 1991

WHEN I RETURNED TO running, I had quite modest ambitions: a mile or so on the 10-laps-to-the-mile track I had marked out behind my house. But that mile became five, and then I began to venture out on the road. The five became ten, and then I discovered the races.

With my first entry blank, I entered a new world. Before me was a cornucopia of excitement and achievement extending from the mile to the marathon. What started as a minor aberration turned into a monomania.

Man, we know, is never content. The jogger who is able to run previously unthinkable distances at previously unthinkable speeds wants to do better and better. The person who thought 3 miles an incredible distance and 10-minute miles an incredible pace is no longer happy with either accomplishment. The entry blank changes all that. Once a newcomer enters a race, there is a new set of standards, a new set of values. Play becomes sport, which is play raised to the highest degree in its demands and its rewards. Sport is play taken seriously. It asks for the individual's best and will commend nothing less.

Racing was an education for me. I quickly learned the facts about two new variables: place and time. I discovered that place was not that important. It would vary with the number of people in the race. The bigger the field, the more people who would beat me and the more people I would beat. Place was secondary.

It was time that mattered. It was those minutes per mile that I carried home with pride or disappointment. It is minutes per mile that bothers almost every runner. That statistic leads to the failure-to-thrive syndrome, the runner who hits a plateau and cannot seem to improve. The complaint now is, "I've gotten this good. Why can't I get any better?" When I failed to improve, it was not that I was training too little. It was that I wasn't doing the right kind of training. I needed the long, slow distance to build up my endurance. But I also needed training of the anaerobic kind for speed and for stamina. This is energy produced in the absence of oxygen. It is the ability to go into oxygen debt and not develop too much lactic acid. The best way to teach my body that ability is to do interval 440s or 880s at the pace I set as my goal.

When I finally accepted that truth, I joined a high school track team and began to do speed work 2 days a week with the milers. Five years after I began running, I ran my best mile of 4:47, and 10 years after I began, I ran my best marathon of 3:01.

What I discovered, and you should know, is that improvement is not linear. It is cyclic. I also discovered that training is not like money. You cannot put it in the bank and save it. You have to go out continually and fight again and again for the desired improvement. If I am to run a 5-minute mile again, it will mean a lot of "bottom" work and a lot of painful "sharpening" work as well.

I spoke of that with Roger Bannister, hoping he knew of an alternative. I asked him about racing a few more 5- and 10-milers or doing stadium steps, or perhaps some real long runs.

"George," he said, "you are avoiding the truth. Interval work is the only answer."

The worst-tasting medicine always works best. But like all cures, it must be taken only as directed.

One summer I had a lingering leg injury and could not run for about 2 weeks. I swam instead. Long distance in the ocean. Interval sprints in the pool.

I would do the length of the pool, about 50 yards, at close to top speed. Then climb out, walk back, and do it again. Fifty yards swimming is roughly equal to 200 yards running on the track. An all-out 50 yards in the water takes just as much out of me, and possibly a little more since I am a runner, as a 220-yard sprint.

The sensations are much the same. With each one there is a gradual buildup of pain. Discomfort first, then the leaden ache in the arms and legs, finally the whole body screaming. And each successive interval raises the base line of that pain a notch or two higher.

One day I was in the final stages of such a workout, feeling and, apparently, showing the ordeal. I was putting myself through. A woman who had been watching came up to me.

"Dr. Sheehan," she said, "I hope you are writing all this down somewhere."

She found the entire episode incomprehensible. Yet at the same time she realized that there must be something here that had value. There must be something worth all this effort and suffering.

There are, of course, physiological reasons for running interval sprints. These sharpening techniques are the final preparation for my assaults on my best times at almost any distance. Intervals raise my anaerobic threshold. They enable me to cruise at a higher speed. Interval quarters done once a week will improve my times noticeably within a month.

But such inducements are not what keep me doing just one more, and then another, and another, testing myself again and again. The physiological formula doesn't require those final two or three. The more painful they become, the less need to do them. So why do I continue? What is actually happening when I do these interval workouts?

As I see it, interval training is as much for the will as it is for the body. I am getting my will ready for the race. I am, in fact, running the race in advance. I am trying to reach that interval quarter that will feel exactly the same as the last lap of a race. And then be able to deal with it mentally as well as physically.

In interval quarters the will is paramount. The will makes me finish one interval. It calls up the energies to do another. William James, who was a student of the energies of man, wrote much on this. He was vitally interested in how·we could mobilize the forces which we contain deep within us.

For James this effort was the measure of man.

"Effort," he wrote, "is the one strictly underived and original contribution we make to this world." Everything else is given to us. Health, strength, talent, abilities of all sorts, whether spiritual or mental or physical. Effort is the only element we can add. "He alone is happy," James wrote, "who has will. The rest are zeroes. He uses, they are used."

Otto Rank, who was Freud's protégé, also wrote extensively on the same subject. Like James, he was concerned with the heroic and the exuberances of man. For him as well, the will was all. The will was our only real resource in dealing with life, which Rank viewed as an irrational situation from which there was no escape. We have to deal with the fact that we have been given this will to immortality, despite the reality that we must die.

We all respond to this paradox in our own way. We ignore it, explain it away, find security in belief in the hereafter, or deal with it at a personal level. This last, said Rank, depended on the will. A person, he thought, experiences his individuality in terms of his will. His personal existence is identical to his capacity to express his will in this world.

I know of few better ways to reach this primitive level where will and effort combine than interval quarters. The answer to life's question becomes simply, yes or no. There is no place for explanations, qualifications, excuses. Will I or will I not continue until I know this is truly the last lap?

I remember one time running interval quarters in a high school stadium during football practice. There were 50 or more football players on the field going through drills. They took no notice of me as I did one repeat quarter after another. That day as always the laps gradually became more and more difficult. After each successive interval my distress became more obvious. The gasping more noticeable. The groaning a little louder.

Finally I collapsed on the grass, knowing there was only one more quarter in me and then only if I could force myself to do it.

I lay there for the longest time. The two minutes had almost expired when I finally raised myself, got to my hands and knees. Then I noticed that practice had stopped and they were watching me, curious to see what I would do. It was as if I were an animal hit at long range and they were waiting to see if I would get up and trot off into the woods.

Then I did get up and started jogging slowly to the starting line.

Behind me I could hear this cheer ringing, and then someone shouting, "Way to go, Doc."

I will not last forever, but I am damn well going to know I have been here. That day, so did they.

—*THIS RUNNING LIFE,* 1980

WHEN I TRAIN, I am pushing myself to the absolute limit. I am testing the furthermost reaches of my body's integrity. I am trying to go beyond anything I have done before. I am seeking the breaking point of my physiology. Should I pass that limit, I should get more than a slap on the wrist. I should get appropriate punishment, some clear signal that I have exceeded my capacities. And I do. It is called "staleness" and consists of a variety of symptoms which·add up to remind me that I am mortal.

When I get stale, I accept this reminder of my finitude. I relax and vegetate. I eat and sleep and nap. Instead of running an hour a day, I take a nap for an hour a day. This routine usually proves to be sufficient penance, and in a week or 10 days I am back running at a suitably lower level.

However, there are runners who find that eating and sleeping and napping are not enough. For them, the fatigue persists; the depression goes on, the zest will not return, the curse will not lift. For these runners, days become weeks and weeks, months—and still running is a chore, and performance is never quite the same as before. They are in the dark night of the soul.

Brendan Foster, a world record holder from Britain, once described a distance runner as a person who went to bed tired at night and got out of bed even more tired in the morning. I think he was wrong. That is the description of a distance runner headed for trouble. When that state occurs, it is time for rest and reassessment.

Plato said we needed a more sophisticated form of training. It is time we heeded his advice.

In running, as with everything in life, there can be too much of a good thing—too much training but especially too much racing. It is extremely hard to resist the excitement and challenge of a race. So the runner can become over-raced just as the tennis player is over-tennised and the golfer is over-golfed.

My mail is filled with letters about this phenomenon: high school seniors who have never achieved their sophomore promise, college runners now unable to get back to what they did in high school, club runners who are getting worse instead of better, runners everywhere wondering why their bodies are breaking down.

It is a mystery, this state of staleness—the heavy legs, the rapid pulse, the frequent colds, the loss of zest, the poor performances. There is no specific test that can pin it down. Nor is there any test that will warn me when I have reached my peak, and the next race or hard workout will send me over the cliff into a state of fatigue and depression.

That knowledge is just what we need. The runner who is in peak condition is only a razor's edge from catastrophe. A personal best time is, to be sure, an occasion for joy and celebration, but it should also make the runner quite cautious about trying to better the performance immediately. I have come to the conclusion that the proper response to running an outstanding race is to take a week off to savor it.

Intelligent runners tend to do that. In fact, the winner of one 56-mile Comrades run in South Africa took 6 weeks off before resuming training. Few of us, however, have that common sense. Few of us read our bodies that well. A great race, we are inclined to think, is evidence of an even greater race inside. With a little more speed work and some time on the hills, who knows what marvelous things can happen? The marvelous things, however, often turn out to be those dismal complaints.

The clearest warning of impending staleness is a bad race. Nine times out of 10, this slump means the runner is overtrained, but the impulse is to go out and train harder. That only digs the pit deeper. The proper approach to this all-too-human problem is to recognize the wisdom of Ecclesiastes, which says there is a time for everything. There is a time to race, a time not to race. There is a time to be elated, a time to be depressed. There is a time to be king of your hill, a time to be at the bottom of the heap. There is a time to train, a time to nap.

When you restore the Biblical rhythm to your days, you will be able to accept staleness. And when you do, it will disappear.

—*THIS RUNNING LIFE,* 1980

———◆———

A FEW YEARS AGO, in a column complaining of having to run races measured in kilometers, I wrote, 'We think in miles. We train in miles. We should race in miles." Now that I'm 70-something, I would like to amend that statement: "I think in minutes. I train in minutes. I race in minutes."

In recommending an attitude that ignores distance, I'm following rules set forth by exercise physiologists. They've always told us that the formula for achieving fitness is a matter of frequency, time, and intensity. The seminal work on fitness resulting from jogging, cycling, and walking, done by Michael Pollack, PhD, and his colleagues, makes no reference to distance whatsoever. Likewise, most fitness programs described in scientific journals, as well as those in the popular press, are based on some formula of frequency, intensity, and time. You won't find any mention of mileage.

Since entering my eighth decade, I can apply this concept to my running. I now realize that running has never been a matter of distance. It has always been a product of intensity over time. The results produced by this equation range from comfort to pain and even agony. The distance I cover while this equation is played out is immaterial.

This wisdom evolved as my ability decreased with age. Expending the same effort (about 95 percent of max) for the same length of time, I cover about one-third less ground than I did 10 years ago. A 10-K has become a very long race. In my early sixties, I would finish in 40 minutes. Now after 40 minutes I still have a mile and a half to go.

In the past, I considered the 5-mile run the optimal race.

Now my 5-mile time is longer than I used to average for a 10-K. So I am inclined to favor the 25 minutes it takes me to run 5 kilometers.

Minutes also become important in hot-weather races. Meet directors usually put the first water stop at 3 miles. That's okay for the front-runners, but for me and my friends, who arrive at that point 25 to 30 minutes after the start, this is a long time. So I'm careful to drink as much fluid as possible just before the starting gun sounds. When I reach the water station, I drink twice as much as I would have in previous years, because now it takes me longer to finish the race.

But race directors don't control my training; I do. And I define my training in terms of time. When people see me out on the boardwalk, they often ask how far I am running. I usually answer, "45 minutes," or on some days, "An hour." My body knows time and intensity. It is not aware of distance.

I run these minutes at a comfortable pace, which allows me to spend most of my time in deep thought. But after running for an hour, my body begins to protest. I stop thinking, and I wish I were home.

When I was younger, I ran my hour at a thinking pace as well, but I covered a lot more ground. Then I knew how many miles a week I ran, but now I don't. I'm putting in the same number of minutes, however, as I have always done. My training formula hasn't changed.

The same phenomenon has occurred in my interval training. Two age groups ago, I did my repeat quarter-miles virtually flat out in 70 seconds. Now I go virtually flat out for 70 seconds and stop wherever I am. I am holding to the same time and intensity formula as before.

Injury prevention follows the same formula as fitness. The books tell us that the frequency of injuries rises rapidly when mileage reaches 40 miles per week. But injuries result from repeated impact at footstrike, and almost all runners, whatever their age or ability, take 5,000 strides on each foot per hour. So the critical factor in injuries is time, and injuries begin at 4 hours of training per week, not 40 miles.

Measuring runs in miles instead of minutes is a big mistake. Using time and intensity as guidelines will make the necessary adjustments as performance decreases with age. As I grow older, I find the running experience has not changed. The secret is to focus on logging in the same amount of time rather than the same number of miles.

—*RUNNING TO WIN,* 1991

I WAS RUNNING ALONG an ocean road when a young man came alongside and asked, "How fast are you going?" He obviously expected an answer in minutes per mile. He asked the question of a novice. I gave him the answer of a veteran.

"Comfortable," I said.

My pace is not a measure of the distance I can cover or how fast I can go. I gauge my intensity with my body—not with a stopwatch or mile markers. I dial my body to comfortable, not knowing or caring about my exact per-mile pace.

In the beginning, I was like the runner who questioned me. I wanted to know exactly how far I had run so I could calculate my speed. I would count laps on a track or even drive my car over my road routes so I could be absolutely sure.

At times this was frustrating. I would lose count of the laps. I used my fingers and got mixed up going from one hand to the other. I couldn't remember if I had run 20 laps or 21 or some such number. Looking back, I can see how ridiculous this scorekeeping was. As I matured, I realized neither distance nor speed mattered—only the time spent at a comfortable pace.

When this runner caught up to me, I did not know whether I was running 8-minute miles or 10-minute miles. Nor did I care. I had put my body on automatic pilot and taken off into my head. This was my thinking pace—one I can hold indefinitely. Some days it is faster than others, but it is always comfortable.

I hoped he would stay and chat, but he sped on. I let him go. Staying with him would have brought me out of the comfort zone. Rarely does my training require that level of effort. I spend time training for thinking or talking, for contemplation or conversation. Neither can be accomplished when I step up the pace.

Pain or shortness of breath has no place in my daily runs. I make no room for pushing to the limit. Those tortures come every week-end. They permeate part of every race. My weekday runs give me time-outs from all stress, physical and mental. They become retreats inside myself or opportunities for a revealing talk with a friend.

The other day, after I finished an out-and-back run with another runner, he said to me, "That was the shortest hour I've had in some time." We had run at a pace congenial to communication. We occu-pied the world on the other side of sweat. There, competence and self-esteem make me feel at my absolute best; thoughts and feelings ordinarily too private to utter come spontaneously from my lips. Recently, when I ran an hour with my daughter, we had the best talk in memory.

How fast must I go to enjoy these unexpected gifts from running? Do they occur only at a certain minute-per-mile speed? No. I just have to run at a comfortable level. Fast enough to dispel my worries about the world. Fast enough to enjoy the workings of my body. And slow enough to let me observe the world around me. Slow enough to escape into the world within.

A comfortable pace exceeds the physical. Comfortable has to do with my mental and emotional state as well. Comfortable touches my entire person. When I am comfortable, I am finally at home with myself. I am an animal happy in its habitat. I have said yes to myself and to life. My comfortable pace allows me to meditate on the chal-lenge of living—and bring back something to help me deal with it. In that way, I get through my life until my comfortable run tomorrow.

—*RUNNER'S WORLD* MAGAZINE, DECEMBER 1988

WHEN YOU TRAIN, THREE things happen to your muscles, and two of them are bad. The prime movers, the power muscles, become short and inflexible. The antagonist muscles that modulate the action become relatively weak. This strength/flexibility imbalance causes or is a major contributor to injuries in our various sports.

When a person is involved in a sport that demands thousands of repetitions of a particular movement, these imbalances are bound to occur. Training of the legs, for instance, results in development of the muscles of the back of the leg, the thigh, and the low back. At the same time muscles of the shins, front thighs, the abdomen, and the buttocks become relatively weak.

These postural weaknesses put abnormal stress on the foot, leg, knee, thigh, and low back. A variety of overuse syndromes can then occur. This is especially true if there is some associated structural weakness.

The short, powerful calf muscle combines with weak shin muscle in contributing to such injuries as shin splints, Achilles tendinitis, plantar fasciitis, and calf cramps.

The muscle imbalance from the knee up causes malposition of the pelvis and a host of problems involving the low back, sciatic nerves, and hip joints.

Prevention is best accomplished by regular remedial exercises. The three muscles on the back side of the body must be stretched. The three opposing muscle groups on the front of the body must be strengthened.

The stretching is easily described and appears quite simple but must be done with great care. At no time should there be pain or discomfort; the limiting point should be simply a feeling of tension.

The first exercise is performed standing an arm's length away from the wall with feet flat on the floor. Lean forward until your chest is against the wall, feet still flat and the body forming a straight line from heel to chest. Hold for 10 seconds. Then return to upright. Repeat 10 times.

The second stretch consists of standing on one leg, knee locked, and placing the other straight leg (knee locked) on a step, stool, or table depending on your level of flexibility. Attempt to touch your head to your knee—you may achieve only an approximation. Again, do not go beyond feeling of tension. Hold for 10 seconds then return to upright. Repeat 10 times.

The final stretch is the backover. Lie on your back on the ground, legs out straight, knees locked. Bring legs over your head toward the floor behind it. Touch floor if possible, but under no circumstances go beyond the feeling of tension. Hold for 10 seconds then return to resting state. Repeat 10 times.

The strengthening exercises involve the opposing muscles. The first two use weights of 5 to 10 pounds (or a paint can with water). Sit on the edge of a table and place the weight over the foot. Now flex the foot upward, keeping the leg immobile. Hold for 10 seconds. Relax. Repeat 10 times.

Next, still sitting on the table and using the same weights on the foot, straighten the leg and lock the knee. Hold for 10 seconds. Relax. Repeat 10 times.

The final exercise is the bent-leg sit-up. Lie on your back with your knees bent and your feet flat on the floor. Now tighten your buttocks and bring your head and upper chest to a 45-degree angle off the floor. Hold for 10 seconds. Relax. Repeat 10 times. Have some-one hold your feet or lock them under a chair, if necessary.

Done on a daily basis, these small groups of exercises will provide considerable protection against the injuries that beset athletes. When injury does occur, they should be used in conjunction with other forms of therapy.

—RUNNING TO WIN, 1991

———————◆———————

SUMMER IS HERE, AND the water fountain is back in operation on the back porch of our beach house. On these hot, humid days, run-ners are regular visitors to this little oasis. They interrupt their miles on the boardwalk to refresh themselves with the clear, cool water, then move on.

The water fountain was my wife's idea. She believes that no one drinks enough water. And she's right. Half of what is the matter with us now, and most of the terrible things that will happen to us in the future, are due to not drinking enough water. We don't follow the time-honored prescription of eight glasses a day to flush out our sys-tems. And runners are prime offenders. They lose more fluid than they take in. For the runner, water loss is continuous and inexorable. We breathe out water, we sweat out water, we lose it through our kidneys. While we carry enough fat to run on for almost a week, and have enough air available to go indefinitely, we can lose water at a rate that can incapacitate us in as little as an hour or two.

As a matter of fact, the average person (and certainly the average runner) is usually in a mildly dehydrated state. We cannot rely on thirst to tell us when to drink. "Listen to your body" is a rule that works in almost every instance—except with thirst. Thirst is a sensation that lags behind the body's needs. Thirst is an unreliable reporter. So fluid balance is an area where common sense takes precedence over body wisdom.

I first learned this when I was an intern. I did my own laboratory tests and soon found that most patients' urine had a high specific gravity, a sign that the body is concentrating urine to conserve water. Most patients, I discovered, drank a little less water than they needed. Later, I saw a report that even patients with kidney stones, who were specifically instructed to drink more water than their bodies told them to, also had urine with high specific gravity. If this is so, what about the runners going by our beach house? Usually, they are dripping with sweat, their T-shirts sopping wet. Some look as if they just stepped out of a shower. If they began their run with a fluid deficit, they are certainly risking dehydration problems from then on.

Most of the boardwalk runners do forget to take fluids before they start. By the time they reach·our house, they're like Samuel Coleridge's Ancient Mariner—"Water, water everywhere, nor any drop to drink." They are ready to appreciate the refreshment one gets from clear, cool water.

Obviously, runners should consume enough or even an excess of fluid before beginning a run. The most accurate way to determine this is to check the specific gravity of the urine. In my medical practice, I used a urinometer, which is no more than a glass tube that holds the urine and a glass measuring device you float in it. There is also a test tape made by the Ames Company that can be dipped into the urine and then read directly. The goal is a specific gravity reading of less than 1.010.

Having sufficient fluid aboard makes everything easier.

The runners who use our fountain have come to know they feel better if they drink water about every 30 minutes. Otherwise, their performance suffers. When dehydration occurs, body temperature rises, greater demands are made on the heart to dissipate heat, and the runner faces the possibility of heat exhaustion or heatstroke.

So pay special attention to fluid intake. Drink enough before the run. And rest assured, water brings relief without bloating. Also, taking time out from a race to stop for a drink will save time later. The runner who stops for water will run faster and longer than those who are in too great a hurry to make a pit stop.

I make my own pit stops at the water cooler—the first just before I start, 10 solid gulps; the second when I return with the sweat dripping off me. With the second fill-up, the water has a special quality. It reminds me of another water source in my youth. In my teens, I played golf in the summer on a course that had a spring on the 13th hole. I remember it was a par-3, the tee high on a hill, and we hit out over some woods to the green below. In the woods on the path to the green was a spring with a constant stream of water. By the time we reached the spring, we were hot and sweaty and dusty and tired. We would take turns with the ladle, savoring the cool, satisfying taste. Stopping at that spring was always the highlight of our round. At the time, I couldn't think of a drink that could compare to it.

But now I've found something almost the equal of that golf course spring—our beach house water fountain after a long run on a hot summer day.

—*RUNNING TO WIN*, 1991

WHEN I BEGAN RUNNING again at age 45, I became my own coach. I had to. At that time, no one was interested in the training of a middle-aged runner. No one was writing about the conditioning needs of aging athletes.

It was left to me to decide on goals and a training schedule. I had to determine the correct frequency and intensity and duration of my workouts. I was an experiment of one. And lacking both instruction and experience, I was forced to learn by my mistakes.

There is a saying among medical students: If you treat yourself, you have a fool for a patient. The same saying applies to coaching. Someone has to keep his head while you are losing yours. Someone must resist the pressures of pride and ambition, of wishful thinking and dreams of glory. Someone must stand back and see things as they are, and must make the difficult decisions. It takes a sound mind to train a sound body. And when ego is involved, sanity is likely to get trampled.

I was no different from many others. I immediately fell into the pit. I committed all the cardinal sins of coaching. My first and most serious error was to set unreasonable goals. I was influenced by my early running success. There is always that initial quantum leap in running capability. The ease with which I progressed from a brisk walk to an easy 2 miles persuaded me that such improvement would follow an upward spiral to infinity.

Once I was running well, I expected to run better and better: break 5 minutes in the mile, go under 3 hours in the marathon, catch up to those youngsters 25 years my junior. I looked for too much too soon.

Unreasonable goals mean unreasonable training. I had hardly broken in my shoes when I got caught in the mileage trap. I was soon putting in more weekly distance than I had done on a championship cross-country team in college. When not accumulating mileage on the road, I did interval work on the track and headed anywhere within a 2-hour drive of home looking for weekly road races.

The inevitable occurred, again and again: staleness, exhaustion, and sickness. I finally realized that the more I did, the worse I became. What I hadn't realized yet was that Hans Selye was right. The body can be trained to greater performance by inducing stress. But the amount of stress and the time allowed for recovery are critical to the success of the process.

I also developed injuries. Again, these came as part of high goals and heavy training. Long mileage, hills, and speed work breed injuries. I went through periods of shin splints and Achilles tendinitis, runner's knee and heel-spur syndrome. Each month brought a new and depressing injury because of overuse. Worse, I tended to ignore them. Like many other runners, I ran hurt. I would not let an injury or an illness force me to miss a race for which I had trained for months.

The run-despite-injury-or-illness attitude is almost universal. The glamour events in road running always have their share of runners who would be better off as spectators. I had a telephone call from just such a runner in South Africa 2 days before the 55-mile Comrades Marathon. He had recently gone through a weeklong fever of such severity that the doctors had seen fit to do a spinal tap to rule out encephalitis.

"Would it be all right," the runner asked, "to run the Comrades?" He had been training for this race for 6 months and could not bear to miss it. When he finished his question, I asked one in return: "Do you have a family?" Only someone alone in this world, whose survival mattered only to himself, would run the Comrades in that condition.

It is difficult when you act as your own coach to understand that running is a lifetime activity. Short-term triumphs matter very little. There will always be another race, another marathon, another Comrades, even another Boston. It is possible to miss the race next Sunday and survive.

I was slow to learn this, of course. I realize now that my early goals were too high. Runners are much like racecars. We have a built-in range of performance. Eventually, I modified my training. I took one day off a week, then two. Now, I do as little as 30 miles a week and find I can still race well, even continue to improve. I limit my intervals to those few weeks before the three or four races a year that I want to run especially well. I accept my cycles. The times when I run well don't spur me to train more. Nor does a bad performance get me out early the next day to put in extra miles.

I still make occasional mistakes as I coach myself. However, there are compensations. Being my own coach has taught me to be independent, to trust my own experience, to learn from my mistakes. Being a coach has made me an expert on myself.

The mistakes I have made in coaching are no more than the mistakes I make in living: unreasonable goals, misguided efforts, short-term views, and the failure to recognize what is important. I see that now. Running not only has made me a coach; it has made me a philosopher.

—*RUNNER'S WORLD* MAGAZINE, JANUARY 1981

ONCE I AM UNDERWAY, I enjoy running in winter weather as much as any other time of the year. The cold doesn't bother me. Once I am warmed up, once my core temperature has risen that necessary one degree, once I have reached my second wind, I run as comfortably as I do in May or September. The drivers, who pass by wondering why I am torturing myself, are no more cozy, snug, and warm in their cars than I am in my running gear. Running in cold weather is not torture; it is fun, invigorating, life-giving fun. All I need to do it is a little willpower and some common sense. The willpower is that extra push that gets me out the kitchen door. The common sense I have acquired through numerous experiments is dressing for winter running. I have learned through experience the rules that govern the choice of clothes for a run on a cold winter's day.

The best way to keep heat in is to use several layers of light material. Such "layering" allows the air between each layer to act as insulation. I like to have cotton next to my skin, then wool if it is cold enough outside, and finally a nylon mesh T-shirt which is both water-repellent and wind-repellent. I use nylon shorts for the same reason.

So I begin with cotton long johns, then follow with a cotton turtleneck shirt. This covers the arteries in my neck. For me, this protection for my neck is essential. No matter how warmly I dress, if my neck is exposed I feel cold.

The lesson I learned quickly was not to overdress. When I do, I sweat so much the clothes soak through, and I immediately lose heat and rapidly feel cold. It is amazing how little clothing is needed on a frigid day. The experts estimate that the amount of clothing needed to sit around in 70-degree temperatures is sufficient for running at

45 degrees Fahrenheit. Some runners prefer to wear clothes made from Gore-Tex, Lycra, and polypropylene.

One way to avoid wearing too much clothes is to use some temporary insulation which can be discarded after the run or race is underway. I frequently use newspapers under my T-shirt for this purpose. As soon as my body warms to its task, I get rid of them. Meanwhile, my overdressed colleagues are stuck with several extra items of outerwear.

Another method of temporary heat conservation is to use the plastic covers that come on clothes from the dry cleaners. I cut a hole for my head and arms and wear it. This is especially effective in difficult wet-cold conditions, those days when it is about 35 degrees and sleeting with winds of 15 to 20 miles an hour.

Covering the head and covering it well is essential. I am told we lose 40 percent of our heat through our head. I believe it. For me, running without a ski mask is next to impossible. The mask warms the air I breathe, and then my exhaled breath keeps my face warm. In fact, one of the most enjoyable things about winter running is being inside that mask. It is also the answer to that frequent question about freezing the lungs.

The experts tell us there is no such thing as freezing the lungs. All the air that is inhaled is filtered, warmed to body temperature, and completely saturated with moisture long before it reaches the lungs.

Still, the mask is what makes me believe what they say. After the mask come the mittens, not gloves. Gloves separate the fingers, allowing heat to escape. I like wool mittens, but when the thermometer starts to hit bottom I switch to down mittens with a nylon cover.

On occasion, I have used heavy wool socks either alone or over mittens and found them to work well.

Oddly, with all this attention to other target areas, my feet have given me little trouble. Tennis anklets seem to be enough. However, I do use leather running shoes, which may give me added protection.

That about does it for my clothing. There is, however, another staple item in my ditty bag which I find indispensable in cold weather: Vaseline. I apply it liberally to my face, cover my ears, then work on my hands and use what is left over on my legs. Even where body areas will be under layers of clothing, I use Vaseline and have the impression it helps a great deal.

There is one other thing I must remember to do before I open the kitchen door: I have to remove my wristwatch. It has a metal band and can become so cold it is painful to wear. On a long run, I usually end up taking it off and holding it.

Now I am ready for the road. I have enough layers of clothing artfully arranged to handle the weather outside. I have taken into account the temperature, the wind-chill factor, the presence of rain, snow, or sleet.

What remains to be determined is which way to run. Shall I go north or south, east or west? At other times of the year, direction is chosen by whim. Here, it is by wind. The rule in winter is to go out against the wind and come back with it.

In running, as in life, if you follow a few simple rules, half the battle is won.

—*RUNNING & BEING,* 1978

WHEN IT COMES TIME for my hour run, my body can't wait. It will accept no excuses. It interrupts my thoughts, interferes with my thinking, and will not let me be. Once that feeling arises, everything, however important, must be put aside. Like a dog going for its leash or scratching at the door, it badgers me until I give in.

My body wants out, and I don't blame it. During the working day, my troubles are psychosomatic. My body is reacting to my mind, and my mind is reacting to the innumerable aggravations and upsets and embarrassments which go with living with people and deadlines and goals and obligations. My body is the victim of the tension and guilt and anger that go with failing to meet the demands of others and, even worse, myself.

Before the sun is at noon, my autonomic nervous system is in disarray, and my visceral brain is about to throw in the towel.

Anything from a late start in the morning to a yet-to-be-opened letter from a lawyer affects that poor body. What I forgot to do or don't want to do or did badly is constantly reflected in the reactions of my body. The knowing observer can see it all: the shifty eyes, the hang-dog expression, the meaningless smile, the body hunched, the head tucked in, the slouching walk.

I know it in other ways. My hands are clammy, my head aches, and my sciatic nerve sings with pain. I am beginning to hear from my intestines. The belches are here, and I sense the stomach filling with acid. Lower down, the colon is in spasm. No wonder my body wants out. It has had enough of manning the barricades.

So the moment I suggest a run, my body goes crazy. It starts jumping up and down (inside, of course) and making joyous sounds (inaudible, to be sure). It begrudges the time needed to get ready. I have, on occasion, been known to start undressing in the car on the way home. My mind and will are little more than onlookers of this dash to freedom.

Still, once out the door my body accepts the leash. It is willing to wait for the second wind. So I trot that first mile, deliberately making it very easy. I allow myself to savor the initial feeling of release, to experience that sensation of escape. And then I am on the river road, away from traffic, alone on that silent road. I slip the leash and let the body go.

The Swedes call it *fartlek,* which means running play. It is simply the body running for fun, running how it pleases, running at the speed the body wants—easy or hard, fast or slow, jogging or sprinting, dashing up one hill and coasting down another, racing from one telephone pole to the next and then barely moving through the grass, feeling it soft and springy beneath my feet.

The body is in command. The mind can do nothing but follow. My soma is healing my psyche. If you saw me now, you would call out, "Looking strong, Doc, looking strong." I feel that way, too—strong and competent and a little proud. For once this day, I am doing what I do best and doing it well.

William James had it right: "To make life worth living, we must descend to a more profound and primitive level. The good of seeing and smelling and tasting and daring and doing with one's body grows and grows."

I can feel that good growing. My body and I go for a long 10-miler every other day now. Listening to it has convinced me that anything every day is too much. There were days, you see, when I took my body out whether it wanted to go or not. It was like dragging a reluctant pooch by the neck. But my body loves those tens. Even a mile from home, when you would think it would slow down and just enjoy, I find my body accelerating.

When I say, "Hey! Slow down and think of tomorrow," what I hear back is, "That's your problem. Tomorrow is my day off."

—*THIS RUNNING LIFE,* 1980

———◆———

IT OCCURRED TO ME while running that there must be an equivalent training program for the mind. "A sound mind in a sound body" implies that physical and psychological fitness must proceed from the same principles, in fact from the same source.

The basis of the sound body is, of course, stress—stress applied in measured and constantly increasing quantities with suitable intervals of time between to allow the body to adapt. What makes this process work, however, is play. What makes us fit must be sport, or we won't participate. What makes us healthy must come from a self-renewing inner compulsion, or we won't persist in it. What makes us athletes must become an essential part of our day, or our bodies will rebel against it. If play is the answer to our physical life, should not play be the answer to our psychological life as well? Does not our mental health depend upon play as surely as our physical health does? Will not the play that made us athletes also make us saints?

I put it to you that it does. There is no question in my mind that the best way to handle psychological stress is play. The surest way to develop a sound mind is through humor. How better, then, to deal with stress than with humor?

Humor allows us to tolerate the intolerable, to accept the unacceptable, to bear the unbearable, even to understand the incomprehensible.

Humor gives us the capacity to live with ambiguity, the courage to take chances, the strength to go forward without solutions.

What humor does is reduce life to the game that it is. It allows us to take a long look at the real world and all that is evil about us, yet to know that it is somehow part of the plan. Only a sense of humor can help each of us face those great unanswerable questions: Why was I born? Why am I here? Why must I die? What must I do to make my life a triumph?

—THIS RUNNING LIFE, 1980

———◆———

I NEVER SUCCUMBED TO the lures of high mileage. I was a member of two intercollegiate championship cross-country teams, yet I don't recall doing more than 5 miles in any given practice. When I returned to running in the 1960s, I found that the veterans I met trained 5 miles a day and ran a race every week. And that's been my practice ever since. Except for races, I remember running more than 10 miles only once or twice.

We forget that Roger Bannister broke the 4-minute-mile barrier on 5 hours of training a week. Bannister later wrote that an additional 10 seconds of improvement would require four times as much training.

Research by exercise physiologist Dr. David Costill confirms Bannister's theory. Dr. Costill found that the greatest percentage of improvement occurs with 25 miles a week. Close to maximum improvement takes place with 50 miles a week. Beyond this—training as much as 200 to 225 miles per week—resulted in no further increase in maximum oxygen uptake or the ability of the heart to pump blood. In fact, training beyond 50 miles a week reduces a runner's anaerobic strength (that is, non-oxygen-using effort), which affects speed and the "push" at the finish.

I discovered these truths on my own. First I found I could run a respectable marathon on 30 miles of training per week. By observing my colleagues, I also figured out that if I doubled my weekly mileage, I could probably improve my marathon time by 5 minutes. But in return, I would risk the staleness, illness, and injury that comes with excessive mileage.

I also had to deal with my body. It likes to run 45 minutes to 1 hour and not much more. When I ran a 10-mile loop, I always spent the last 15 to 20 minutes wishing it were over. By then, the optimum time for creativity, thinking, and problem solving had passed. My body wanted to be home. (And so did I!)

I refer to this productive time for thinking as the "third wind." A "second wind" occurs about 6 to 10 minutes into the run, which physiologist Walter Cannon described as "an almost miraculous refreshment and renewal of vigor." Then, about 35 minutes out, there is this third wind, and with it comes a rush of ideas, memories, and experiences associated with whatever topic I have chosen to think about.

—*RUNNING TO WIN*, 1991

———◆———

I'VE NEVER RUN A mile I didn't like. Every mile I run is productive, either for my body or for my mind. Every minute spent on the roads is a reward in itself. I follow my own schedule. I run because I want to, not because some expert tells me I have to. When I read about some of these high-mileage programs, I ask myself two questions: "What would I gain?" and "What is the cost?"

Any gain from high mileage follows the law of diminishing returns. The more miles I put in, the less I have to gain. The cost, on the other hand, has the opposite tendency. The more miles I log, the more illness and injuries are likely. Even worse, I run the possibility of staleness and burnout—frightening possibilities, since I am determined to run as long as I live.

Yet runners maintain the notion that the more they run, the better they will get. Some years back, I got a call from a woman runner who had sustained numerous injuries and periods of staleness and overtraining. "Am I fated never to be able to run over 70 miles a week?" she wailed. She wouldn't listen to my answer that her body would do best on a lot less.

Bill Bowerman, thought by many to be the greatest American coach, has made his views on the subject known: "The idea that the harder you work, the better you're going to be is garbage." Perhaps that's why those many unneeded miles on the road are called "junk miles," of little value to the body or the brain.

—*RUNNING TO WIN,* 1991

IF AN INDIVIDUAL DECIDES to exercise, or go into training, or become an athlete, just how should he go about it? In other words, what is the fitness formula? What factors go into the equation that provides us with energy and the ability to do work?

Most experts in exercise agree on the specifics. Few take exception to fundamentals of exercise physiology as they are now understood. You can be confident that attention to the following four factors will make you fit.

MODE OF EXERCISE: Large muscle mass must be involved in the exercise. The majority of the benefits of exercise occur in the muscles; therefore, the more muscle used during the exercise, the better. Walking, jogging, swimming, and cycling are the staple methods. As are, of course, aerobic dancing, cross-country skiing, rowing, backpacking, rope skipping, and other activities that might come to mind.

You are looking for stamina, so conventional weight building is not recommended. Muscle men do very poorly when they get on a treadmill and go on to exhaustion. Only by turning lifting into an endurance activity, by using very light weights and innumerable repetitions, will you achieve fitness through weight lifting.

DURATION: The average workout should be at least 30 minutes, with a cumulative total of at least 2 hours a week. This activity should be continuous, as it is in running and swimming. Otherwise, as in tennis and other racket sports, it is best to have a friend hold a stopwatch on you to see how much of the time you are actually in motion.

This "30 minutes" eliminates any attention to miles or laps. There is no need to count anything except minutes. The training effect has to do with time—and the next variable we must consider:

INTENSITY: Most exercisers want to know how fast they should go. At what speed should the activity be performed. The answer is simple: Listen to your body. Go at the effort that the body says is comfortable—somewhere between fairly light and somewhat hard. This factor is based on the Swedish physiologist G. A. Borg's theory of Perceived Exertion, the idea that the body knows what it is doing.

"Most individuals," writes Dr. William Morgan, the sports psychologist, "are capable of rating the perceptual cost of physical work in an accurate, precise, and consistent manner." Most of us can rate exertion better than any test procedure, because this perception involves processes that are not as yet accessible to our technology.

So when you exercise, use Perceived Exertion. Dial your body to comfortable. Put it on automatic pilot, and then forget what you are doing. If this is all too new to you, you could also start by using the "Talk Test": the ability to converse comfortably with a companion and exercise at the same time. This will keep you in the correct aerobic range until you relearn the ability to read your own body.

FREQUENCY: The usual recommendation is to exercise every other day. This gives the body a chance to recoup. Glycogen replacement in the muscles will usually take 48 hours. Other neuroendocrine stresses probably take this long to adapt as well. Rest, as Olympic runner Noel Carroll has pointed out, is when the training effect takes place in the body. This is the time when the body adapts to the applied stress.

I prefer going 45 minutes or so instead of 30. My mind seems to open up more with the longer runs. When I stop at 30 minutes I feel I am missing something. So I usually do 45 minutes or an hour, two or three times a week. A friend of mine (a walker) once told me of similar feelings. "The first 30 minutes is for my body," she said. "The second 30 minutes is for my soul."

Running is a low-budget sport. Except for shoes, everything you need is already in the house. Once you have bought a good pair of shoes, the only other expense should be entry fees. The total outlay for the year should average little more than pennies a day.

It will, but only if you learn to deal with your injuries. Running is an inexpensive pursuit on paper, but not on the roads. Once mileage builds up, most runners develop injuries. And most injuries develop doctor's bills. Costs begin to mount. In the course of treating shin splints or runner's knee, a person can run the gamut of health-care specialists and incur bills that exceed the monthly rent.

I follow two rules in treating my running injuries. First, I treat myself. I do this even though I could see my colleagues without charge. I have discovered that I know more than they do. Not because I am a physician, but because I am an experienced runner and now know things I was not taught in medical school. Given some surgical felt and a pair of scissors, I can shape any number of devices to put in my shoes and help my troubles.

I have also discovered a number of materials and appliances that have been useful in treating my various injuries and overuse syndromes. A little diligent searching in drug stores, running shops, and surgical supply houses has uncovered most of the equipment I have used over the years. A partial listing would include the following:

ARCH SUPPORTS: These range from Dr. Scholl's Flexos, available in drug stores, to the heavier and more expensive ones displayed in shoe stores and surgical supply places. Dr. Scholl's 610's, Spenco, and other serviceable ones are generally available.

ORTHOTICS: These differ from arch supports in providing correct placement at all points of the foot strike. They are especially needed when pronation is severe. Mine are made for me by a sports podiatrist. There are, however, cheaper over-the-counter ones available.

SHOCK ABSORBERS: The first and still the favorite is the Spenco innersole. A new entrant untried by me is sorbothane, a much heavier material.

HEEL LIFTS: I avoid compressible sponge rubber. Mostly I use surgical felt, which tends to bottom out but usually not before it has done its job. For permanent heel lifts inside the shoes, the best are leather, available in shoe repair shops.

AIR STIRRUPS: These new and quite marvelous devices allow a person to run with a sprain or even a stress fracture. They cast the leg, preventing lateral movement but allowing both plantar and dorsiflexion.

KNEE STRAP: Another new and effective device. A simple band that goes just below the kneecap and reduces symptoms in most knee problems. It acts on the same principle as the tennis elbow strap. It reduces the movement of the patellar tendon.

ZONAS TAPE: Made by Johnson and Johnson and not sold in drug stores. It must be obtained at surgical supply houses. It tears easily, molds to the skin, and is superb for the treatment and prevention of blisters.

TINCTURE OF BENZOIN: This is sticky stuff that can be sprayed on the skin before you apply the tape.

HEEL COUNTER SUPPORTS: These are plastic bands that can be cemented around the heel of the shoe to give better protection against pronation. They can convert a shoe from being the cause of the injury to becoming the cure.

HOT AND COLD PACKS: To be used on injured area before (hot) and after (cold) running. Just as good, and perhaps better, is the ice-massage Popsicle you can make yourself with a paper cup and a tongue depressor placed in the freezer.

SAND WEIGHTS: These are a luxury but do make strengthening exercises for the shin and quads more convenient and a lot easier. Much less awkward than the paint can, the usual home trainer.

SACROGARD: A small sacroiliac belt for about $10 which maintains the pelvis in proper position. No replacement for a girdle of muscles but will do part of the job until you do the rest.

SURGICAL FELT: With this and a pair of scissors you can become your own podiatrist. You can make almost anything needed to support the foot. These can then be taped to the foot or a Spenco innersole.

The self-treating runner may use all this equipment and fail to make the one change necessary for relief. A change in shoes. I have found that when these measures fail it is usually the shoes that have caused the problem. The heels are worn down, or the heel no longer controls the foot. Getting a shoe with excellent rear foot control can be decisive.

My second rule? If these efforts fail, see the best. I go to someone who has learned how to treat injured runners through treating thousands of injured runners. The books on this have yet to be written. It is worth the travel and the expense to see the expert.

It pays, as they say, in the long run.

—*HOW TO FEEL GREAT 24 HOURS A DAY,* 1983

What Dr. Sheehan Means to Me

BY NINA KUSCSIK, THE FIRST WOMAN TO
OFFICIALLY RUN THE BOSTON MARATHON

WHEN I ENTERED THE running world by running the Boston Marathon in 1969, I learned about the New York Road Runners and all the local races right here in New York.

Right after Boston, I started running races with the New York Road Runners Club. The races were mostly in the Bronx, and the awards were given out in the men's locker room, which I was allowed to enter. I met and learned so much from these runners. Dr. George Sheehan was there with us, and I learned that he believed and supported the idea that just like men, women could also benefit physically and psychologically from the pathways that road running provided.

My favorite memory of Dr. Sheehan came not from running, however, but from his speaking.

He was so humble and would always get very nervous before speaking at clinic lectures for runners. He usually paced back and forth a bit to calm down. But once he started talking, he was great and the lectures were always so focused, with really important information for runners to remember and use in their training and their races.

For the Boston Marathon, there was always a preparation speech the evening before the race. In 1976, with Dr. Sheehan scheduled to speak, the weather forecast for the next day predicted a temperature of 96 degrees. Dr. Sheehan was nervous as usual, pacing back and forth a bit on the stage. Then he began his talk with these words: "Someone's going to die tomorrow." He immediately got everyone's attention. The audience was extremely silent and listened carefully to his advice for the next day's race. The thermometer did touch 96 that day, and I think only one runner went to the hospital and was discharged soon after.

6/ *Racing*

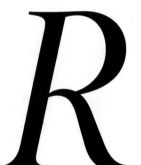acing is a true experience. Only the conditions are

artificial. My entire self is engaged in a genuine struggle against time and distance

and those around me. All my strengths, physical and emotional and moral,

are called upon to decide the issue.

HOW TO FEEL GREAT 24 HOURS A DAY, 1983

"WHAT STRIKES ME ABOUT this whole scene," said my friend who is a playwright, "is how gentle everyone is." We were standing at the finish of the Berkshires Masters Ten-Kilometer Run watching the runners stream by. Beyond the grass homestretch on the soccer field was a small grandstand packed with cheering friends and families. Now and then the applause would rise to another peak as a woman or older man dashed the final yards to the finish.

Only moments before, I had come through that finish line wrapped in that silent struggle with myself, deep in the private torture that occurs in the last stages of a race. I had gone through those final 6 or 7 minutes where just maintaining my pace is a notable act of courage. I had heard the same applause. Gotten my time and number. Shook hands, touched others, been embraced. And now stood filled with those wonderful sentiments that fill my soul after a race.

And as I looked into myself and looked at those around me, I realized my friend was right. Gentle was the way to describe it. Gentle and perhaps one word more. Peaceful. A poet friend of mine had used the word. She had never, she told me, seen a face more filled with peace than mine after a race.

The peace is a positive quality. It is not merely the absence of stress or strife or conflict. It is a peace that is active. A peace that is strong. It is a peace that has certainty. A peace that tells me that I am good and holy and complete.

It is also a peace that is rare. All other acts carry within them a counter reaction. There is the depression that follows exultation. The sadness that comes after ecstasy. Not so with the race and the peace that follows. This peace is the fruit of the race. Something born of that suffering, that testing, that exhibition of character, that attainment of class.

And with it comes the relaxation, the elimination of desires, the end of craving, the death of ambition. For a time pettiness and the lesser appetites and all the meanness are wiped·out. I have put on the new man.

Earlier I had been more concerned with records and performance. While I was warming up a runner came up to me and said, "You'll set a new record, for sure." I thought not. It was my third race in a week and within that week I had been forced to slow to a walk at the 3-mile mark in a training run because of fatigue.

As I had jogged up and down the soccer field where the race was to start and finish, I felt my thighs rubbing together, a sure sign of exhaustion. I stopped thinking then about records and concentrated on the thought of doing my best. I was going to do poorly, I knew, but whatever it was it must be my best.

I need not have worried.

It turned out to be one of those days when everything went well. It was an easy out-and-back course with no hills. The weather did its part: The day was one of those beautiful, dry, clear days in New England, the sky an uninterrupted blue.

Right from the start I felt good and began to feel even better after the first mile. On the way back I felt so strong it was a matter of controlling my speed lest I sprint the entire last 3 miles. I had my age group won and was beginning to think about the record.

The sequence was much like one a psychiatrist-runner had outlined in a letter to me, describing a half-marathon. "As I started the run," he wrote, "I recalled the lines from Wordsworth's 'Happy Warrior.' By the time I had reached halfway I thought of Kipling's 'If.' By the ninth mile I began praying. That carried me until close to the finish, when simple physiology became dominant."

I was reliving that experience along with everyone else in the race. The first half was the Happy Warrior, "playing in the many games of life the one where what he dost most value must be won." Then as I neared the last few miles it became Kipling and the task of "filling every minute with sixty seconds of distance run."

By this time I had the record in hand, but I could not back off. It was no longer my record, it was everybody's record. I was no longer running for myself. I was running for the 430 people in this race and every runner who would look at what a 60-year-old had done and feel proud. Despite the pain I had to break that record by the greatest margin possible.

Then as I searched desperately up ahead for the final turn into the soccer field, it was prayer. The usual prayer of the runner: "Let this cup pass." In the end, of course, it was the body gradually reducing its function, but the will refusing to accept anything but collapse. Trying, in fact, to make the finish and the collapse coincide.

Out of that common experience came the scene that was unfolding before us. This spontaneous meeting of bodies and souls as runner after runner came from that common ordeal. There is no purer embrace, someone once wrote, than that of the vanquished and the victor on the battlefield.

Here was its equivalent, except there was no vanquished. All of us were victors. All of us had gone through levels of effort, levels of pain, and hence levels of performance which were, by standards of our everyday existence, superhuman. All of us were record breakers. We embraced as equals.

The race is the key. The race and everything that happens in it. Mostly, that is pain. Pain that is in time and therefore never ending. Pain that is the negative eternity Hegel wrote about. And because I have lived with this pain and accepted it and offered it for all my fellow runners, I have gained this peace. The peace that is Hegel's positive eternity. The peace that is outside of time and therefore unending.

The last finisher was in and it was time for the food and the awards.

We stood in line for chowder and beans and franks and got our soda and beer. Then we sat at long tables eating and drinking and exchanging stories of the race we had just run and others we could remember.

And a gentle peace filled that Sunday afternoon in the Berkshires in New England.

—THIS RUNNING LIFE, **1980**

THE RACE IS A true experience. Only the conditions are artificial. My entire self is engaged in a genuine struggle against time and distance and those around me. All my strengths, physical and emotional and moral, are called upon to decide the issue.

The race is, as Santayana said, "a great and continuing endeavor, a representation of all the primitive virtues and fundamental gifts of man." Because it involves these primitive virtues and these fundamental gifts, the race is an uplifting event. It tells me previously unrecognized truths about myself. It fills my subconscious with the experience of the "good me." It makes me a hero and floods my innermost life with proof of that fact.

Our highest need is to be a hero. We need heroic experiences to saturate our subconscious, to fill up our psychic reservoir. It is imperative that this "deep well of cerebration," as William James called it, contain good news rather than bad—that what later comes to the surface is positive rather than negative.

But to be a hero, we must find what best allows us to do something heroic. We must find that arena, find that event. In this duel with life, we are allowed to choose our own weapons. We have the right to fight from high ground.

James wrote of this situation in a letter to his wife: "I often thought that the best way to define personal character would be to seek out the particular mental or moral attitude in which, when it came upon him, he felt himself most deeply and intensely active and alive. At such moments, there is a voice inside which speaks and says, 'This is the real me.'"

That is the voice I hear at the race. The race is, for one thing, absolutely true. Everything is seen and felt exactly as it is. The pain is real. The suffering is real. I am challenged. I respond to that challenge. And when I come to the finish line, I am completely spent yet completely happy. I have forgotten momentarily all the bad things about myself.

But the race is more than the moment. The subconscious is being purged and rinsed and cleansed. It is being emptied of all the mean and embarrassing things I have accumulated during my life. My bedrock concept of myself and the world is being refurbished. I am replacing all the depressing memories, all the dirt and debris, with something that is bright and clean and positive. I am hearing the good news.

This is most necessary because the subconscious is the source of all our creativity. Creativity in the arts or in thought or in life situations depends upon a subconscious that contains what is good and true and joyful. It must be kept free of everything that is not.

Hemingway once wrote that he never read criticism of his works because they made his subconscious murky and muddy. And, he said, he had to be kept clean if he was to write.

We don't have to read critics to make our subconscious murky and muddy. All we have to do is go to work, or go to school, or go to church, or even perhaps go home. There are critics all around us. Rarely do we hear anything that would make us feel good about ourselves. Our subconscious is constantly being crammed with evidence of our shortcomings and failures.

The race reverses that. It tells me I am a success. It makes me feel good about myself. And later in the week, this experience percolates out of my subconscious when I am at play—on my training runs, where I am in control, feeling virtuous at an 8-minute-per-mile pace.

Then I write my column, or plan my day, or think in new directions—all because of this new "me" that has come into being.

Our problems are solved creatively, or even left unsolved creatively, only by a profound and thorough alteration of our inner life.

The race is my transforming experience. It causes a profound and thorough alteration of my inner life. The training run is the play in which this experience finds its aesthetic expression. The experience of the race germinating.

Then the freedom of the body and mind takes the event and its meaning, and produces art—the outer form in which life finds expression and support. Whether this is a poem or a statue, a letter or a garden, a recipe or a relationship, makes little difference. Whatever the expression, it will be a new representation of you when you are deeply and intensely active and alive.

Now you can say, "This is me," and be proud to say it.

—*HOW TO FEEL GREAT 24 HOURS A DAY,* 1983

———◆———

I HAD JUST FINISHED the Battle of Monmouth 5-mile race and was standing near the finish line shouting encouragement to the long line of runners following me. Where the race ended, there was a large digital clock so the runners could see at a glance what their final time was. From where I stood, however, a few feet before the finish line, the clock was not visible to them. I was there to alert them to their times.

"Come on!" I yelled to one runner. "You can break 35 minutes!" Then later, "Take it in, you're 39:30!"

And even later, to an aging and overweight and very tired athlete who then broke into a broad smile, "Way to go, you've got 45 beat!"

If you are a runner, you know how important it is to break those 7- and 8- and 9-minutes-per-mile barriers. If you are a runner, you also know that for me and the 300 other runners this race was not play; it was sport. We tend to use the words interchangeably, but there are essential differences.

Running is play; racing is sport. Play is the preparation; sport is the performance. My training is play; my race is sport in its purest expression.

You can see two of the basic elements of sport in the finish line and the digital clock. Sport proceeds within certain limits of time and space. In sport, there is an ending and then a score. Winning and losing are secondary to this absolute need for a final outcome.

In most things in life, there is no score, no objective, tangible, clearcut measure of success. Ambiguity and doubt cloud day-to-day living. It is not enough to be told how good one is at writing or doctoring or lecturing. There is something inside me that wants figures and statistics and facts. For that, nothing can beat the race. The race is the supreme reckoning: a mark down to tenths of seconds, an exact place among hundreds of entrants, a course verified for accuracy, records for comparison, age-group prizes. Who could ask for a better ending?

This finish also guarantees another start. There is always another race and another and another, each pure and complete in itself. Sport is the perpetual second chance. If I fail this week, I may succeed the next. If this digital clock does not give me the desired answer, perhaps the next one will.

Play is only the preliminary to this world of quantifiable excellence. Play has no closure, no urgency, no rules. Play is doing a leisurely 10 miles on a country road. Play is suffering through a set of interval quarters, or sprinting to one telephone pole and jogging to the next. Play is 5 miles of conversation with a plunge in the surf at the end. Play is freewheeling, uninhibited, with no boundaries of time or space.

Sport is, of course, altogether different. When I race over a previous training route, I am now aware that every step matters. A grade unnoticed during a creative reverie now presents a critical test of my pace. A hill not seen as a challenge becomes a pass-fail situation. Long stretches of scenic delight on a boardwalk are now miles of barely tolerable pain.

It is in this encounter with time and space that the runner is forged. The race makes me that athlete. All my potential becomes actual. I leave nothing behind, nothing in reserve. There is only the now, the here, and me in the unity of this effort. Like most common people, I become uncommon only in my sport.

The nervousness and self-defeating tension that accompany many precision sports are rarely felt in distance running. Where skill and strategy and chance are prime factors in the outcome, a player is likely to choke. Running, however, is not that type of a sport. In running, effort alone is the measure of each competitor.

The danger in running is worrying too little rather than too much. I frequently come to the starting line with little thought of what lies ahead. The race is a festival. It is meeting old friends and making new ones. The exchange of gossip and entry blanks for coming races fills the available time from dressing until the race starts.

So I forget the warm-up, I neglect the stretching, I fail to get psychologically prepared for the challenges only a few minutes away.

Then, the gun goes off, and I am overwhelmed by the sudden demands on my body—the swift onset of discomfort, the immediate aloneness that comes with every race.

When I get on the line, I realize that the issue is 90 percent settled.

My recent training, whether I am over or under or at my peak, the state of my health cannot be helped. These factors are out of my hands. They are behind me. I need no longer worry about them. I have to remember only two things: one, not to do anything stupid, and two, not to quit.

My aim in those few minutes before the start must be to create physiological and psychological readiness. The physiological preparation is simple. Ten minutes is usually enough. It takes me just 6 minutes of easy jogging to get my second wind. I then break out into a light, warm sweat. That means I have raised my body temperature one degree, and most of the blood is going to the muscles and skin the way it must for all-out running. I then do a few spurts at close to full speed, a few minutes on stretching, a minute concentrating on form and belly-breathing, and I am physically ready for the gun.

The psychological preparation is just as simple and to the point. The essential is solitude, a brief period alone with myself. First, I go over the course mentally, deciding where the bad spots will be. Then, I concentrate on what is really at stake here. I am in this race to do my best on this course, on this day. It is at that moment just before the gun sounds that I make those resolutions men make before going into battle. I accept what is to come with full knowledge of what it may contain.

Once into the race, I try to do the best with what I have. There is an old baseball adage: "Don't beat yourself." I must be careful not to run the first mile too fast. The race must be run evenly. Too much speed in the beginning and I will pay dearly at the end. I listen to my body, not the watch. After that first mile, I know exactly what I can do. I push to the pain threshold and hold the throttle there.

There have been races where this pace has been so slow and painful I have felt like quitting. I have wondered if there would be a way to drop out without anyone noticing. When this happens, I say to myself, "George, it is not your fault. You are doing the best you can." When I can identify with effort instead of performance, there is no need to quit.

I recommend this attitude. Over the years, I remember winning and losing races, but mostly I remember giving the race my best shot. I will not deny that my few virtuoso performances have helped tide me over some barren stretches. But I know that some of my best races where those in which I ran poor times. It is an old story: We hate to suffer, but afterward we are glad we did.

—*THIS RUNNING LIFE,* 1980

◆

I HAVE A LOVE-HATE relationship with hills. I hate running up hills, but I love the feeling of accomplishment I get when I reach the top. I hate the pain going up, but I love the relaxed sprint down. I'm always looking for a flat course so I can run my best time, yet I look for hills too because I want to meet the greatest challenge.

Hills come in all heights, lengths, and grades. Their impact depends not only on their shape but also on their location along the course. No matter where they are, they tend to separate runners rapidly. A group tightly bunched going into a hill is likely to descend in single file a halfmile farther on.

There are some awesome hills at the beginning of races. The worst I have ever run on was in Wheeling, West Virginia. After the gun went off, we took a little quarter-mile tour of downtown Wheeling, and then came the hill. It was a mile and a half long with a relatively steep grade. Halfway up, I had forgotten about the race. It was just me and the hill, just me and the space of ground between where my back foot pushed off and my forward foot landed.

A limited focus always helps. The mountain climber's rule is "Don't look down." The runner's rule is "Don't look up." One upward gaze and I am overcome by the immensity of the task. The attention must be all inward—to monitoring the pain, correcting the form, and living in that little area. I cannot live in the future that is the top of a hill.

In a race on a flat course, I have to maintain contact with the runners around me. I cannot ignore anyone passing me. On a flat course, I am running all-out from the gun to the finish. It is as close as running can come to being mano-a-mano, an eyeball-to-eyeball confrontation. Hills make for a different race. All runners differ in their ability to take hills. So the hill becomes my competitor, not the other runners. I pay no attention to whom I'm passing or who is passing me.

When I train on hills, I use a trick the weight lifters use. They find the weight they can lift just 10 times. If they can lift it only nine times, it was too heavy. If they can lift it 11 times, it was too light. I find the pace that just gets me to the top without stopping. If I have to quit on the way up, it was too fast. If I am able to keep going past the crest, it was too slow.

One time when I was hill training using this method, I came to a hill and gauged it just right. I ran completely out of gas right at the top. Only it wasn't the top. There was another rise that I could not see from below. I refused to stop and continued up, gradually getting slower and slower. When I finally reached the top, only I knew I was running. A passing motorist might have suspected I was shadowboxing.

When the finish of a race is uphill, it seems as if the effort and any consequent pain is doubled or trebled. The worst of these uphill finishes for me is the Cesar Rodney half-marathon in Wilmington, Delaware. One year, I came to that final torment a yard or two behind a fierce rival of mine. He was, we both knew, in 21st place. This fact was to determine our finish. There were, we both also knew, only 20 prizes. So there was nothing at stake at that point except one of us beating the other. I charged by him, took a dearly bought 10-yard advantage, and beat him handily. He told me later that he saw no point in battling to death over 21st place, so he eased in.

At the post-race ceremony, the meet director announced that they had somehow come up with one more trophy, so I got an award for 21st place. God loves runners who refuse to quit on hills.

—THIS RUNNING LIFE, 1980

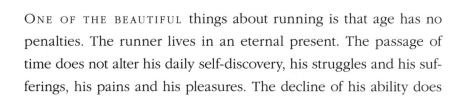

ONE OF THE BEAUTIFUL things about running is that age has no penalties. The runner lives in an eternal present. The passage of time does not alter his daily self-discovery, his struggles and his sufferings, his pains and his pleasures. The decline of his ability does not interfere with the constant interchange between him, his solitude, and the world and everyone around him. And neither of these happenings prevents him from challenging himself to the ultimate limit, putting himself in jeopardy, courting crisis, risking catastrophe.

Because he refuses to look back, the runner remains ageless. That is his secret, that and the fact that his pursuit of running is in obedience to, in Ellen Glasgow's phrase, "a permanent and self-renewing inner compulsion."

In my fifties, I am aware of all this. Like all runners, I live in the present. I am not interested in the way we were. The past is already incorporated in me. There is no use returning to it. I live for the day. Running gives me self-expression, a way of finding out who I am and who I will be. It makes me intimate with pain. I know the feeling of too little oxygen, of too much lactic acid. I have, always within reach, the opportunity to test my absolute barriers, to search out the borders set up by straining muscles and a failing brain.

But what about performance and competition? What about time and place? How does the aging runner handle the stopwatch? How can he feel really competitive during a race? The answers are (1) age-rated performances, and (2) age-group races.

For less than the entry fee to the Boston Marathon, you can get a computer printout of your age-rated performances for every standard running distance. With this point scoring, you can compare your results not only with your own achievements from year to year, but with world class (1000 points), or national championship (900), or high school dual meet (600–700) performances.

Age-group racing normally begins at age 40 for older runners (there's a similar program for the very young), with classes split down to 5-year increments.

Together, they make age 55 as exciting as 21. They make every race important, and therefore stimulating and absorbing and exhilarating just like mine on one weekend.

The first was the 40-and-over mile. Normally, I would be over my head in the 40-and-over race. Some of these runners arrive at the line with the icing of their 40th birthday cake still on the corners of their mouths. But this time only one really good runner, Joe Bessel, showed up. Bessel won by a hundred yards to polite applause. But the crowd was on its feet and shouting for three of us fighting it out down that last furlong, the longest homestretch I have ever seen.

I just outlasted the other two in 5:19 (840 points) and afterward received my plaque from Ben Jipcho (an 1100-point miler). Now you can say what you will, but there are not too many ways a 55-year-old can equal taking a second place, running the equivalent of a 4:17 mile, and getting his prize from one of the world's best milers—especially when Ben Jipcho says "Fantastic . . ." in handing it to you.

The weekend, however, was not over. A 5-mile race with 300 entries was the next day. Here I moved back into the 50-and-over category, and my initial appraisal at the starting line disclosed there was no one to worry about. I could concentrate on my form, my time, and my point score. Winning the 50-andover would take care of itself.

So I was in a state of happy agony nearing the finish, knowing I was the winner in my division, when I saw Rod Nichols up ahead. I had always thought of Rod as a very good runner working out his salvation in the 40-and-over group. But I suddenly noticed that Rod was getting quite bald, and it occurred to me that Rod had been around the running scene for a very long time. He began to look more and more like a very competent 50-year-old.

At considerable cost, partially paid for by the panic I felt at this thought, I caught up to him. Easing alongside, I casually gasped, "How old are you, Rod?"

"I'm 75," he replied in a tone just short of exasperation, and then added, "I'm 44."

I relaxed. I didn't have to beat him. When he gets to be 50, I thought as I cruised around the high school track to the finish, I'll be in the 60-and-over.

—DR. SHEEHAN ON RUNNING, 1975

◆

FIVE MINUTES BEFORE THE Fourth of July 10-Kilometer Pepsi Challenge Race, the loudspeakers began to pour out "Rocky's Theme." There was a noticeable increase in movement on the plaza of the George Washington Bridge. Thousands of runners began walking and jogging to the starting line. The race was only moments away. The next half-hour for some, an hour for others, would be what the Greeks called the *agon,* the struggle. Johan Huizinga in his book *Homo Ludens* described it as play. We runners know better. We call it sport.

"The occasion," said Huizinga, "is sacred or festive." Today it was both. We were celebrating a secular feast. It was a day of holiday and history. A day that said all men were equal and all men were free. And we were putting the seal on it by freely taking an oath on the race that was to follow. Giving our word of honor to do our best.

There was a brief silence. Then the anthem. And now we were

ready for what was to come. "It is an activity," Huizinga went on, "which proceeds within certain limits of time and place, in a visible order according to rules freely accepted and outside the sphere of necessity and material utility."

We were to proceed for 10 kilometers (about 6¼ miles) over the bridge into Manhattan and end up at Baker Field, an athletic facility of Columbia University. We knew the rules and accepted them. Runners are a law-abiding lot, but in the race we accept rules that are generally unenforceable. Cheating is not merely unethical, it is unintelligible. It destroys both the runner and the race.

One reason for this obedience is time. Time matters as much as space. Indeed, the real enemy is the digital clock at the finish line. That clock is the closure, the end, the judgment. And it has, as you can see, no relation to necessity or utility.

In those last moments I can feel the electricity in the crowd. There is a continual stirring. An excitement that leaps from one runner to another. "The mood," wrote Huizinga, "is one of rapture and enthusiasm." I feel that mood fill me. "Enthusiasm" is a strong word for strong feelings. I have them. Passion and daring and commitment to what is ahead. And rapture. I am seized by the whole event. The rest of the world falls away. Up until now I have felt reluctant to suffer, but now that is set aside. I cannot wait for that suffering to get underway.

The gun sounds, and we stream down an incline and spill out onto the bridge. The Hudson is on either side and in front Manhattan, and the entire span empty of everything except runners. I am running the first mile too fast, as I always do. I am filled with the exultation that Huizinga said accompanied the action. I am carried away by the race and the day and those around me. I feel larger than life and capable of anything.

A brief 6 minutes and the feeling is over. From now on another emotion identified by Huizinga will dominate—tension. Uncertainty about myself and the outcome will fill the rest of the race. I am in control, yet I am not in control. What will I face and will I be able to face it? I'll be running with that question from here to the end.

We come off the bridge and run upriver past the Cloisters. The going is fairly easy until a steep half-mile hill leading to the toll booths on the Henry Hudson Bridge, the turnaround point. That hill is my moment of truth. I am paying for the fast pace on the first mile. I hold nothing back, but my pace gets slower and slower. People are passing me, and my thighs can take no more pain. This is the race right here.

The top finally comes and then the long merciful downhill. Now I am passing those who passed me going up. I am feeling better than at any other time since the start. The race, I suddenly realize, is mine.

And that was the way it was through the finish. The digital clock read 38:38, my best time of the year. Others had done personal bests also. Baker Field was filled with happy runners in groups talking about the race and how it had been to run. All around me it was as Huizinga described it. "Mirth and relaxation follow," he said.

Eventually we went to a small Irish bar a block or so away and sat drinking beer and telling each other what wonderful people we were. Not, of course, in words but with our eyes and our gestures and that bearing that comes with running the best you can on the Fourth of July.

—HOW TO FEEL GREAT 24 HOURS A DAY, 1983

I HAD DISCOVERED WHAT every runner looks for. A race with a small field, a flat course, and trophies in my age group. It was a Sunday event in a little seacoast town with less than 200 entrants and only a handful in the 50-and-over group.

Then I saw him. He was already waiting at the starting line stripped to the waist, wearing a digital stopwatch and the telltale 500 number. He was lean and muscular and built for endurance. And not a gray hair on his head. I had found a race and gotten myself a tiger.

I knew then it would be no different from every other Sunday. The stage was set for the usual drama. Age-group racing does that. The confrontation with runners my own age makes every race a race within a race, a play within a play. Every race is a stage, and I become one of the actors.

The race is always a race against the clock. It is also a race for the best place in the multitude that faces the starter's gun. But when there is a prize for people of my vintage, the race becomes pure Elizabethan drama.

In Greek drama it is man against the superhuman. The tragedy results when the hero or heroine sins against the gods. Our current theater is man against the world. The individual interests against the common good. The question is, Which is the stronger, the one standing alone or the one who gives to others? But the Elizabethan drama is man against himself. The plot unfolds and is determined by the flaws and faults of the protagonist. The ambition of Macbeth, the irresoluteness of Hamlet, the jealousy of Othello makes the play.

In the next 30 minutes or so this bare-chested, well-trained, competent 50-year-old runner was going to test me. He was going to search out the flaws in my character. He and I were about to produce, write, and act out our own drama. It would be, as George Santayana wrote of athletics, a physical drama, in which all moral and emotional interests are involved. "The soul is stirred," he said, "in this spectacle that represents the basis of its whole life."

You might wonder why at my age I do these things. I could easily have been at the beach or sitting over a late breakfast reading the *New York Times*. I could have been enjoying this summer Sunday like millions of others in this land. But no, here I am with but moments to the start, tying my shoes for the third time, taking the last ounces of my cola, exchanging greetings with those around me.

I have left behind the self and the equilibrium I have established over the years. I have come to the uncertainty and tension and the possibility of disaster that this race represents. I have put myself in a most difficult and trying situation when I could be peaceful and content at home.

Why do I feel this compulsion? Mainly, I believe, because human nature abhors equilibrium. There is nothing more boring than ease and routine. We cannot stand for long the slow succession of uneventful days. We are never quite content with the status quo. It is nature that aims to achieve stability, nature that constantly seeks homeostasis. But human beings will not let things rest. We must be in motion.

So I take this hard-won equilibrium, this self that I have made, and then establish a vacuum of deeds not yet done, achievements not yet mine. I say nay to all that has gone before, and I come to the race. I impose another test, another trial, another challenge to be experienced before I can claim to be me.

The playwrights know this sequence well. The equilibrium is first destroyed. Then there are moves and countermoves. There is the clash of wills. The issue is joined. The inevitable then occurs. The flaws of the individual are revealed. And they determine the outcome.

When the equilibrium is restored, what must be done has been done. The play comes full circle, revealing what has always been potential in the situation and the people in it. Replay the drama and it comes out the same. Rerun the race and it does also. Only the growth and development of the characters can change it.

There were by now only seconds to go. I stood just behind my rival waiting for the curtain to go up on our private struggle. The gun went off. The play had begun.

When the gun sounded, we went off as if tied together. Two 50-andover runners oblivious of the rest of the field. What was now of importance in this 6-mile race in a little seacoast town would occur between us. The moves and countermoves, the clash of wills which would mark this drama, would be our moves and counter-moves, and our personal clash of wills. The exposition, the confron-tation, the climax and the denouement would all occur in the less than 5 yards that would separate us for the entire race. And the new equilibrium we would find at the finish line would come from who we truly were.

The race does what every good drama does. It tells the truth. Each move, each event, is an actual happening. And everything that hap-pens has an effect on everything else. In race as in drama, there is no unimportant information. From gun to finish line my every action would reveal the inner man who prompted it.

The stranger who was my opponent and rival would also be col-league and friend. Together we would write and act out this drama. Together we would explore this new experience. Together we would gain a new appreciation of ourselves. Together we would make this struggle an image of our inner struggle to make sense out of our lives.

We went through the first mile in 6 minutes. The exposition was already taking place. His best pace was my best pace. The issue was now joined. He made the next move. A slight acceleration in pace. He was using the classical strategy in the confrontation between my speed and his endurance. He was trying to break away from me or at the least take the sting out of my kick at the finish.

My tactic was simple. Sit in behind. Let him do the work. Take him at the end. His had become equally simple. Increase the pace until I let him go. The pressure of this speed eventually became unbearable, so I took the lead in an attempt to slow it down. He would have none of that and immediately went out in front once more.

And so went those first few miles. It had become a matter of the body and the will. Emotion can help, but reason is useless. After the first rush the race is a matter of character and talent. One runner rarely out-thinks another. The runner knows what must be done and then musters the courage to do it.

He knew his role; I knew mine. His, a continued striving to leave me behind. Mine, a persistent refusal to allow that to happen. So on I went, the arms getting heavy, the chest desperate for air, the legs now filling with pain. He was calling on his body for even more effort, and I attached to his right shoulder and was paying the price.

This was the perennial struggle between human wills and within individual human wills now seen plain. We had gone through the exposition and the confrontation. Now we were in the last mile. He still led with me a step behind. Neither of us would give an inch. We matched stride for stride. I was running on virtues and values I never knew I had. I just would not give up. Nor would he.

I was now no longer merely racing against him. I was racing against me at my best. That was what he had come to represent. He was my alter ego. The best possible me. And only my best effort would beat him. He was in a similar predicament. He had not been able to shake me. I was still there off his right shoulder as I had been almost from the beginning. It was a signal to do more or less.

We made a turn then, and far down the road I could see the banner over the finish line. My friend mustered his final challenge. His pace went up a notch or two. Mine did also. And we came down that last stretch head to head, chest to chest, like a team of matched horses.

By now he was flat out and so was I. With less than a hundred yards to go we were still neck and neck. When I thought of that later I realized we had both won. We had done what had been asked of us and surpassed ourselves in the doing. This tense struggle of wills and bodies had told us truly who we were.

What happened after that was anticlimactic. With 50 yards to go I pulled the trigger and surged forward. I was running on muscle fibers I had not used and he did not have. Pain and exhaustion and shortness of breath were no longer deterrents. He was no match for this madness. So I won the 50-and-over.

I had beaten him, but it really didn't matter. Seconds later we were shaking hands and congratulating each other. We stood there happy and content and more than a little proud. We had made the theoretical fact that we were born to be heroes a reality.

—*RUNNER'S WORLD* MAGAZINE, JANUARY 1982

◆

WHEN I WAS IN school, I ran from the day classes began in September until they closed the doors in June. Now I run from the beginning of the year until its end. The Road Runners Club schedule on the kitchen bulletin board has over 140 races extending from January to December.

So distance running is the sport for every day of my life. There is no need to pack my gear until running starts again. It begins every day. And every time of year is a time for running. I love all of that ever-recurring cycle of the year.

But, like the lover who loves the girl he's near and clings to the kiss he's close to and fancies the face he faces, the season I love best is the one that's here. Soon I will see winter as Paradise, then spring as another Eden, and later summer as the Promised Land. But for now, autumn is my season in heaven.

The October air does that. Crisp, clear, invigorating. Carrying every sound. Demanding attention. And the weather perfect for running. The runner is as sensitive to the weather as a Stradivarius.

And it is autumn that makes me go best. I am living the life my youth had promised me. Living at the top of my powers. No wonder that Yeats, who saw spring as youth and summer as adolescence, saw autumn as manhood.

And autumn is heaven because there are races to do that best, to run at that peak, to manifest that manhood. And make no mistake, it is in action that we are in heaven.

Heaven is not quiet, said Yeats. There the lover still loves, but with greater passion; the rider still rides, but the horse goes like the wind; and the battle goes on. The runner still races.

And for now, in this forever that is autumn, cross-country is the best of all races. That is where I began. In autumn with cross-country. It was my first taste of running and it is good to taste it again. Cross-country is free running at its best. Just me and the land. Me and that crisp air. Me and the leaves underfoot. Me and the silent hills. That's cross-country. Just me and the breathing and the leaves crunching underfoot on those silent hills. Nature has given up the ghost. Everything around me is dead or dying and I feel reborn. I am at my best.

And it is a best, a rebirth that I experience alone. Nature is the only spectator. In other seasons, in other races, there are people to cheer and encourage or just to watch. Curious onlookers. But not in cross-country. Within minutes, I am alone with my fellow runners.

Minutes later and I am separated even from them. Yards ahead or yards behind, they are out of my line of thought, beyond the horizon of my mind.

I am alone on the back hills of Van Cortlandt. And the course that tested me as a teenager is testing me again. And again I suffer on hills that made me suffer when I was 18. Again I fly down hills I flew down in bygone years. And again I come out of those hills facing an all-out fight to the finish with any runner close to me.

And that was the way it was at Van Cortlandt last week. Nine miles, three times over those back hills. The first 3-mile loop oddly the most painful. Then the second loop not quite as bad. And finally the third time actually running at the hills and conquering them. So that when I came out on the flat, the man I had to beat was only 30 yards ahead.

Only in another autumn, in another season in heaven, will I relive that finish. An impossible quarter-mile sprint and then holding on to the man I had just beaten so I wouldn't fall down. Hearing his heart pounding against my ear and my own beating in unison. Knowing only that and a world suddenly filled with friends saying nice things to an aging man who felt ageless in autumn.

—RUNNING & BEING, 1978

What Dr. Sheehan Means to Me

BY AMBY BURFOOT, *RUNNER'S WORLD* EDITOR-AT-LARGE
AND 1968 BOSTON MARATHON WINNER

EARLY IN MY RUNNING career, George Sheehan chased after me. Many years later, I pursued him. We both got what we wanted.

On April 20, 1968, the day after I won the Boston Marathon, Robert Lipsyte wrote a *New York Times* sports column about a 49-year-old, self-described "main-line jogger" who had just completed his fifth marathon. "I view the Boston Marathon as a Greek tragedy," this runner told Lipsyte after finishing in 3:30:05, roughed up by the day's heat and the infamous Boston hills. "There is Hubris, and there is Nemesis."

Though George Sheehan was not yet a famous writer and book author, his voice and perspective rang loud and clear as the Catholic church bells that had dominated his youth.

Twenty-five years later, I was executive editor of *Runner's World* magazine, and Sheehan, its best-loved author, was fading away from prostate cancer. I hounded him for a final interview, which I knew his legions of fans would treasure. He kept refusing, perhaps to protect his privacy and his failing health.

Finally, several months before his death, Sheehan agreed to come to the *Runner's World* offices in Pennsylvania. I was a bit shocked to see that he needed physical support from two of his sons to guide him into my modest office. But after they left, closing the door behind them, it became instantly obvious that Sheehan still possessed every fiber of his brilliant mind.

I asked all the big questions about cancer, fear, courage, competition, decline, death, and the authenticity of one's life experience. He answered every question without a moment's hesitation. "Things come out of racing for reasons we're not sure of—things like justice, courage, and wisdom," he said at one point. "When you race on a regular basis, you gradually come to embody those things."

After an hour, I could see that he was growing weary, so I sprung just one last question on him. I had always been amazed at his competitive fire, much greater than my own. Sheehan seemed to run to the point of collapse every time he raced. What had he learned from all this? I wanted to know.

"I learned the ultimate truth about competition," he said. "I had been racing against the clock, my opponents, the weather, the hills and all that. Finally I began racing *against myself.*

"And then I learned what it means to become a runner. It means there's only one person in the race, and you are it."

7/ The *Marathon*

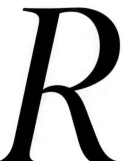unning 26 miles is a feat that truly stretches a human being. At the 20-mile mark, someone has said, the race is half over. Almost anyone can run 20 miles, but the last six are the equivalent of 20 more. Here the runner finds himself pushed to the absolute limit. And therefore needs to call on those hidden reserves, to use all the fidelity and courage and endurance he has.

RUNNING & BEING, 1978

WHEN I RAN MY first Boston Marathon, the race was little more than a club. We were 225 strong. But many of us were present only because of a dare or as a joke. Some were overweight and out of shape, attired in gym suits and tennis clothes. Others wore sneakers instead of running shoes. And, I recall, either that year or the next, a runner who led me all the way to Framingham wore a derby.

That first year at Boston, I finished 96th in 3 hours and 7 minutes and because of this considered myself one of the top hundred marathoners in the country. Now, with nearly the same time, I am not even in the top 5,000. Back then, there were about seven marathons a year; now there are over 200. The Boston field has swelled to 2,200 and is kept manageable only by limiting entrants to those who have run under 3 hours the previous year.

Women and men over 40 are required to beat 3:30.* Where have all these people come from, and why do they do it? How did this mania arise, and what keeps it multiplying among the populace?

I can only answer for myself, and even my answer changes from day to day. For this day, then, I will tell you what I discovered in running. Then why I eventually came to run marathons. And finally, what the continuing fascination of the marathon is. Runners, you see, do not run one marathon. They run them again and again. They are much like surfers seeking the perfect wave.

Why I began running is no longer important. It is enough that it generated a desire to run. Then the running itself took over. Running became a self-renewing compulsion. The more I ran, the more I wanted to run.

One reason was the energy. "Become first a good animal," Emerson said. I did. I came to know my body and enjoy it. Things that previously exhausted me were no longer an effort. Where once I fell asleep in front of the TV set, I was up roaming the house looking for things to do. I was living on a different level of performance.

Then I discovered, or rediscovered, play. Running, I found, was fun. Running became an hour of play and enjoyment away from my daily routine. And in that hour of play I discovered, or rediscovered, myself. Finally, after 45 years, I accepted the person I was.

It would seem that this should be enough—the fitness, the play, the

* EDITOR'S NOTE: This is now 3:15 for men 40 to 44, 3:45 for women; qualifying time escalates in 5-year age groups from there.

self-acceptance. But it wasn't, and never will be. I wanted to be challenged, wanted to be tested, wanted to find my limits and then surpass them. Merely running and enjoying and creating were not enough.

From here on, I think more of the answers will be found in the philosophy of William James than anywhere else. However I phrase it, it comes down to one of the Jamesian expressions: "The nobler thing tastes better. The strenuous life is the one we seek." James was not a writer for those who would simply cope, for those who would groove through life. He believed in effort. He thought the decisive thing about us was not intelligence, strength, or wealth. Those are things we carry, he said. The real question posed to us is the effort we are willing to make. And that available effort is always, he kept saying, much more than we suspect. We live far below the energy we have and therefore must learn how to tap these reservoirs of power. For this, he said, we need a "dynamogenic agent," a "moral equivalent of war." Like war, this would provide a theater of heroism, an arena where one could demonstrate courage and fortitude, a setting where one could be the best one would ever be.

For me and others like me, that is the marathon. We are all there in the works of William James. He is the psychologist who tells us we can be more than we are. The philosopher who appeals to everyone who values his own experience. The thinker who saw happiness in the struggle and found the meaning of life in the marriage of some unhabitual idea with some fidelity, courage, and endurance.

Which is as good a definition of a marathon as you are likely to find. I tell you all this, and still you might not understand. What is so special, what is unique about this 26-mile, 385-yard distance? Why this and not some other race?

The answer is the wall, the physiological breaking point that comes at the 20-mile mark. Runners claim that at this mark the marathon is only half over, that the last 6 miles are equivalent to the 20 that went before. It is nearer the truth to say that the 20-mile mark is where the marathon begins—there at the wall.

The miles that have gone before are just the foothills to this Everest. The wall is where the runner begins to come apart. Either as suddenly as it takes to write this sentence, or slowly and inexorably as the final miles turn into a cauldron of pain.

Any reasonably fit runner can go a 20-mile race. Were I to get up next Sunday and see in the *New York Times* that there was a 20-mile race in Central Park, I would be likely to pack my gear and go. But if that same morning I discovered there was a marathon in town, I would draw a bye.

I would not be prepared to go that extra 6 miles, to handle the wall. Exactly what happens there is not known, even to the experts. Is the exhaustion, the seeming impasse, due to low blood sugar or lactic acid accumulation? Is it due, perhaps, to dehydration or high body temperature? Is it the result of a loss of blood volume or, as many runners suspect, depletion of muscle glycogen? No one seems quite sure. Whatever the reason, the runner's homeostasis, the equilibrium of his internal milieu, begins to break down. And the final 6 miles must be accomplished in some way unexplained by medical science. From the wall on, the runner goes it alone.

One exercise physiologist, Dr. David Costill, director of the Ball State University Human Performance Laboratory in Muncie, Indiana, ran the marathon as an experiment because he did not think the wall existed. When he came to that point, however, he said, "The sensations of exhaustion were unlike anything I had ever experienced. I could not run, walk, or stand, and even found sitting a bit strenuous."

So there it is. It begins with running. Until one day you progress to where you want to be challenged by the marathon. And then you meet the wall. No matter how many times you attack it, you always think you can do better, find more energy, more fortitude, more courage, more endurance. You always think this time you will be the hero you were meant to be. Fifty marathons later, that's the best explanation I know.

—*RUNNER'S WORLD* MAGAZINE, MAY 1978

———————◆———————

WHEN I RETURNED TO running some 20 years ago, it had nothing to do with health and fitness. I wanted to relive my competitive years in college. I wanted to feel again that competent, responding body, the excitement of the race, the struggle down the homestretch, neck and neck with an opponent.

I wanted once more to be a hero.

I did not realize then that this drive toward immortality is universal—that I would be followed by millions of others Americans. But I and the other runners who followed me were simply repeating something that had occurred over the ages: men and women answering the ascetic impulse, the inborn need to be heroic.

William James felt that this drive to asceticism was characteristic of the twice-born—those who saw the evil in the world and knew it could only be dealt with on the individual basis, through meeting pain and guilt and death squarely. Mankind, James said, has taken it as reality that the world is made to be a theater for heroism.

If so, we are like so many out-of-work actors. There were few chances, it appears, to find such a part. The call to do an heroic deed occurs rarely, if at all, in day-to-day life. American poet James Dickey once said that you could go throughout your entire life in these United States without ever finding out whether or not you were a coward.

I now have the chance offered to me every week. The race has become my theater for heroism, and of all the races there is no better proscenium—no better stage—for heroism than a marathon.

Each marathon is a stage on which I must write and act out an epic drama—one that, as American philosopher George Santayana said of the football game, involves all the values and virtues of the race. And while the marathon stirs my soul, and every marathon stirs my best, none stirs the heroic more than the Marine Corps Marathon.

The race begins in Arlington National Cemetery. The start is at the foot of the hill where the Iwo Jima monument stands; the finish of the race is at the monument itself. As we make our final preparations, we can see across the Potomac the various monuments we will pass on the course. Surrounded by the graves of heroes, we visit tributes of other heroes along the way.

Getting to the starting line in battle trim is itself a heroic enterprise. Marathon training, for someone who works for their daily bread or raising a family, is little different from going to Marine boot camp.

In one of this earliest works, *Meditations of Don Quixote,* Spanish philosopher José Ortega y Gasset discusses the hero. "The hero," he wrote, "is someone in continual opposition to the status quo." As I stood on the line at the Marine Corps Marathon, I was surrounded by such people—no longer satisfied with the status quo, desperately involved in the heroic project of becoming themselves.

I had met many of them the evening before at the clinic I give here every year. Some came up and visited after the program finished. We talked about tomorrow and the 3-hour barrier, of what we hoped to do. The year before, a man in his early thirties with a sturdy build but quite trim came up to me and said, "Last year I was three-oh-seven." Close, I thought; this year he might enter that charmed circle of marathoners who have broken 3 hours. What did he expect this year? I asked him. "I'd like to get down to 168." He was talking pounds, not minutes, but it meant the same thing: His preparation had transformed him into the classic athlete, the hero waiting-to-be.

Around me at the starting line, I am sure there were many such stories. Raw recruits now fashioned into warriors. Ordinary citizens, whose previous lives had held little more than boredom, frustration, anxiety, or depression, now filled with martial virtues. Common-variety human beings, ready to take on the most grueling challenge devised by man.

And I do not exaggerate. World-class runners approach the marathon with trepidation. Olympians fail to finish. Record holders collapse. This contest has consequences in pain and fatigue and exhaustion unrivaled in sport. And all the more because the agony is self-inflicted. At any moment the runner can yield to the body's demand for relief. The end of the marathon—the end of heroism—is always just one step away. You can stop anytime you like.

But on this day, the heroes were out. At the halfway point, I turned to the runner next to me and said, "I have never seen such mass competence in my life." I had reached Washington's Union Station in 1 hour and 35 minutes. My pace was just as I planned—7:15 a mile. If held to the end, this pace would usually guarantee me a finish in the top third of most marathons and especially this one—a marathon for the ordinary runner.

But on this day it was evident that the ordinary runner was no longer ordinary. The runners, almost 12,000 in number, seemed like

Marines themselves. They'd taken basic training, gone through their own equivalent of boot camp, and had been, in effect, their own drill instructors. They were combat-ready and showed it.

When the cannon boomed, they'd set out in full cry, streaming past me right from the start. I covered the first mile in under 7 minutes, but hundreds upon hundreds had gone flying past me in that short stretch.

When I slowed my planned pace, those numbers increased. There were thousands of ordinary distance runners, a people's army, ahead of me at the halfway mark. These were ordinary human beings, people you would recognize as neighbors or friends. The Marine Corps Marathon is known for its organization but not for its runners—it's a marathon of first-timers and those at the back of the pack, people who run before work in the morning or after it at night, people who a few years back viewed a walk to the store as an inconvenience.

But now these first-timers and back-of-the-pack runners were easing past me looking like experts—and experts is what they had become. A race-tested veteran of 20 years, I was positioned far in the rear and still losing ground. I was having my consciousness elevated with every step. Here were thousands of people running for more than 90 minutes at a speed that in the past would have winded them in a minute. They were going at a rate they had previously reserved for emergencies like crossing the street or catching a bus—and even more, planning to maintain it for over 3 hours.

Forget that disaster might lie ahead. Forget that many would eventually slow down. Forget that some might even have to walk. Forget that the last 6 miles would take its usual toll. There at Union Station, all I could see was evidence of heroism and the marvelous endurance of the human body.

At mile 17, we set out on Hains Point, and I began to see evidence of the marvelous power of human will. I had yet to pass a tiring runner. I was, however, now moving with a flow that was slowing just as I was. I had lost the lift in my legs. My stride was shortened. I had become conscious of my calves and my thighs, my shoulders and my arms. Soon the consciousness would turn to outright pain.

Runners were now taking longer at water stations, and were slower to start up again. But start up again they did, and they continued to crank out the miles. Their bodies were faltering, but not their minds.

Mass competence had become mass determination.

An hour or more of that ordeal and mass determination became mass courage. Every runner was having the same experience: The body had forgotten how. The will could not remember why. The heart supplied the strength that kept us going. And the driving force was the heroic passion that we almost unknowingly brought with us to this struggle. This race has become a commitment beyond pain or exhaustion or indeed any argument the body or mind could bring to bear.

We had begun this race in the burial ground of ordinary men who had become heroes—soldiers who in the end had found in themselves a competence and determination and courage they never knew they possessed. When we returned, so had we.

—*RUNNER'S WORLD* MAGAZINE, NOVEMBER 1984

———◆———

THE ATHLETIC EXPERIENCE CAN be divided into three parts. One is the preparation, the training of the body. Two is the event, the challenging of the self. And three is the aftermath. And for the runner, the ultimate athletic experience is the marathon. It takes training and challenging and creating to the absolute limits.

Running has been described as a thinking person's sport. The reference is to the predominance of middle-class, highly educated people who have taken up this activity. But it is also true that it is a sport that requires extensive study of the workings of the body. Runners in training acquire extensive knowledge of how the body operates best. In coming to one's peak, a good working knowledge of exercise physiology and nutrition is necessary.

But the application of that science is both intellectual and intuitive. Runners have an expression: "Listen to your body." Basically, it means that your body can tell you things all the sophisticated hardware in the world never will. Runners understand that biofeedback machines only amplify messages that should be heard without them. They develop biological wisdom: Experts in their own bodies, they become good animals.

This listening and learning is often done by playing with the edge of self-inflicted pain. Doing hills and speed work, for example, means repeatedly pushing to the limits of tolerance of oxygen debt. This is painful. There are times, however, when even training like this can be a pleasure—days when I get tremendous enjoyment out of the effort and the sweat and competence I feel. Like Thoreau, I occupy my body with delight.

In training for the marathon, I grow in physical wisdom. I learn how my body works best. I read the texts, of course, but then I take these bookish theories out on the road and test them. I filter them through my exercising body and come up with my own truth. I prepare myself for an exploration to my outer limits—the marathon itself.

The marathon is the focal point of all that goes before and all that comes afterward. The long-distance race is a struggle that results in self-discovery. It is an adventure into the limits of the self, representing for runners what has been called the moral equivalent of war—a theater for heroism, where the runner can do deeds of daring and greatness.

Life is made in doing and suffering and creating. All of that is there in the marathon—the doing in training, the suffering in the race, and finally, the creating that comes in the tranquility that follows.

This stage on which we can be bigger than life is a place where we can exhibit all that is good in us. Courage and determination, discipline and willpower, the purging of all negative impulses—we see that we are indeed whole and holy. We have been told time and again we were born to success, but a truly run marathon convinces·us of that truth.

The marathon fills our subconscious with this gospel. Taking a well-trained body through a grueling 26.2-mile race does immeasurably more for the self-concept and self-esteem than years with the best psychiatrist.

Robert Frost once said that to write a poem you have to have an experience. To do any creative act, you must have an experience. Any race is such an experience, but the marathon is that experience raised to the nth degree. It fills the conscious and unconscious with sights and sounds, feelings and emotions, trials and accomplishments. And in the end, we know creation.

—*PERSONAL BEST,* 1989

LATER, AFTER THE HOT tub had soaked some of the pain out of my legs, I hobbled to the bed and stretched out, enjoying being horizontal.

Downstairs, John, our number-six son, put it on the rest of the family watching the Lakers–Bucks game. "If he's going to feel that bad," he asked, "why does he do it?"

Upstairs, I was asking myself the same question. Why suffer this way? Why run marathons when nine out of 10 of them end in a contest of the human will pushing the human body beyond endurance? This one had been no different. The first 10 miles to Sea Bright, New Jersey, had been a lark. Moving steadily along the coast with that strong south wind at my back was a fine way to spend a Sunday morning in January. Past Sea Bright, I had even picked up my pace, still feeling good and full of running.

The first hint of disaster came at the turnaround in Sandy Hook Park. The 15-mile-an-hour wind, hardly noticed as an ally, became a constant alien presence. Reducing my speed and increasing my effort, it would give me no respite for the next 2 hours. Still, the legs felt fresh, the breathing good, and the form under control. Sea Bright reappeared and disappeared in my wake.

Then, as quickly as it takes to write this, the cramps came. They started in both calves, then spread to the thighs, cutting my stride in half and making each step a painful decision. It was ridiculous, I told myself, to even think of finishing with 7 miles to go. No one who knew how I felt right now could expect me to finish.

But I kept going. My progress getting slower and slower as I tested a variety of running forms that might permit movement without torture. Nothing helped, but the thought of quitting gradually receded from my mind. When the pain was particularly bad, I would breathe, "Oh, God"; more a statement than a prayer. And I took to counting my steps. Counting. Counting by ones seemed the highest mental activity I could perform. It also reassured me that I was moving and would after 4,500 or thereabouts steps arrive at Convention Hall in Asbury Park.

Somehow in all this torment, Allenhurst came and went. Deal Lake appeared, then the Conventional Hall, and then three of the longest blocks in the world to the finish. Three hours and 45 minutes after it started in ecstasy, the agony ended.

The marathon, I thought, as I lay there feeling warmer and healthier by the minute, is just not my race. True, I had not trained adequately for this one. Had not run over 10 miles in one stretch since April and the last Boston. It was foolish to expect a good one on that amount of work. In the old days, maybe, but now, with age coming on and the desire dying, it might be best to let the marathon go.

There were times in the beginning when the marathon, any marathon, seemed an impossible dream. When any race over 5 miles was beyond my imagination. My goals were more immediate (a 5-minute mile) and practical (physical fitness).

Subtly, insidiously, running became much more. Became, as exercise did for Oliver Alden, George Santayana's Last Puritan, a necessity. "To go a single day without two hours of rigorous outdoor exercise," wrote Santayana, "was now out of the question. It would have meant physical restlessness and discomfort indoors and the most horrible sensual moodiness in the inner man."

For Alden, the 2 hours of sculling or horseback riding brought him into genuine communication with nature such as he never found in either religion or poetry. And was able to turn him for the moment, Santayana declared, into the gladdest, the most perfect, and yet the most independent of people.

Couldn't that "escape, that wordless religion," be enough? Why get into 26-mile runs with the certainty of bone-weary fatigue and the possibility of the ignominy of walking to the finish line? Wasn't the marathon equivalent to Alden's Puritan ethic, from which he escaped only when rowing on the Charles or galloping his horse on a brisk New England day? Another mindless duty, another needless challenge, another unwanted privilege. All demanding success and achievement.

Downstairs, Kareem Abdul-Jabbar was not looking to escape. He had engaged Wilt Chamberlain in hand-to-hand combat and was revealing what Fordham's Charley Yelverton once said was the principle of being an athlete—"the principle that makes you dig your guts out no matter what kind of game you're in."

I still don't know. "You can very well afford to dangle about enjoying the fresh air and admiring the sunset," the captain of the Harvard crew had told Alden, "but we've got to train. We're not in the crew to have a good time, but to win the Yale race." But perhaps you could have both. Perhaps what I needed was more marathons, not fewer. Needed the pain, the torture, the indescribable fatigue of a marathon in February and another in March. The Boston in April would be a breeze, another of those daily afternoon runs when you know who you are and where you're going. And I would come to the finish as I would come to my back door, warm and relaxed, still strong and full from running, enjoying the fresh air and admiring the sunset. Now, where was that February entry blank?

—RUNNING & BEING, 1978

———◆———

IF YOU WOULD BE a marathon runner, study William James. Technique and training can safely be left to lesser teachers. You will soon find the proper shoes, know what to wear, how to eat, what exercise to do, how far to run. What you need most is to know it is possible, possible for you, possible for any common man.

And then you must learn it is not only possible but necessary. And that there are ways to make what is possible and necessary, however difficult it appears, a source of joy and happiness. James is the man who teaches this. He is the psychologist who speaks to all who would be more than they are. He is the philosopher who appeals to everyone who values his own experience. Everyone who suspects there is more to each one of us than meets the eye. He is the thinker who said that how to gain, how to keep, and how to recover happiness were the certain motive of all we do and are willing to endure.

James is the scientist who dealt in happiness. He went beyond science into the human heart, into those recesses where lie our values and ideals and with them the energies needed to accomplish them. For James, life was meant to be a struggle. Life, he said, was built on doing and suffering and creating. Its solid meaning was the same eternal thing—the marriage of some unhabitual idea with some fidelity, courage, and endurance.

Sweat and effort and human nature strained to its utmost and on the rack, yet getting through alive, he wrote, are the sort of thing that inspires us.

"Man must be stretched," he wrote. "If not in one way, then another."

The marathon is one way. Running 26 miles is a feat that truly stretches a human being. At the 20-mile mark, someone has said, the race is half over. Almost anyone can run 20 miles, but the last six are the equivalent of 20 more. Here the runner finds himself pushed to the absolute limit. And therefore needs to call on those hidden reserves, to use all the fidelity and courage and endurance he has.

Would James have considered the marathon an absurd waste of these energies, of these great human resources? I doubt it. Indeed, who better than James to speak to marathon runners? He always championed the life of sanctity or poverty or sport. He was always caught up with the athlete or the saint, whom he saw as the athlete of God. He always admired the ascetic way of life, which is no more, as the original Greek word would have it, than athletic training.

"Asceticism," he stated, "is the profounder way of handling human existence."

This type of discipline, he thought, would allow us to live to our maximum. And find in ourselves unexpected heights of fortitude and heroism and the capability to endure suffering and hardship. To discover, if you will, the person we are. Reaching peaks we previously thought unattainable.

And how better to reach this state than by the rules of habit formation that James suggested? To lead life well and attend to the major things, we must, he said, make as much of our daily activity as possible simply habit. Otherwise we will consume both energy and time making decisions.

The marathoner who would be successful can learn how to get the correct habits from James. Put on the right course, his training will be no problem. The 30 to 50 miles a week he needs to run a respectable and suitable painful marathon will be a matter of course. He will suit up and get out on the roads without agonizing about wind or cold or weather. Or about more attractive things. Or the priorities of family or society.

Begin, said James, with firm resolve. Start with high hopes and a strong and decisive initiative. Do not permit exceptions, he warned. Unraveling a string is easier than winding it up. Practice must become an inviolate hour. Nothing should come between the runner and running.

Next, seize every opportunity to act in the direction of this habit.

Further, do not talk about what you are going to do; do it. And finally, he said, keep the faculty of effort alive by a little gratuitous exercise each day.

The marathoner schooled by James comes to the Hopkinton Common on Patriots' Day at the height of his physical powers, willing to pay the price in pain and even agony the marathon demands. But James also wrote on other things that occupy the runner on the way to Boston: mystical states, the primacy of religion, and the problem of truth.

And in the end, when the race is half over, when there are 6 miles to go, because he is mind and soul as well as body, the runner will find new ways of looking at himself and his god. "Experience," said James, "is a process that continually gives us new material to digest."

And for the marathoner there is no greater experience than the marathon. And no better companion on that run than William James.

—*RUNNING & BEING,* 1978

◆

JAMES JOYCE TOOK THE 10 years of Homer's *Odyssey* and compressed them into a Dublin day. He looked into the mind and heart and body of the hero Ulysses and created Leopold Bloom, who is everyman.

And saw in the lotus-eaters, Cyclops, the gift of the winds, Circe, Hades, the Sirens, and even the nymph Calypso those inner and outer events that happen to everyone, every day. And then he put all of it into the waking-to-sleeping day of his Irish Jew. It takes 18 hours. The Boston Marathon does it in three.

Like many sports, the marathon is a microcosm of life. The marathoner can experience the drama of everyday existence so evident to the artist and poet. For him, all the emotions are heightened. Agony and ecstasy become familiar feelings. The journey from Hopkinton to Boston, like the journey from Troy to Ithaca, reveals what happens to a man when he faces up to himself and the world around him. And why he succeeds or fails.

Ulysses succeeds not because he is a superior athlete, although he is. He can build a boat and sail it. He can wrestle, run, and throw a discus. He can flay, skin, cut up, and cook an ox. But all these skills do not explain his eventual success. His secret is that he endures. He takes life as it comes and says yes.

This trait is so commonly displayed at Boston, it seems universal. I believe every human must have this capacity and could find it if he tried. And there is no better place to discover it than a marathon. For the truth is that every man in a marathon is a survivor or nothing, including the winner.

Winning is, in fact, unimportant. "Brief is the season of man's delight," sang Pindar in his ode to an Olympic winner. And many a winner has learned the truth that his laurel is indeed, as Housman wrote, a garland briefer than a girl's. There is, then, no happy-ever-aftering for a marathoner, no matter what his age. Tomorrow is another race, another test, another challenge. And then there is another race, and another.

What, then, of Ulysses? Was he content to live as an aging and idle king? Others besides marathoners have thought not. Dante saw him calling on his old comrades, urging them to further adventures.

"Consider your origin," he tells them. "You were not formed to live like brutes, but to follow virtue and knowledge."

Such pursuit would be in action. The Greeks developed the whole man. They saw no happiness in creature comforts, no wisdom in meditation.

We aging marathoners already know that. We learned it at Boston. And so, when Tennyson takes up Dante's idea and has Ulysses speak, we hear ourselves: "And though we are not now the strength which in old days moved earth and heaven, that which we are, we are— made weak by time and fate, but strong in will to strive, to seek, to find, and not to yield."

Not to yield says it all. The enduring, the surviving, does not stop with age. We may even grow more skillful at it as the years pass. So we do not envy youth. We ask no quarter of life. We accept no favors. We are men following virtue and knowledge. "Though much has been taken," wrote Tennyson, "much abides." We will live and endure. We know, better than others, "how dull it is to pause, to make an end, to rust unburnished, not to shine in use." I do not intend to pause, or rest, or rust. Descendant of Ulysses, brother of Bloom, I will survive.

—RUNNING & BEING, 1978

THERE IS NO EASIER running for me than the first few miles of the Boston Marathon. I come to that race at my peak. I am lean and fit and ready. And the excitement of the day lights a fire. So I am almost pure energy when the gun goes off at high noon on the Hopkinton Common.

The start is all laughter and talking and wishing people well. The pace is a pleasure. Smooth and comfortable and little more than a trot. I move at a speed just above that of my warm-up ("In the beginning always hold something back," Adolph Gruber, the Austrian Olympian, once told me). So these miles are like no others in any race. Down the long hill out of Hopkinton and through Ashland and over the gentle slopes to Framingham, I coast along. The running is automatic. I feel nothing but the elation of being in this company.

The miles pass as if I were watching them out of a train window. But miles change, somewhere the holding back must end. I pass the 10-mile mark and enter Natick. The miles, no longer effortless, become an effort that comes easily. My style remains sure and smooth and economical. I increase my speed, but it is still well below the 6-minute miles of those cruel 10- and 12-milers in Central Park. I try for maximum efficiency. Careful to push off my toes and get those extra few inches a stride that make the difference in a 3-hour run.

Soon I am at Wellesley, the halfway point. The miles again change. Now each mile is running at my best. It is now becoming hard work. Not disagreeable, but an exertion not previously felt. I am still surprisingly fresh and moving well. Better now than I have moved before or will move later. Still, the body is beginning to tell me this is no lark.

No longer child's play. Not just a long run in the sun. And now at the 17-mile mark come the Newton Hills, a 2-mile stretch which includes the four hills that make up the world-renowned Heartbreak Hill. I will take these on the grass divider behind the crowds that line the street.

The grass dampens the shock on my lower legs and thighs. And I shift to shorter steps as a cyclist would shift to a lower gear to maintain the same workload. Even with grass and mini-steps, miles over hills are most difficult. Quite suddenly, what in the beginning seemed like something I would accomplish with ease and even distinction comes down to survival. A question of whether or not I can keep moving. These two short miles seem interminable. And then, just as suddenly, I am at Boston College and it is, as the crowds insist, all downhill from there. Downhill or not, we marathoners know that at Boston College the race is only half over. I am quite a different runner from the one who stood on the line at Hopkinton. The steady pace has used up my muscle glycogen, my precious fuel supply. The Newton Hills have built up my lactic acid and the heaviness in my muscles. The downhills in the early going have inserted ice picks in my thighs. My blood sugar is getting low. And although I have drunk everything in sight, I have not kept up with my fluid loss.

Descending the hill from Boston College, I feel these inner events for the first time. And I know again that the last 6 miles at Boston will be the worst 6 miles I will ever run. From now on, pain is a constant companion. The slightest downgrade is a torture to my thighs. My legs get heavier and heavier.

The same effort that made a romp of a 7-minute mile outside of Hopkinton barely gets me through a 10-minute mile on Commonwealth Avenue. I experiment with strides and body positions to see if there are any muscles still willing to respond.

By now I can see the Pru Tower, and then come the unkindest miles of all. Miles where I must will every step toward a goal that never seems any nearer. I spend a mile in agony and bring that tower not one inch nearer. Minutes pass, and the Pru and with it the finish and the relief from pain and my chance to get into a hot tub seem just a mirage.

But somehow I reach Beacon Street and I know I have made it. Like a horse who smells the barn, I am suddenly refreshed. The last mile brings with it a joy, an elevation of the spirit that makes everything that went before worthwhile. And worth doing again next year. One mile at a time.

—*RUNNING & BEING,* 1978

———◆———

THE FRIDAY NIGHT BEFORE the 1981 New York City Marathon, I spoke at a spaghetti dinner given by a local running club. Before the talk to the 100 runners and their families, I had loaded up on the bread, beer and pasta. I had joined in the excitement and anticipation they all felt. Then, in the question-and-answer period that followed the talk, someone asked me if I was going to run the marathon. Without hesitation, I answered yes.

Before that dinner, I would have said no. For the previous week, I had thought of any number of legitimate reasons not to run, the primary one being that I had not gotten in the necessary training.

Most marathon training programs prescribe a gradual buildup over 3 to 6 months, to where the runner is doing at least 60, and preferably 70, miles a week. I have always run marathons on a good deal less. In fact, I have *never* run 70 miles in a single week and don't intend to. Three hours of easy running and a race each week has been my pre-marathon routine over the years.

But this year my training had dipped far below even my minimum.

Travel, colds and injuries had cut into my time on the roads, and when I was healthy I had raced so much I was too tired to train. My mileage the last month before the New York City Marathon had been less than what most runners had done in a week to prepare for this race.

Then there were the calf cramps. In several recent races, I had experienced some ominous warnings in my calves: cramps that were severe enough to slow me down on two occasions. Suppose I got a cramp in some godforsaken spot in Brooklyn or the Bronx, and I had to stop and walk in?

Even if I were able to run without injury, it would undoubtedly be in some undistinguished time. Later, whenever the subject of the New York City Marathon came up, I would have to apologize for my time. I once ran the White Rock Marathon in 3:28 after a long layoff. Quite respectable under the circumstances, but few people let me explain the circumstances. So rather than be a bore, I just told them my time and let them think I was over the hill and slipping.

I had this all in mind when I rose to speak that Friday night. I had even investigated the possibility of other races that day, a 5-miler, perhaps, or some easy 10-kilometer run. But the closest event I could find was in Richmond, Virginia.

Then as I looked around at those runners in New York City, I knew I had to join them. The worst feeling in the world is that of missing something, the feeling that everything is going on somewhere else.

Those people in front of me were what William James called "the faithful fighters." They were silently repeating to me the words of Henry IV when he greeted the tardy Crillon after a great victory: "Hang yourself, brave Crillon. We fought at Arques, and you were not there."

That night, I knew I wanted to join in the fight. It was easier to risk pain, embarrassment, failure and the possibility of walking home through the Bronx than to miss this great struggle.

So on Sunday I was at Fort Wadsworth with the 14,000 other marathoners, getting my number verified and fortifying myself with coffee and doughnuts. All of my reluctance had gone; I was impatient to get underway.

The first 20 miles were delightful. You have heard of automatic writing that flows out of the writer from some mysterious source? Those first 20 miles were automatic running. Almost effortlessly, the 7-minute miles spun on and on. At 10 miles, the digital clock read 1:10:10; at 20, it was 2:20:10—an almost incredible consistency. Then I passed a sign that said, "Salazar, 2:08:13, World Record." It was an inspiration—he had gone for it; so would I.

But the last 6 miles were every bit as painful as they are said to be. Try as I might, my pace kept slowing. My form began to go. I lost the strength and flow that had marked the early going. Now the pain became constant in my legs, and on the hills it filled my arms and chest.

I was constantly losing time to the clock. With a mile to go, I was uncertain about finishing. But those around me were still running, so I assumed I could and must. By now I was on Central Park South, heading for Columbus Circle.

That avenue has a slight upgrade with poor footing, and is always strangely devoid of spectators cheering the runners. I find this stretch the most trying of the entire marathon. Here pain and exhaustion fuse with an intense desire to give up. I want to say, "Enough is enough. This whole enterprise is a mistake. It is too much for me." But then I made the turn into the park and heard the cheering up ahead. There they were, thousands of people lining the road and filling the grandstands and calling out my name. That was all I needed. I went up that last terrible hill to the finish line as if it didn't exist. So hang yourself, dear reader. We ran at New York, and you were not there.

—RUNNER'S WORLD MAGAZINE, FEBRUARY 1982

———◆———

WHEN EMERSON WAS 61 he wrote in his journal: "Within, I do not find wrinkles or a used heart, but unspent youth." I am now 61 and know exactly what he meant. Yet I'm not sure what led Emerson to make that entry, just what it was that alerted him to his continuing potential for growth. For me it was the announcement of the qualifying times for the 1980 Boston Marathon.

Specifically the stipulation that runners over 40 must better 3:10 in order to enter. There were no further provisions for age. No exemptions for those over 60. No indication that the committee realized the toll that years take on the body.

My initial reaction was outrage. I had not run under 3:10 in 3 years and did not expect to do it ever again. I was content to be, and indeed deserved to be, emeritus. I was entitled to privileges and prerogatives that went with that status. I had run in Boston since 1964 and should be allowed to run there as long as I pleased. Asking me to turn back the clock was ridiculous.

Other 60-year-olds were taking the same position. One of my aging friends had written a long letter to Will Cloney, the head man, asking for leniency. Pleading that Cloney make an exception for the old-timers. Otherwise some grand old men, he said, would be excluded. This grand old man felt the same way. When I read the letter I thought, "Right on!" It was unseemly to treat us heroes that way. We had paid our dues. We had been there and back. Yet here they were asking us to re-enlist and do it again. At 60 I was through with combat. I wanted out. Just give me a standing ovation. Then a quiet corner where I could put my feet up, drink some beer, and give advice. At 60 everything is or should be settled. No more tests. Behind, the best I could do; ahead, the enjoyment of having done it. Suppose I could even beat 3:10; why should I? What would that prove?

Eventually it was the thinking that did me in. I began to see that the Boston people were right. They were, in fact, doing me a favor. Offering a challenge and, given the proper response, an opportunity for rebirth rather than retirement. They were forcing me to face the crisis of the 60-year-old, which is no less than a third adolescence.

The feelings I had were much like those I had experienced at 20 and again at 45. Of being capable of more, but being afraid to try. Of being capable of more, but shrinking from the necessary hard work and discipline. And above all dreading being told what I was capable of because then I had to go out and do it.

The third adolescence is as difficult as the other two. The young fear failure. The middle-aged have come to doubt success. The elderly know both are false and it is effort alone that counts. For the elderly adolescent the major problem is getting geared up to go out again. It doesn't seem worth it. The lesson, then, is never give up. So I knew it would not be just for this once but again and again. People may retire you, but life never does.

Emerson, of course, had no doubts. A year later we see him going full tilt into the future. "When I read a good book," he wrote in the journal, "I wish that life was 300 years long. The Chaldaic Oracles tempt me. But so does algebra and astronomy and chemistry and geology and botany."

So I yielded to the Boston group. I accepted their unfair standard. I knew then this goal was good for me. It would make me the best marathoner I could be. It would lead me through this crisis to a new flowering, a new growth.

My first try was the New York Marathon. I ran well, placed well, won the 60-and-over. But my time was 3:14, still not good enough. Two weeks later I was in Washington for another attempt, this time the Marine Corps Marathon.

Looking back now, it is remarkable how easy it was. The course was flat, the weather perfect. A little band music before the start. The Festive Overture of Shostakovich, then the "Battle Hymn of the Republic" followed by the National Anthem. I had to be restrained from jumping the gun.

There was no need. I breezed through the first mile in 6:30. Then found a young medical student named Victor who claimed to have a clock in his head. "I am going to run 7 minutes a mile," he said, "until I come apart." He turned out to be a metronome. And his pacing was all I needed.

There were a few anxious moments at the 23-mile mark when I thought I might be hitting the wall. Then they passed and I was in control the rest of the way.

The last mile was against the wind and the final 600 yards uphill, but I never had any doubts of the outcome. I crossed the line 783rd in a field of more than 7,000. My average time for the mile: an unprecedented 6:54. After 16 years of running and 50 or more marathons, I had run the Marine Corps Marathon in Washington, DC, in the time of 3:01:10, an all-time personal best. The next day I gave a lecture on running at a college in upstate New York. Shortly into the question-and-answer period, someone asked me what I thought of the qualifying times for Boston.

I stood there gazing around at the audience of students and faculty and townspeople. Surveying this assemblage of adolescents, some 20, some 40, some 60. Looking out at all that unspent youth. Then I drew myself up and stood as tall as a 60-year-old can without appearing arrogant.

"Eminently fair," I said.

—*RUNNER'S WORLD* MAGAZINE, JUNE 1979

THE NEXT DAY, PEOPLE kept asking me how I had done. At first, I answered that I didn't finish. Then I began saying that I couldn't finish. What I should have said was, "I hit the wall." I should have told them right off that I hit it. Then they might have understood.

In any case, that is what happened. In this 1980 Boston Marathon, I finally hit the wall. After years of reading about it, hearing about it, lecturing about it, I had totally and irrevocably hit the wall. After 17 years of successful Bostons, I failed to finish. I reached the Prudential in a trolley, not on foot.

Just past the 21-mile mark, coming down the hill at Boston College, I knew I was finished. There had been, however, a hint of disaster all day. I had come to Boston on the strength of my best-ever marathon and was attempting to duplicate it—a dangerous thing to do at any time but particularly with the temperature in the 70s. There was a cloudless sky, so the sun was contributing another 10 to 20 degrees. The following wind virtually eliminated heat dissipation by air conduction.

On such a day, initial pace is of paramount importance. When there is excessive heat stress, speed increases dehydration, elevates body temperature, and, of prime importance, rapidly uses up the muscle glycogen stores. On such a day, I should have been thinking of running 30 seconds a mile slower than my usual time. Instead I was thinking of running 30 seconds a mile faster. I had always prided myself on prudence in such circumstances, but like many other runners I was already thinking about qualifying for next year. Instead of running according to our bodies, we ran against the clock. It was the most competitive Boston Marathon I ever ran.

At around the 15-mile mark in Newton Lower Falls, I began to feel uneasy about the outcome. The long downhill there was much more difficult than in other years. Then, on the upgrade, I discovered I was losing the drive in my legs. There was no bounce. I had no lift. I could hear my foot strike, a sure sign of losing form and coordination. I was like a pitcher who had found there was no steam on his fastball. I was in trouble.

Nonetheless, I negotiated the Newton Hills and got past Heartbreak without too much additional difficulty. It was on the long descent past the crowds at Boston College that I began to come apart. My pace slowed until was running in slow motion. My arms were moving more than my legs. All the way to the foot of the hill, I ran—rather, moved in a grotesque caricature of running—all the while hoping that I would be all right once I got on the flat and could run again.

Going downhill at that point is always bad. The front thigh muscles always protest. Each step becomes extremely painful. I had gone through that before and then recovered to run well to the finish, so I hoped that would happen again when I finally reached the bottom.

"Now," I said to myself, "it will be better." But it wasn't. If anything, it was worse. The pain was still there, and now an overwhelming weariness. The muscles had become lifeless. They had lost not only power and coordination but shock absorption as well. Every step not only hurt my thighs but was doing terrible things to my knees.

Nevertheless, I persisted. With each step my pace became slower, but I refused to walk. There was simply no question of walking. No matter what happens, I told myself, I will not walk. I had never walked in Boston, and there would be no first time.

I could hear the crowd encouraging me. Some called out, "Looking good." Others yelled, "You can make it." The more perceptive shouted, "Tough it out" and "Hang in there." Now and then, I would hear what seemed to be the rallying cry for this year's run: "Go for it."

It was going for it that had gotten me into this state. Had I run prudently during the first half, I would now be taking it in, running my body and heart out but finishing. Now I was reduced to this private little hell, my eyes fixed on my shadow in front of me, watching this pantomime. I was apparently running but actually not. I was moving up and down, but not forward. I was virtually running in place. And all the while, I was losing any sense of the crowd and the race and where I was. My life became that one thought: Keep running.

Then I felt a hand and looked up. There was a friend beside me. She was watching the race, and seeing me in this state, she had rushed out. "Don't you want to walk, George?" she asked. She was a mother talking to a child. By now she had her arm around me, holding me up. I was still running, and there she was standing there holding me up. I was no longer moving forward, but I was not going to walk.

"George, don't you want to walk?" she asked again. She had come out of the crowd to save me from myself. I looked at her standing there, her face full of sympathy and care and love. I knew it was the end. "Nina," I said, "all I want is someone to take me home."

Then a trolley appeared as if she had summoned it, and she got me on it. When I boarded it, the 20 or so people inside sent up a cheer. That upset me at first. "Why cheer me?" I asked them. "I didn't even finish."

It apparently didn't matter. Someone came up and offered me orange juice, and someone else gave me his seat. So I rode to the Prudential, beginning to feel good about the whole thing. The wall, I thought, can be a peak experience.

——*RUNNER'S WORLD* MAGAZINE, JUNE 1980

FOR A FRIEND OF mine the setting was the Scottish Games at Grandfather Mountain. The marathon there is one of the most difficult in this country. Its 26.2 miles through mountainous country test a runner as almost no other race does.

My friend survived that test and ultimately conquered the course. And when he came to the last climb where the finish was supposed to be, he heard the sound of bagpipes. Now, as everyone knows, the skirling of bagpipes stirs passions and emotions inaccessible in other ways. So my friend, already overcome by reaching the end of this ordeal, was in tears when he breasted the hill.

And now he saw he was on a great plain encircled by the camps of the various Scottish clans. And each sent up a great shout as he passed them. What place he took, he sometimes forgets. But he will never forget when time stood still on that plain atop Grandfather Mountain and all around him were happy cheering people and the sound of bagpipes.

All this has, of course, nothing to do with winning and losing. Winning and losing is what you do in team games. The runner is not in a game; he is in a contest. And that is a word whose Latin root means to witness or testify. The other runners are witnesses to what he is doing. And therefore, anything else than all he can give is not enough. When you race, you are under oath. When you race, you are testifying as to who you are.

The distance runner understands this. He is the mildest of men. Quiet and even-tempered and rarely given to argument. He avoids confrontation and seeks his own private world, but in a marathon he becomes a tiger. He will go to the end of his physiology to find who he is and what he can do. Put himself deeper and deeper into a cauldron of pain. What is necessary becomes possible, however absurd the effort may be.

But such interrogations, if they are to mean anything, should be infrequent. If the marathon is to measure a man, it should synchronize with the cycles of his growth. Maturity is an uneven, discouraging process. Becoming who you are is not done on schedule. There are years when nothing seems to happen. But one must still say that marathons can make memories like no other event in your life. And that could be an argument for running one every month. When rocking-chair time comes, you'll be all set.

—HOW TO FEEL GREAT 24 HOURS A DAY, 1983

LIKE MOST DISTANCE RUNNERS, I am still a child. And never more so than when I run. I take that play more seriously than anything else I do. And in that play I retire into the fantasyland of my imagination anytime I please.

Like most children, I think I control my life. Believe myself to be independent. I am certain I have been placed on this earth to enjoy myself. Like most children, I live in the best of all possible worlds, a world made for running and racing, where nothing but good can happen. And, like most children, I am oblivious to all of the work done by other people to make it that way.

This is more than faith. Faith is the Breton peasant praying for rain and then taking an umbrella with him when he leaves the house. Faith is a nun friend of my grandmother's who periodically herded 30 to 40 orphans onto a train at Poughkeepsie and set out for Coney Island without a penny in her purse. "God will provide," was her motto. That's faith.

Faith is an act of the will made by an adult. The child acts before will and reason and dogma. He simply knows. And the child in me knows that I am in a game that will always have a happy ending. That I can enjoy the anxiety leading up to the race, and the tremendous challenge in the running, and the sweetness or bitterness of the ending, knowing that, whatever happens, I am already a hero, a winner. Knowing that in the end, whatever the crisis, there would always be someone to take care of me.

I hadn't realized this (although it may well have been evident to my family and friends) until the 1976 Boston Marathon. The official temperature on Patriots' Day was 92 degrees, a level listed as dangerous for livestock and death-dealing to runners. Any thinking adult would have sat this one out. But there I was with 1,800 others dressing at the Hopkinton High School gym.

Then, walking to the starting line, I passed a gasoline station with a thermometer on the wall. It read 116 degrees. I passed by undeterred. At the starting line there were hoses to fill our cups to douse our heads and caps and the shirts we wore. The family of man was already operating. The people were already taking care of their children.

And that was the way it was. The whole thing was absurd. The race should have been postponed or set for later in the day. There was no way for a runner to go those 26 sunbaked miles to Boston relying on official help. Yet I set out knowing I would get whatever help I needed. Knowing I would survive.

For one thing, Boston Marathon crowds are special. I recall my first Boston and how astounded I was that people called me George all along the way. They stood in groups with one person picking the names out of the *Globe* so that when I got to them there would be cries of "You can do it, George," or "George, you're looking strong," or, in the late stages, "Keep it up, George, there's only 3 miles to go."

What that can do to a childlike runner previously known only to his own family is unbelievable. I felt capable of anything, even completing the Boston Marathon.

This year the crowd outdid itself. Within 2 miles we were running in the rain. It was 92 degrees with a cloudless sky, and we were running in a rain provided by hose after hose after hose. There was water everywhere. Mile upon mile of people and children offering water to drink and pour on me. Swarms of young boys giving out Gatorade, with the same enthusiasm they had shown an hour before supplying the leaders. Others with buckets of ice. Some with the traditional orange slices, many of the children just holding out their hands to be touched by the heroes passing by.

From Ashland on, there was nothing but applause and cheers. Then came the reception from the girls at Wellesley, and farther on the children in the Newton Hills outdoing each other to get us ice and water. And there I saw this solemn 4-year-old, just standing with a tiny cup, hoping someone would stop. I did and drank the 2 ounces and told her, "You're my honey." Boston is like that, a voice, a face, a child that you remember forever.

I was in Boston now and should have been home free. I wasn't. I was running a poor marathon, and when you run a poor marathon you not only hurt, you hurt longer. I had been out on the roads longer than any time in my 14 years of running. But through all the pain and not knowing whether I would finish, dragging out those last terrible miles, I always felt safe. I knew I was surrounded by friends and family and those who would take care of me no matter what happened.

And knowing too that if I stopped they would say, "You gave it your best, George." Knowing that whatever I did, I would not disappoint them. There would always be a meal and a soft bed and a good day of running tomorrow.

Only the child still lives in a world where such days are possible. The year my daughter entered college in Boston, she came to see me in the marathon. She was, she told me later, the only calm and rational person among those thousands that jammed Prudential Center.

They cheered and yelled and applauded every finisher. They cheered the young, cheered the old, cheered those from Harvard, cheered those from California. And they cheered even more wildly when someone they knew came into sight. Through it all, she stood as quiet and as staid and withdrawn as an Episcopalian at a revival meeting.

Then I arrived. I made my turn into that long, wide plaza, which at that moment was completely empty except for me and the cheering group. The finish line was still an eighth of a mile away, but it didn't matter. The race was over. The crowd's cheers told me that I had made it. And this was my victory lap. Almost an hour behind the winner, having nailed down 312th place, I was suddenly renewed and refreshed. I was running my homerun home, and every stride I took revealed my joy.

Then I saw a figure break out of the crowd into the white expanse that lay between me and the officials at the finish. It wasn't until another 50 yards that I recognized who this yelling, waving, cheering person was. My daughter.

The finish of any marathon can be that kind of emotional experience. Somewhere along the way the runner has been challenged. He has met pain fairly and overcome it. He has had a real deliverance. And at the end of that ordeal, both runner and spectator are aware that something very special has happened. Sometimes this awareness is expressed in ways that neither runner nor spectator will ever forget. For me that occurred in Boston.

—HOW TO FEEL GREAT 24 HOURS A DAY, 1983

———————◆———————

NEAR THE 23-MILE MARK of the New York Marathon, the course turns off Fifth Avenue into Central Park. The runners face a short but fairly steep and demanding hill, and then the course follows the undulating road through the park toward the finish.

I entered the park in the grip of the inexpressible fatigue that comes at that stage in the race. I was once again engaged in the struggle between a completely exhausted body and a yet undefeated will. I ran toward that hill, realizing that finishing was still problematical, fearing that I might still have to walk, and knowing that no matter what happened those final 25 or more minutes would constitute my most painful experience this side of major surgery.

I ascended the hill past a small group of onlookers. One of them recognized me and called out, "Dr. Sheehan, what would Emerson have said now?"

I had to laugh, even in that pain. It was a particularly deft shot at someone who had used other people's words to express his own truth, and I was now in a situation that clearly no one else could describe. But the question also went to the question of why I run marathons.

The case for distance running cannot be stated simply, even by its adherents. No matter how often I'm asked, even in more favorably circumstances than the 23-mile mark of a marathon, my answer is always inadequate.

I am not alone in this inadequacy. At that same marathon, a questionnaire was distributed asking the entrants why they ran. The series of suggested answers had been made up by scientists of the body and mind. There were 15 possible choices, the last one being, "Don't really know." The range of answers indicated the researchers' own indecision, their inability to put their fingers on their personal motivations.

I think it instructive, however, that only three of the answers— "Improving physical health," "Improving sexual capacity," and "Acquiring a youthful appearance"—had to do with the body. All the others (except the final disclaimer of not knowing at all) were psychological benefits.

Runners apparently take as a given truth that physical health is a byproduct of running but not the real reason they run. I am aware of that also. I am my body. What I do begins there. But I am much more besides. What happens to my body has an enormous effect on my heart and mind. When I run, I become of necessity a good animal, but I also become for less obvious and even mysterious reasons a good person. I become, in some uncanny way, complete. Perhaps it has something to do with a sense of success and mastery over this art of running.

The scientists tried to express this in their suggested answers. Do I run, they asked, to relax, to relieve boredom, or to improve my mental health? Is it possible, they inquired, that I do it to achieve recognition or to master a challenge or to find an additional purpose in life? Perhaps running, the questionnaire went on, is something I do for friendship and association, or because I am unhappy and unfulfilled without it.

What we were being asked was the familiar "either/or." Is it process or product that pushes us? Is it what happens while we run or what we achieve through running that motivates us? Is running for the body or the spirit?

My running is not either/or. It is all these reasons and more. Running is indeed product. It is done for the goal—the ability to run a marathon, the having done it. But it is the process as well. Training is not only a means; it is an end in itself. The achievement is not the whole reason. There is also what goes on before the attainment of that achievement, what goes on before the mastering of the challenge, what is gone through in finding an additional purpose in life.

My running is both process and product. Sometimes, it is all meaning and no purpose. Other times, it is all purpose and no meaning.

Sometimes, it is work, other times play, and there are even times when it is an act of love.

We who run are different from those who merely study us. We are out there experiencing what they are trying to put into words. We know what they are merely trying to know. They are seeking belief, while we already believe. Our difficulty is in expressing the whole truth of that experience, that knowledge, that belief.

So I wish Emerson had run marathons, and somewhere around the 23-mile mark a friend had asked him, "What's it all about, Waldo?"

—*RUNNER'S WORLD* MAGAZINE, JUNE 1979

What Dr. Sheehan Means to Me

BY ROBERT LIPSYTE

I'M NOT SURE WHO discovered whom at the 1968 Boston Marathon—me, trolling for a story, or George, hunting for a major media outlet—but we collided like magnets and stuck for the next 25 years. He became a recurrent character in my *New York Times* columns and in my books. Within minutes of that first meeting, he described the race to me as a Greek tragedy. He had me at "hubris."

And that was the word for George too. Overweening pride. To the very end. A few months before he died in 1993, on a sunny summer day as runners he had undoubtedly inspired moved past his beachfront window, he told me how he manipulated his life-prolonging cancer medication so he could compete more successfully in local races. A little less of it gave him more speed but shortened the time of his life.

He reveled in the control. He said, "In the contest, what the Greeks call the *agon,* you find out you have what it takes and you're altered by the experience. To meet the challenge of death is now my race."

George was important—is still important—to people who pay attention to what he says (not always to what he did). He gave a moral spine to running with his spiritual implications and he infused ancient philosophers with miles of fresh air, all the while sending out legions of people now more connected with the health of both their bodies and their minds.

George was not dogmatic. After taking my running history and scoping my body type, he suggested I become a bike rider. For that too, I'm grateful.

8/ *Challenge* and the Pursuit of *Excellence*

*L*ive if you will a life without risk. Avoid the forge, the fire, the flame. But know that joy and happiness and the good life come only as unexpected interludes in the endless, stressful, tense, and restless journey to become the person you are.

DR. SHEEHAN ON RUNNING, 1975

I'VE BEEN A DISTANCE runner for almost 30 years, and I'm still trying to explain this self-renewing inner compulsion. The more I run, the more I want to run. The more I run, the more I live a life conditioned and influenced and fashioned by my running. And the more I run, the more certain I am that I am heading for my real goal: to become the person I am.

If Francis Bacon had written on running, he would have put it this way: "Running maketh the whole man." I see that whole person as being part animal, part child, part artist, and part saint. Running makes me all of these. It makes me a whole person.

I begin as body. "Be first a good animal," wrote Emerson. I am. I have that animal energy, that ease of movement, that good tight body, that sense of occupying just the right amount of space. I am pared down to bone and muscle. My skin taut, my eyes clear, I have become my body. I occupy it with delight.

The tests prove what I feel. My biological age is that of a person 30 years younger. I have the oxygen capacity and physical work capacity of a 40-year-old instead of someone over 70. My pulse is slow, my blood pressure normal. My body fat is a mere 5 percent. Yet I am no different from others my age who run with me. Running proves that man at any age is the greatest marvel in the world.

Next comes the child. Running makes me a child, a child at play. That is the aim of life: to become an adult while remaining a child at heart. Play is the key. When we play, we do things because we want to, without thought of payment.

Play is something we would do for nothing, something that has meaning but no purpose. When I run, I feel that. For that hour a day, I am a child finally doing what I want to do and enjoying it. When I do, I realize what happens to the body is simply a bonus. I must first play an hour a day, then all other things will be added on.

One great addition is to make myself an artist. Being an artist is, after all, only seeing things as if for the first time. When we do, we see the real meaning of things, the solutions to our problems. Running gives me that creativity. It provides the meditative setting. It opens up areas in my mind I seem not to use otherwise.

At the minimum, it places me where these things can happen. A physician friend of mine expressed it this way: "I decided to run at a pace that would allow me to (1) enjoy my surroundings; (2) let me think a bit; and (3) be alone for an hour a day." I agree. On the roads at a pace I could run forever, I find what that "forever" is all about.

Finally, running has given me the chance to be a saint, to be a hero. Like everyone else, I want to be challenged. I want to find out whether or not I am a coward. I want to see how much effort I can put out . . . what I can endure . . . if I measure up. Running allows that.

I can run the classic race, the mile, and know the terrible pain that accompanies that third quarter-mile and the almost total oblivion of that final 100 yards to the finish. I can suffer, die, and be born again in a 6-mile race over hills on a cross country course. And I can compete with myself in the marathon, the race Roger Bannister called the "acme of athletic heroism."

There are as many reasons for running as there are days in the year, years in my life. But mostly I run because I am an animal and a child, an artist and a saint. So, too, are you. Find your own play, your own self-renewing compulsion, and you will become the person you are meant to be.

—RUNNING TO WIN, 1991

"WHERE HAVE ALL THE heroes gone?" asked novelist Edward Hoagland in the *New York Times Magazine.* And his question taken up a day or two later by sports writer Bob Lipsyte.

"Help! Wanted: Hero or Heroine" was the name of the Lipsyte piece.

Both pointed out that the traditional heroes no longer held our respect or admiration. Hoagland observed that experts and physicians, soldiers and statesmen aren't heroes to anyone at the present time. And Lipsyte saw no one in the soldier-statesman-athlete pool who could fill Carlyle's definition of the heroic man: the messenger sent from the infinite unknown with tidings for all of us. There seemed to be no one ready to seize fire and run with it.

In Hoagland's view, the hero has died from familiarity. "One must love one's heroes," he wrote, "notwithstanding their pains, self-doubts and inconsistencies—which is much more difficult with overexposure."

There you have it. The transistor did them in. TV and the electronic age have freed future generations from the cult of these public successes and private failures. Our communication marvels have shown us that heroes not only have feet of clay, they have lives of clay. This has given us a clue to who are the real winners and losers in this world. More than anything else, we have come to see the hero as a man simply trying to become what he conceives himself to be.

We know that the major battles in life are waged unseen and unnoticed. We the people truly dream the impossible dream, fight the unbeatable foe, and bear unbearable sorrows. We are on that quest, no matter how hopeless, no matter how far. And we know it is only in pursuing that quest that we will finally come to rest fulfilled.

So we are all heroes to some degree. We become more so as we base our actions on ourselves and ourselves alone. "Heroism," wrote Ortega, "is the will to be oneself." The hero's will is not that of family or custom or society, but his own. His life is a resistance to what is customary and habitual, to business as usual. The hero takes himself and his place in time and creates his own drama.

Hear Ortega again on this. We come into this world, he says, to play a part for which neither script nor role has been established. It is for us to compose and act out the drama of our existence. No one else can or should do this for us. There is no hero, past or future, who can be used as a model.

Where have all the heroes gone? They've gone with the simplicities and the pieties and the easy answers of another era. Our lack of heroes is an indication of the maturity of our age—a realization that everyman has come in to his own and has the capability of making a success out of his life. Success rests with having the courage and endurance and, above all, the will to become the person you are, however peculiar that may be.

Then you will be able to say, "I have found my hero and he is me."

—*DR. SHEEHAN ON RUNNING,* 1975

◆

"IF YOU RUN MORE than 15 miles per week," said Kenneth Cooper, MD, of the Cooper Institute for Aerobic Research in Texas, "you run for something other than aerobic fitness." That statement, and Cooper's implication that many runners are obsessive about mileage, are both true. Aerobic fitness is the ability to do work, and if all you want or require from exercise is the ability to do work, Dr. Cooper is right:

15 miles is enough.

But how far do we have to run for all the other things running brings—sanity and self-worth, for example? That's not so easy to say. Self-mastery and self-esteem cannot be calculated by a treadmill, nor can the value of a spiritual insight be determined by a blood test. But all three are common consequences of exercise. We must not ignore the psychological, creative, and spiritual dividends people gain from exercise.

Some runners, for instance, require 5 to 10 miles a day to maintain their sanity, serenity, and good humor. A female friend, who walks an hour a day getting to and from work, told me she still likes to run 5 miles when she gets home. "I need it for head time," she said.

The reasons for running and other forms of exercise go far beyond fitness. Some people run for philosophical reasons, not finish lines. Running is an entry to another world, a pathway to experiences that cannot always be articulated. Whether you call them peak experiences or mystical events, runners continue to seek them.

"There are other and greater realities," said philosopher William James. And it's true: There is more to life than what our senses tell us, and people have sought in many ways to find out precisely what. James, for example, experimented with nitrous oxide. Running is a significantly safer way to pursue the same thing—new understanding.

James also spent considerable amounts of his time investigating psychic phenomena. And it is important to note that the fitness movement has taken place at a time of resurgence in interest in psychics. We now have around us what is called the New Age movement—people focusing on aspects of the self that are beyond scientific proof. They are going into the right brain, into nonlogical areas of the mind to explore the possibilities.

Even television is showing the effects. Advertisers are asking us to "be all you can be," "master the possibilities," and "perfect the experience." These are slogans that James would have loved. One of his greatest works is *The Varieties of Religious Experience*. This book, composed of the Gifford Lectures he gave in Edinburgh, is no less than a continuous account of human beings going beyond the ordinary human experience—a New Age bible of sorts written in the last century.

Fitness can be an attempt to go beyond the ordinary human experience. It begins with exploring the limits of the body, and it then explores the limits of the mind. Ultimately, it explores the limits of the whole person. One discovers from hand-to-hand combat with the self—or through a transport to indescribable areas of the soul—that there are indeed other and greater realities.

And, frankly, I'm not at all sure you can find this other life on Dr. Kenneth Cooper's 15 miles a week.

—*PERSONAL BEST,* 1989

MOTIVATION IS THE NEED, drive, or desire to act in a certain way to achieve a certain end. Basic needs are strong motivators. When I am hungry or thirsty or cold, or when I am in obvious danger, I am impelled to do something about it. I am willing to attack the problem head-on: I do what must be done.

Whereas drives push, desires pull. I have desires for many things. I want self-esteem. I would like to be a hero. I wish to have peak experiences. I pray for that perfect communion with another person. And as I sit here at the typewriter, I am trying to write a perfect essay.

Making allowances for differences in vocation and avocation, I presume you would say much the same. Our needs, drives, and desires—the stuff of our lives—do not vary to any great degree. Yet our motivation does. I see about me people who, in philosopher

William James's expression, lead lives inferior to themselves. And I suspect that I do the same. We could all be artists and athletes and heroes. We could all care for orphans and widows and visit the sick. We could all be catchers in the rye, each in his or her own unique and particular way announcing the Creator's intentions at our births. We could be our best. But we· are not.

Our only excuse is ignorance. We are unaware of our capabilities. We do not realize that each one of us is the marvel of the universe. We should read the geniuses of our past. Heed Emerson: "I preach the infinitude of the common man." We sell ourselves short, and our lives as well. When our horizons narrow, our goals do also. We settle for a comfortable passing grade. We groove through life, effortlessly passing our days. But the intensity of our art—our life—and therefore our joy, passes as well. But that is part of the bargain.

I know of one crew coach who retired because he had a different breed of rowers. "They are no longer," he said, "looking at the hills." When people look at the highest goal, the intensity of motivation increases in two ways. First, in the strength of the desire to achieve. Whatever is necessary will now be done. One look at the grandeur of the Matterhorn gives the true mountaineer all the inspiration he needs! The year's preparation that precedes his climb is now automatic. The climb becomes the reason for existence.

My end is not simple happiness. My need, drive, and desire is to achieve my full and complete self. If I do what I have come to do, if I create the life I was made for, then happiness will follow. The problem in motivation is not the dedication and effort and sacrifice needed to get what we want, it is knowing what it is we could and must want to begin with.

—*PERSONAL BEST,* 1989

THE DECLARATION OF INDEPENDENCE states unequivocally that all men are created equal. Yet every day I find reason to believe this to be untrue. I run in a race and half the field beats me. I attend a seminar and can't follow the reasoning of the speaker. I read a book and I am unable to understand what is evident to others. Daily I am instructed in my deficiencies. I do something, physical or mental, and realize how far I fall short of what other people accomplish.

Despite the Declaration, we are apparently not born equal. I cannot aspire to win the Boston Marathon. I most certainly will not receive the Nobel Prize for literature. I am surrounded by people who know more, do more, and make more than I do. But, like many others, I identify myself with my performance. I become my marathon time. I become my latest book. I become the last lecture I gave.

I am all those things, of course. They are part of the self. They are the various ways I have of expressing who I am and what I believe. These are the operations that reveal the body-mind machine that I am.

But I am more than a body-mind complex. I am a soul as well. I share with everyone on this planet one power infinitely more important than talent: willpower. In this power of the soul, all of us are created equal. Each one of us is capable of the ideal or moral action, which William James defined in this way: "It is the action in the line of the greatest resistance."

Anyone so inclined can decide on ideal action. The will considers the question, Will you or won't you have it so? And in that decision you can be the equal of anyone else. "Effort is the measure of a man," wrote James.

How well we know that. I am never content with contentment. I am uneasy when things go easy. "Don't take things easy," said a great physician, "take things hard." Doing one's absolute best becomes the criterion.

"I am writing the best I can," said the author of some bestselling popular novels. "If I could write any better I would. This is the peak of my powers." It matters little that she cannot write any better. It matters, more than life, that she is doing it with all her might.

Running in races has made this whole subject plain to me. I am thinking now of Palmetto Road, the long steep hill at the 5-mile mark of the Bermuda 10-kilometer run. For most of the race, I am running in the lee of a gentleman my age wearing plaid shorts. Just before the hill I pass him and go into second place in my age group.

It is a short-lived moment of triumph. The hill suddenly puts urgent demands on my body. I forget the imperative of beating anyone in my age group and especially one in plaid shorts. It becomes the hill and me. My legs are heavy and filled with pain. My breath comes in short gasps. I am bent over almost double. The battle shifts. It becomes me against me. My will in a duel with my mind and my body. A contest with that part of myself who wants to stop.

All around me, runners are engaged in the same struggle. Pushing themselves as if their lives depended on reaching the top of this hill. The leaders have already finished, and the race, you might say, is over. But not for us. A spectator who could see this race for what it truly is would see not bodies but wills straining to reach the crest. Here indeed is "action in the line of the greatest resistance."

A jockey, speaking of a champion horse, said, "He makes the effort and makes it more often." The uncrowned champions at the back of the pack do the same. Unconcerned with what others are doing, driven by the need to do our best, we make the effort and we make it more often. And for those few moments, we become the equal of anyone on this earth.

—PERSONAL BEST, 1989

———◆———

ONE YEAR WHEN I was in Boston for the marathon, I saw an advertisement in the *Boston Globe:* "Runners Wanted!" The Dana Farber Cancer Institute was recruiting runners to participate in their research studies.

"We are engaged," the ad went on, "in our own difficult kind of marathon, a long road to discover solutions to complex problems about the cause and cure of cancer. . . . We need people with qualities you possess: dedication, discipline, energy, and the belief you change things for the better."

Those qualities come with the athletic experience. Whatever the sport, it develops not only the body but the mind and spirit as well. Sport is an essential element in education. The Greeks knew this centuries ago, and it's now becoming apparent to those who, long after graduation, have returned to the task of becoming athletes.

The athletic experience consists of three parts: the training, which the Greeks called *askesis;* the event, or *agon;* and the aftermath, which the Greeks termed *arete,* which can be variously translated as "excellence" or "vigor" or "virtue." The goal of Greek education was to create a citizen-soldier. This education, said Plato, was what develops virtue from childhood, what makes one able to rule the state or defend it.

The ultimate aim is self-mastery. If we are to dominate events, we must first dominate ourselves. Self-rule comes naturally to the athlete. Training, or askesis, brings with it the virtues of prudence and moderation. The lifestyle of athletes con forms to the laws of the body. "Breaking training" is physical sin. When I became a runner, I became my body and accepted its laws. This does not, of course, go unrewarded. Athletes perform at the peak of their powers. They have the energy the Dana Farber people seek.

Basketball player Bill Bradley, in speaking of his months of pre-season in training, developed self-mastery: "I didn't buy the argument that I was going to lose because I wasn't working hard enough. I might lose because I wasn't fast enough; I might lose because I wasn't tall enough; but I wasn't going to lose because I wasn't ready."

But self-mastery goes beyond preparation. The race becomes the agon, where the self is developed. "The race to be run, the victory to be won, the defeat that one risked suffering," writes Michel Foucault about the Greeks, "these are processes and events that took place between oneself and oneself. The adversaries the individual had to combat were not just with him and close by; they are part of him."

How well the runner knows that. At first, it appeared that I was fighting hills and terrain, heat and humidity, and the distance I had to race. But it was soon apparent that these were not my opponents. My opponent is me—the real me who would let this cup pass, the true self who is willing to settle for "a good try," and not the last desperate and painful and revealing plunge into the black hole of who I am.

The importance of this element of sport has not been lost on philosophers. After observing a football game, the philosopher George Santayana wrote, "There is then a great and continuous endeavor, a representation of all the primitive virtues and fundamental gifts of man." In the race, the runner searches for these virtues and values, the martial virtues now liberated from the attendant horrors of war. We have then, as Santayana states, "a drama in which all moral and emotional interests are involved. The whole soul is stirred by a spectacle that represents the basis for life."

Is this an exaggeration? Poet Robert Frost, attending a baseball all-star game, compared athletes to artists and rejoiced in their display of prowess, courage, knowledge, and justice. We see again and again the elevation of the whole person. Educators forced to reevaluate the athletic experience come to the same conclusions. A faculty committee at Dickinson College in Carlisle, Pennsylvania, in considering the role of sports in the students' lives, wrote: "The agon is not a matter of winning or losing. It is the willingness to compete. Let us not forget that the agon is freely accepted—it is a matter of committing the self to act and bear the consequences of action."

And there are other rewards seen by these educators: "To experience sport and analyze it critically is to be involved in an enterprise with dramatic and intense personal immediacy rarely, if ever, offered by more traditional studies." The report goes on: "Sport is an easily accessible laboratory of dedication, sacrifice, courage, mastery, order, cooperation, leadership, companionship, solitude, loyalty, and authority."

Therein lies the final part of the athletic experience—the transformation of the self—brought about by these learning experiences. The deposition into the subconscious of the good news about the self— an entry into the world of William Blake, where we become "chariots of fire" and for which the best word is "exultation." We now are what we became in the race and ready for whatever the day brings.

What the day brings, as everyone learns sooner or later, is recurrent challenge. The agon is a daily experience. The Greek philosopher Epictetus told us that almost 2 centuries ago: "If anything laborious or pleasant, glorious or inglorious, be presented to you, remember now is the contest, now are the Olympic Games, and they cannot be deferred." There will never be a day when we won't need energy, dedication, discipline, and the feeling that we can change things for the better. The people at the Dana Farber Cancer Institute know that. And we should, too.

—*RUNNING TO WIN,* 1991

UNTIL I TOOK UP distance running, I found it easy to take it easy. I had no difficulty following the warnings of the experts. "Avoid stress," cautioned the physicians. I did. "Reduce your tensions," advised the psychologists. I did. "Rest that restless heart," counseled the clergy. I did.

Doing these things requires no effort when you are lacking what Santayana called America's ruling passion—a love for business— when you are a lifelong non-joiner whose greatest desire is not to become involved, when almost everyone you meet is less interesting than your own ideas, and when your inner life has more reality than your outer one.

Running has not changed that. I am still a small-boned loner built for flight and fantasy. I cannot manufacture an interest or talent for business or institutions or people. Beyond these limitations, however, I now accept no limitations.

It may be common sense for the common man to consent to be

ordinary. But now everything instinctive, everything intuitive, everything beyond logic tells me otherwise. It tells me that compared to what I ought to be, I am only half awake. It tells me that, as William James did, I am using only a small part of my mental and physical resources. Running gave me these insights. It made me an athlete, albeit an aging one, and started my ascent toward a new goal.

Now I accept stress, and even seek it out. I no longer avoid the tension between what I am and what I perceive I can be. I no longer ignore the gap between what I have achieved and what I should accomplish. I realize that I have yet to live the perfect day, the day worthy of reliving. And I know Maslow was right when he suggested that equilibrium and adaptation and self-preservation and adjustment are negative concepts.

When I run my hour on the roads, I accept no negatives. I may start with a leisurely pace, but soon the hills come and I must attack them. Every hill is a challenge. No pain, no shortness of breath will stop me until I reach the top completely spent. And even then I wish the hill would go still higher.

Surely this is a mad act. Health doesn't demand this. Health is, in fact, something passed through on the way to this seemingly unnecessary area of fitness. This area is also quite dangerous because just beyond t he possibility of doing as well as I am able lies the dread condition of overtraining, with its exhaustion and fatigue, its apathy and depression. And just as stress on the body can affect both heart and head, so the tension that upsets the psyche takes a similar toll on the body.

But if these dangers exist, the converse is also true. When you complete yourself physically, it benefits you totally. And the energies exist to accomplish this. The real problem is to discover how these energy reserves can be set loose.

My method is running. It is the hub of my creative wheel. At those moments, I am athlete, poet, philosopher, even saint.

Running introduces risk, and takes me beyond tranquility and harmony and the smooth workings of ordinary day-to-day living. When I run, I recognize my essential inadequacy, my insufficiency of body, mind, and heart. And I realize the only answer is in pushing myself to the limits on the roads, or in struggling for the right word to express the truth, or in searching for meaning for myself and the universe.

Still, the experts may be right. Stress is a killer. Tensions do cause neuroses. Uneasiness of the heart can lead to despair. But without them, we remain inferior to our true selves. Live if you will a life without risk. Avoid the forge, the fire, the flame. But know that joy and happiness and the good life come only as *un*expected interludes in the endless, stressful, tense, and restless journey to become the person you are.

—*DR. SHEEHAN ON RUNNING,* 1975

———◆———

THERE IS A TENDENCY these days to see mental pressure as something to be avoided. We view mental health as a state in which we are free from the feeling that there is something wrong with us; free from the need to become more and more; free from the tension between what we are and what we should be. Mental health, we are led to believe, is to be once and for all free from pressure.

Actually, it is quite the opposite. Mental health comes with the ability to live with these feelings, these needs, these tensions. These pressures are as essential as they are unavoidable. They are our way to salvation.

It is, appropriately, a salvation that requires religion. William James pointed this out in his Gospel of Relaxation. Religion, he stated, was the sovereign remedy for worry. The really religious person, he said, is unshakable and calmly ready for any duty the day might bring forth.

We common folk know this. There is an expression we use about people "getting religion." We apply it when people finally realize their sport or study or project requires hard work and discipline and dedication, and that it is likely to be filled with failures and false starts. Yet knowing this, they discover the will to decide, and the strength and energy and faith to persevere. They know you've gotta believe.

Religion generates the same attitude as play: the certainty that whatever happens, things will be all right; that there is no final defeat in this world, and within the rules and the rituals we can be as free and inventive as we please.

Play in a sense anticipates religion. It takes us past our basic needs, beyond being fed and housed and kept warm. Play can give us self-knowledge, although in the process we may get cold and wet and go without food. Play is also a theater of heroism. In play, we become capable of facing what must be faced, of enduring what must be endured and somehow coming through in the end.

William Faulkner, in accepting the Nobel Prize for Literature, said, "man will not merely endure: He will prevail. He is immortal, not because he alone among creatures has an inexhaustible voice, but because he has a soul, a spirit capable of compassion and sacrifice and endurance."

That is my project—that this person, however weak, however

cowardly, however fearful, however anxious, should somehow not only only endure, but prevail. But first, I gotta believe.

—*THIS RUNNING LIFE,* 1980

———◆———

LONG BEFORE STRESS HAD become our major problem, decades before those who doctor our physical and social ills had recognized its importance, almost a century before authors and publishers had found it to be a profitable and inexhaustible subject, William James had made it a central theme of his lectures.

James was a Boston Brahmin—an aristocrat by birth, position, and intellect. He had known stress first-hand. He had been exposed to what must be our greatest danger—security. His initial response had been to contemplate suicide. Rejecting that, he had gone on to develop his own universe. It was a world filled with uncertainty, choice, hypothesis, novelty, and possibility. It was an incomplete world, a world in the making, in which man was the most important ingredient. It was a world which demanded no less than his best, a world which required the strenuous life, and was filled with challenge and stress.

In 1900, when James was writing, life was not easy except for the privileged few. Over one-third of Americans were farmers. Two-thirds of the remainder had manual jobs requiring considerable physical effort. Even the white-collar workers did a considerable amount of walking during the long hours of their workweek.

Now, of course, all is changed. Technology has freed all but 3 percent of us from the farms. It has reduced and in most cases removed the manual labor of almost half of the work force still in service jobs. The result is that only about 5 percent of Americans are at jobs that keep them physically fit. The rest of us are gradually succumbing to this new leisure economy. The privileged few have become the privileged many. The common man has become an aristocrat.

Now, challenge and insecurity must be sought. They are not thrust upon us. We have to go back to fundamentals. We need to feel danger, chase after conflict, seek stress. Our aim is "a sound mind in a sound body." Stress is simply the resistance we encounter in seeking that health for our body and truth for our soul. James said all that at the turn of the century. Every one of us, he thought, needs muscular vigor not to fight the old heavy battles with nature, but to furnish a background of sanity and serenity and cheerfulness to life.

Today, only the athlete knows that feeling. Only the athlete feels the inner peace and confidence that James said wells up from every part of the body of the well-trained human being. James, the intellectual and aristocrat, saw clearly the importance of the body. He knew it was the substrate upon which every other value, mental or spiritual, must take root.

—THIS RUNNING LIFE, 1980

What Dr. Sheehan Means to Me

BY GEORGE SHEEHAN III

FEW GUEST SPEAKERS DREW the enthusiastic crowds that Dad did. Bill Rodgers, Frank Shorter, Joan Benoit, Jeff Galloway, Alberto Salazar, and Joe Henderson were certainly worth the price of admission (usually in tandem with a pasta dinner). But when I think of it, they were specialists. Training tips and racing tales were at their core.

Dad was more of a triple threat.

Here was a runner who was, at once, a philosophic thinker, an accomplished athlete and, very importantly, a physician. Any medical advice he gave was hard earned.

As a speaker, throw in his relaxed outfit of blue jeans and a sweater—and a killer sense of humor—and, well, the crowds tell the story.

Case in point: a Marine Corps Marathon pasta dinner and talk back in the mid-1980s. I was there, sitting in a ballroom with 600 runners, some on the floor and others against the walls. Suddenly our hero pops up on the podium 20 minutes in advance of his talk. He tells the crowd he'd be glad to answer any question on injury or training.

First up is one on the bane of the running life—knee pain. Dad tells them the cure is related to their foot strike; for various reasons it is out of balance. Remedy: Consult a podiatrist. This was his usual biomechanical approach to injuries.

Now, I raised my hand.

He called on me: "Next." My pedigree was unknown to the audience. "What about hip pain?" I asked. Again, he took a structural approach. "Hip problems," he said, "are related to one leg being longer that the other. You have to get them measured. But don't go to doctor."

That response seemed to puzzle the crowd. He kept them waiting. And when he finally gave his common sense advice, the crowd exploded.

"Go to a tailor, they do it for a living!"

9/ The *Spiritual*

*T*he most dangerous thing a man possesses is a logical mind.
A logical mind is practical and pragmatic. It knows the price of everything and
the value of nothing. It reacts appropriately to danger and inappropriately to love.
It accepts work but not play, understands science but not religion.
The logical mind ends where a sense of humor starts.

HOW TO FEEL GREAT 24 HOURS A DAY, 1983

THE REPORTER IN ANCHORAGE was skeptical. "Is it true," he asked, "that you have called running a religion?" I had come to Alaska feeling insecure, not certain of what I had to offer these pioneer people. My talks were not yet formulated in my mind. To me, it looked as though Alaskans were already fit, and now I was· being challenged on the other values I might claim for a running program.

I thought about the question. If I hadn't called running a religion, I had certainly implied it. I had repeated Jim Fixx's story of the woman who described her husband by saying, "Ted used to be a Methodist, but now he's a runner." And I had compared running to Oliver Alden's pursuit of sculling and horseback riding in George Santayana's *The Last Puritan*. "A wordless religion," Santayana had called Alden's regimen.

But Santayana thought of religion not as truth, but as poetry. And he was an observer of athletes, not an athlete himself. He had come up with a poetic phrase and missed the point. And so had I. But fortunately, now I knew the answer. I looked at the reporter and said, "Running is like Alaska. Running is not a religion, it is a place."

This idea had been germinating in my head during the flight from Seattle. I had read an account of a 7-month stay in a Trappist monastery by Father Henri Nouwen, a Belgian priest well known in literary and academic circles. His book *A Genesee Diary* gave me a new insight into the true nature of the running life.

Nouwen's problems are remarkably similar to mine. The things that drove him to retire to the monastery are the same as those that plague me day after day. He was caught in an ascending spiral of activity. Each talk, each article, each book ignited requests for more talks and articles and books, every ring of the phone another demand on his time.

This way of life is addictive. Withdrawal symptoms occur whenever requests and letters and compliments diminish or cease. So the victim has little choice except to continue and even escalate the activity.

"While complaining of too many demands," Nouwen writes, "I felt uneasy when none were made. While speaking of the burden of letter writing, an empty mailbox made me sad. While fretting about my lecture tours, I felt disappointed when there were no speaking invitations. While desiring to be alone, I was afraid to be alone."

The priest who had been teaching and lecturing and writing about the importance of solitude, inner freedom, and peace of mind had become a prisoner, locked into unceasing activity. Finally he made the decision to step back. The time had come, he said, to restore some solitude, some stillness, some isolation to his life. He needed to take a long look at himself and his role in preaching the word of God. So he took a leave of absence and entered the Trappist monastery at Genesee, near Rochester, New York. It was, he found, a perfect place to retreat and restore himself.

The monastery is a place for the body. Father Nouwen was assigned to work in the bakery, helping to make bread, the monks' commercial enterprise. Later, he was chosen to gather stones to build a new chapel.

But the monastery is also a place for the mind. Father Nouwen had his own little sanctum for meditation. Even at work or in the company of others, talking was kept to a minimum. The only demands on his mind were those he made himself. And of course, the monastery is a place for the soul. "The monastery," says Father Nouwen, "is not built to solve problems, but to praise the Lord in the midst of them."

The monastery is a place for ordinary people, for sinners as well as saints. The work sometimes chafed. Relationships were strained. Thought came slowly. Prayer seemed impossible. Nouwen was still Nouwen. But all the while, he knew he was there because of an inner "must." And he stayed because, he says, "I knew I was in the right place."

And all the while, the priest expected to come out a different person, more integrated, more spiritual, more virtuous, more compassionate, more gentle, more joyful, more understanding. "I hoped that my restlessness would turn into quietude, my tensions into a peaceful lifestyle, my ambivalence into a single-minded commitment to God."

But upon leaving, Father Nouwen knew there had been only a lull in the battle with himself. He was the same man, with the same problems. So he asked the abbot for advice. "You must put 90 minutes aside every day for prayer," the abbot told him. If Father Nouwen was to take Genesee home with him, he would have to take time for this daily dialogue with himself and his God. Without constant renewal, what he had experienced at the monastery would vanish. Otherwise, for the rest of his life, he would awake in the morning with the same tendencies, the same desires, the same sins that he conquered only the day before. Only a return each day to the monastery would save him.

Running, I told the reporter, is just such a monastery—a retreat, a place to commune with God and yourself, a place for psychological and spiritual renewal.

—*RUNNER'S WORLD* MAGAZINE, SEPTEMBER 1987

———◆———

"THERE IS NO SUCH thing as a runner's high," wrote runner and radiologist David Levin in the *Journal of the American Medical Association*. "Anyone expecting a high or mystical experience during a run is headed for disappointment. I don't attain them, nor do the marathoners with whom I am acquainted."

Levin is pro-running. He averages 60 miles a week and has run seven marathons, including a 2:38 performance in the 1981 Boston Marathon. He is no stranger to the running experience. The reasons he runs are many and varied. They do not include the runner's high.

He sees this state as a figment of someone's imagination, a myth perpetuated largely by those who stand to gain financially from it. This euphoria—if it occurs at all, he says—comes when the run is over and you know you don't have to face it again. Running for Levin is tough, tedious, tiring, and often painful. The payoff comes from being a runner, not from running itself.

I believe all the particulars in Levin's article. I know he is speaking his truth. But he has made the dangerous leap from his personal experience and the experiences of his friends to that of all runners. He has concluded that if his group does not get a runner's high, no one else does.

I suspect that dogged, determined, 60-miles-a-week marathoners are actually the last ones to ask about mystical experiences. For them, running is indeed tough, tedious, tiring, and often painful. But for those of us who do half that mileage, who train at 2 minutes over our race pace, who run to think, and reserve pain for the race—for us, the runner's high is an integral and essential part of our lives. It draws us again and again to escape our humdrum, ordinary, and commonplace real lives. And in its absolute form, it is undoubtedly what sociologist Abraham Maslow described as "peak performance."

In his later years, Maslow qualified his definition of this phenomenon. He originally thought it occurred to few people and then under very special circumstances. He discovered that this was not so: Any number of activities could result in this feeling. There were, in fact, multiple methods of achieving a sense of timelessness, of oneness with the universe.

He also recognized that there were lesser versions of this variety of satori—"plateau" experiences, where the emotional response was calmer, the experience more a feeling of peace of being in control.

"They seek retreats for themselves," wrote Stoic Marcus Aurelius, "a house in the country, seashore, and the mountains. But this is altogether the mark of the common man, for it is in thy power whenever you shall choose to retire within thyself." My day's run becomes that retreat. There I discover the truth of the meditation of the great Stoic Epictetus: "Nowhere, either with more quiet or freedom from trouble, does a man retire than into his own soul."

My body permits this to happen. At 2 minutes over my race pace, my body is virtuoso. It requires no guidance, no commands, no spur. It is on automatic pilot. My mind is free to dissociate, to wander on its own. On some days, this brings on another type of high—a creative one. My mind becomes a cascade of thoughts. The sights and sounds, the touches and tastes, the pains and pleasures of my entire life become available to me. I am able to read a journal I never knew I'd kept.

At times, these thoughts center around a common theme, the one I am then in the process of writing. Other times, there is a kaleidoscope of new and exciting arrangements of past experiences. I sometimes return from the run with an entire column that arose de novo after I reached my second wind.

Then there are the days—or perhaps the day—when I have that elusive runner's high. By strict definition, mystical experiences are rare. The French philosopher and scientist Blaise Pascal admitted to one. St. John of the Cross was said to have had only three. But by Maslow's standards, mystical experiences can be quite frequent. Children probably have them daily, since childhood is a state of enlightenment much like that sought by the Zen masters: "There are no categories, no words, no time."

Athletes, whatever their level of performance, are also a favored group. "There is no word in English for that feeling," said pitcher Mark Fidrych, describing his emotions in his comeback attempt in a minor league game in Pawtucket, Rhode Island. He was talking about how he felt when the crowd spurred him on in the last few innings.

Words fail when we are attempting to describe what is, by definition, mystical—beyond words. The runner's high is such a state. But if there is one word that approximates it, it is ecstasy—ecstasy in the original Greek sense of "standing outside." Running takes me out of the world and my role in it. For a brief hour, it gives me the freedom to do everything or nothing, to become or just to be, and all without censure or praise. I am, for those 60 minutes, a new Adam, number one in my own universe. And I taste the immortality I thirst for every minute of my waking day.

—*RUNNER'S WORLD* MAGAZINE, MARCH 1984

"DO YOU BELIEVE IN personal immortality?" a Unitarian friend asked me at lunch the other day. Not an everyday subject, but if you have Unitarian friends (being nonjudgmental, they are the best kind) you become accustomed to such questions. Even at lunch. Unitarians, it appears, are ready to discuss the Eternal Verities anytime, day or night. In fact, my friend assures me, they would rather go to a discussion about heaven than to the actual place.

This time I was ready for the hard question. Just the previous day personal immortality had changed for me from a childhood belief and an undergraduate theory to actual fact. It had become a reality.

On my afternoon run I had suddenly overreached the confines of time and space. I had become the perfect runner moving easily and surely and effortlessly toward infinity. My 10 years of almost daily running had brought me to an area of consciousness, a level of being that I never knew existed.

For the runner, running has always been a form of contemplation and meditation; an activity with the saving grace, as Santayana said, of football, of purging, rinsing, and exhausting the inner man; a time when the movements of his body in concert with his mind and heart gave him an appreciation of what was good and true and beautiful.

But it is now evident it can do even more. Running that day became for me, as I'm sure it has for others, a mystical experience. A proof of the existence of God. Something happened and then, in the words of a recent letter writer to *Harper's* magazine, "One simply knows, and believes, and can never forget."

There is no way of documenting this. Such states are difficult to describe and impossible to analyze. Conversely, there is no use denying them. "Mystics," wrote William James, "have been there and know." The mystic, James declared, is invulnerable. He is also, for the most part, unchallenged. Although we may not have been there ourselves, we suspect what he says is true. We simply do not know how to make it true for ourselves.

That way now seems open. Where once it was so that not more than a thimbleful of meditation was going on in America, we are now becoming a nation of meditators. And in our newfound leisure we are discovering the salvation and liberation that exist in play. For it is sport that is finally giving the common man a true picture of himself. Freeing him from authority and allowing him to find and fulfill his own design. For the runners this meant the realization that solitude is the staff of life and not a mark of failure. That, for him at least, community is a myth. He became able to pursue his asocial ways. To change his life to accommodate to his inner reality. (When a psychiatrist-marathoner friend asked me recently, "What was it like before we started running?" I could not remember. If there had been a life before running, it was imperfect and unfulfilled.)

Play is truly the answer. "There are many routes," wrote poet Jonathan Price, "in fact, any way the serious world calls play." So it is running for those who are runners. Other forms for other people. What route you take depends on yourself. I cannot bring visions of immortality to a nonrunner by dragging him along on my afternoon runs. What you do must absorb you utterly and intensely; and to do that it must be your game, your sport, your play. "How we play," writes George Leonard, "signifies nothing less than our way of being in the world."

For the dancer, the dance brings this feeling for life, this intimation of immortality. ("When a jump works," says Jacques d'Amboise, "it feels like forever. I'm riding on top of time.") Others get the same sort of experience from skiing, surfing, karate, golf, football, or what have you.

How long it will take is another story. One must go through discipline to get to freedom. Be assured it does not occur to beginners. Only when how you do a thing surpasses the thing you are doing can you break through the barriers to these levels of consciousness, your own inner depths.

But then when they ask you the real question that is bothering everyone in this age, "Is this all there is?" you can answer, "You've got to be kidding."

—*RUNNING AND BEING,* 1978

ALCOHOL CAN TAKE YOU places the sober man may never see. Sobriety, wrote William James, diminishes, discriminates, and says no; drunkenness expands, unites, and says yes. "The sway of alcohol over mankind," he concluded, "is unquestionably due to its power to stimulate the mystical faculties of human nature."

This is what alcohol can do: can give you a glimpse of yourself in your own particular world, of you as part of the cosmos. Drink also reveals the person you are. Whether you are the solitary schizoid, thinking great thoughts and living in fantasy. Or the gregarious manic-depressive who wants to be part of a warm and eternally friendly group. Or the muscular paranoid, ready to settle any disagreement with his fists.

What alcohol cannot do is bring these insights into purposeful action. Having glimpsed the person he is, the drinker must now find an alternate and fruitful path to his truth. To do this, he must first disentangle himself from alcohol and then rescue himself from the lies of his daily living. So it is frequently the ex-alcoholic, who has been there and back, who experiences the new birth. It is the former lush who finally unites his divided self. It is the reformed drunk who accepts the person he is without reservation. And pursues that perfection however mediocre or even abnormal it may appear to someone else.

Becoming an ex-alcoholic, however, is not easy. Drink may be futile and ultimately degrading, but only the fortunate drinker discovers this. And it is the even more fortunate one who then comes upon a new and healthy path to the summit of his physical and mental powers. Before the liver goes, the heart enlarges, and the brain begins to deteriorate, he must get the message that there is a better way to experience himself and the universe.

My own drinking habits changed because of two such fortunate events. Back in those days when I was living it up on Saturday nights, I had always supposed that drink made me brilliant. I thought that someone should be writing down everything I said, preserving these great ideas and clever bon mots for posterity.

Then, one night, someone took 50 feet of home movies of me under the influence. What I saw on the screen looked like the Missing Link rather than the intellectual I imagined myself to be. Here was photographic evidence that when drunk I was incapable of thought, much less of expressing it. Because of that film, I quit serious drinking. Not so much to become the person I was, but simply to rejoin the human race.

Distance running, my next discovery, was a positive factor and the decisive one. Negative injunctions never work. Lives are changed by dos, not don'ts. And if one is to stop drinking permanently, one must be actively involved in becoming what one is. Distance running did that for me. It reintroduced me to my body. And my body, I found out, had a mind of its own. It would no longer accept anything less than the best. Having gotten into trim, it refused to be tampered with. Having reached the peak of its powers, it dragged my mind and my will along with it.

Now the hour a day on the roads began to provide the altered states of consciousness that alcohol supplied so fleetingly. Running, I learned, gave me a natural high. What happens in those moments I am not sure. Andrew Weil, the author of *The Natural Mind,* calls it the integration of the conscious and unconscious spheres of our mental life. "This integration," he states, "is essential to the wholeness (health) of body and mind."

I'll give him no argument there, but this I know: whatever it is, it starts with the body. By first reaching a fitness that reveals the real person inside my body (just as does the sculptor find the statue inside the stone). And then through this body, this mirror of my soul, this key to my personality, this telltale of my temperament, I see myself as I really am.

I don't drink much anymore. I am never the life of any party. The hostess who invites me knows within the first 5 minutes she has made a mistake. I usually wander into the kitchen for a cup of coffee and then find a large book and a quiet place to read until the festivities are over. I have found out who I am. And I have no intention of impersonating anyone else.

Some people liked me better when I was drinking.

—*RUNNING & BEING,* 1978

———————◆———————

Is HAPPINESS A 5-MILE fix? Are those runners we see on the roads these early mornings and late evenings there in pursuit of the life, liberty, and happiness the Declaration of Independence said was the right of all men?

The answer, according to Edwin Land, the genius who heads the Polaroid Corporation, is probably yes. "Addiction," says Land, "is a necessity and an opportunity." And distance running is clearly an addiction of major proportions.

Land's particular obsession is not running but scientific experiment.

Unless he performs one good experiment a day, "the world goes out of focus, becomes unreal."

Land came to realize the universal nature of addiction when he discussed his reaction to the scientific experience at a university seminar. After hearing the recital of an experiment's sequence of intuition, mystery, excitement, and the final relief and nobility, a bearded youth in the front row turned to a companion and said, "Why, it's just like heroin, isn't it?"

You don't have to tell a genius more than once. Land pounced on the idea and came up with one of the more sensible statements made on the drug problem in memory. Scientific experiment, he reasoned, must be an addiction and must do what heroin is trying to do, but constructively.

The addict is not escaping from reality but is trying to find himself. Runners are doing the same thing, but in a constructive, continually satisfying, and maturing way.

Running's addictive qualities are unquestioned. Doug Hardin, former Harvard cross-country captain, once said that his daily workouts regulate his whole life—his eating habits, his social schedule and his academic future. And why not? "They ranged," he said, "from deepest drama to mere routine, keen excitement to utter boredom, great sensual pleasure to extreme agony." Hardin himself considered distance running not as a sport but "an obsession."

This obsession with running is really an obsession with the potential for more and more life.

—*THIS RUNNING LIFE,* 1980

"WHENEVER I HAVE A problem that upsets me every time I think about it," a runner said to me, "I take it out on the roads. Then I am able to come to grips with it without my emotions getting in the way."

I told him I had made the same discovery. In almost two decades of running, I have never been mad at anyone during my daily run. My hour of solitude on the road has never been marred by what William James called the "coarser emotions."

Exercise has the effect of defusing anger and rage, fear and anxiety. Like music, it soothes the savage in us that lies so close to the surface.

It is the ultimate tranquilizer. Why is this so? What is it about exercise that blocks these destructive feelings? How does it take us out of a world that is an adversary situation and replace it with one that is one for-all-and-all-for-one, a world filled with sanity and good humor?

The best explanation, it seems to me, lies in the James-Lange theory of emotions. This is one of psychology's most unlikely hypotheses and one usually given little credence. Yet as with most ideas espoused by James, time gives us more and more evidence that he was right.

According to James, I do not first get angry and then exhibit that anger in my body. The actual process is the reverse. My body gets angry, and then I become angry. My body perceives the object or idea that causes anger, reacts with the usual physiologic.al phenomena—rapid pulse, flushing of the face, etc.—and only then do I feel the emotion of anger.

When I first read this explanation, I found it incredible. The truth, as I saw it, was obvious: I saw or remembered or dreamed up an object or idea that frightened me or angered me, causing me to feel guilty or to know hate—and then my body reacted to that feeling. The James-Lange theory was, in a word, absurd.

Now I think otherwise. James seems to be correct. If my body does not react to the object or idea, I now realize that I don't feel these emotions. It is not until the physiological effects occur that the emotion becomes apparent. If the usual signs and symptoms of rage are blocked, then I will not feel rage in my mind.

Such blocking can occur in two ways: first, by flooding the various systems of the body with activity so that there is no reserve to produce the reaction identified with the emotion; second, by substituting some positive emotion in its place. (Act happy, look happy, speak happily, said James, and you will be happy. Act like an enthusiast, and you will become an enthusiast.)

When I run, both of these events take place. Running completely occupies my body. It fills every cell. I am all movement, effort, sweat. I become the running as the dancer becomes the dance. The entire functioning of my body is focused on this one action. There is no room for the coarser emotions. Only the higher and more subtle feelings are now able to enter my consciousness.

And indeed they do. Now I can imagine myself a hero and have my body feel heroic; think of myself as a success and find failure unimaginable; know that part of me is good and whole and true, and feel faith flooding through me. My body takes me through the friendly vistas of my river road to even friendlier vistas of my soul. My mind can now think what it likes. It runs ahead of me, investigating things along the way. It is no longer impeded or affected by the negative emotions my body usually creates.

My body usually creates the typical physiological patterns that I know as anger or fear, guilt or rage. And for me, running is the best way to prevent these particular patterns from developing. When I run, I am absolved from those feelings that destroy rather than create, that lead to darkness rather than light. I am cleansed of the passions that arise when I see the world as Them or Us, or rail against Fate, or attempt to change things over which I have no control.

Is running necessary for this? Of course not. The Stoics knew this centuries ago. There is no better guide to tranquility than Marcus Aurelius, no better antidote to anxiety than reading Epictetus. But for those of us made of lesser stuff, the pragmatist James has shown an easier way.

We have discovered an alternative path to peace and serenity. We are coping with life—and quite well, thank you—on the move.

—*HOW TO FEEL GREAT 24 HOURS A DAY,* 1983

◆

THE MOST DANGEROUS THING a man possesses is a logical mind. A logical mind is practical and pragmatic. It knows the price of everything and the value of nothing. It reacts appropriately to danger and inappropriately to love. It accepts work but not play, understands science but not religion. The logical mind ends where a sense of humor starts.

Almost equally dangerous are our appetites and emotions. Unchecked appetites change us from free men to slaves. The negative emotions of hate and envy and despair can kill the good life as surely as a bullet.

What we need is something to synthesize these forces—something to bring harmony to these opposites, create unity out of this diversity, fuse the body, mind, and spirit into the unique person each of us is.

Surprisingly, philosophers have suggested that this is best accomplished in sports. "Man at his utmost," "self-completion (through excellence)" and "self-actualization through self-extension" are a few of the descriptions they give of the effect of sports on the athlete.

The surfer is not merely seeking the perfect wave, the skier the perfect slope, the runner the perfect race. Each is seeking his own perfection, seeking to purge the negative emotions, seeking to quell the animal appetites, seeking to keep the brain at work on things the brain should do, but most of all seeking a total acceptance of himself and his universe, a loving of himself and his fellows and his Creator. For the athlete, sport is not a religion; it is a religious act that brings together work and play, love and religion.

I would be less certain of this ·if I had not read William Gibson's *A Season in Heaven,* an account of his experience studying Transcendental Meditation in Spain under Maharishi Mahesh Yogi. Gibson went because TM had transformed his son who had been drowning in "eddies of self-hatred" into a smiling, loving person.

Scientists tell us that TM is a physiological method of obtaining relaxation and a hypometabolic state. Dr. Herbert Benson of Harvard University has· reported a lowering of blood pressure, a decrease in oxygen intake, and a slowing of the pulse while deep in TM. Many other advantageous metabolic changes are also known to occur. ("I had a letting-go inside," writes Gibson, "which was the first waking rest I'd had from myself in 50 years.")

The key to this is the mantra. This is a simple Vedic sound without meaning (Benson claims any word may do). What it does is throw the reasoning brain off the scent while you descend into the absolute moving away from the stresses that surround you, the disharmony, the diversity, the opposites, all the evidence you have of your mortality. The mantra allows you to get out of that bind into unity.

This unity is the promise of TM: a body free from stress and a mind open to boundless energy, intelligence, creativity, skill in action, and better behavior toward others. This result comes gradually. Recruits to this method initially feel an increase in energy, both mental and physical. They make complete turnabouts as to drugs and alcohol and tobacco. There is even some talk about celibacy. Only later comes the religion that sees God as It.

For Gibson, the religion that opened up to him was his own. A nonbelieving Catholic since the age of 14, he returned home as a daily Mass-goer. He was able, he said, to convince his logical mind to leave his nonrational religion alone. He had found in TM a solution to his own conflicts, and also an antidote to the counsel of our best minds—"despair, impotence, and self-loathing."

I have also gone the TM route—brought the flowers and the fruit and the $75 required to attend a series of four lectures. I agree with much of what Gibson writes, and I am interested in his spiritual odyssey. But I'm inclined to think, at least for me, that running offers more.

What sport does additionally is to bring the body and mind on this trip into what Maharishi calls "cosmic consciousness," the level where we deal in absolutes only, and because running does that, it takes me totally body-mind-soul into this new experience. I am man fully functioning, and there is no one on God's earth I would trade places with at that moment.

One of the more effective ways of relieving stress is the relaxation response. This is an altered state of consciousness in which the mind and the body are deeply relaxed. At the same time, your awareness of the world and its worries diminishes and you are temporarily at peace. The methods used to attain this state are primarily those of Transcendental Meditation and the technique described by Dr. Benson in his book *The Relaxation Response.*

From personal experience, I can tell you they work. The TM and Benson procedures are simple and, except for the mantra, identical. It is suggested you sit in a comfortable chair, relax your muscles and eyes, breathe deeply and slowly with your belly, and then repeat your mantra or the word "one." This is done in tempo with your heart beat (if as slow as mine) or with your breathing. Distracting thoughts are not fought; they succumb to the recitation of the word.

To many, these measures seem quite superficial. They depart from the traditional psychological approach of changing physiological responses by unmasking the psychological factors and feelings that produce them. Stress, say these experts, must first he understood, then dealt with.

Relaxation responses, of course, do the opposite. They treat the effect, not the cause; the result, not the reason. What they seek is oblivion, a mind cleansed of thought, muscles relaxed to jelly. This type of meditation is not active or passive; it is negative. It is the way of detachment, of elimination, of emptiness.

What happens, then, is a reaction that prescinds from the cause of our hurry and worry, that cares not why or how we become tense or anxious. There is no need for psychoanalysis or psychotherapy, no need for insight and acceptance, no need to ask the Great Questions or to debate the answers, no need to study our unconscious or subconscious or even our conscious. Just follow the simple instructions and drift away.

These procedures return me to my resting state. When I use them I am in effect hunkering down, turning my tail to the wind and riding out the storm. These techniques give me a respite, a timeout, a period when I can get my breath, regain my composure, remember my game plan.

That last, I suppose, is most important. One basketball coach told me that about timeouts. "There is not much you can do," he said, "except remind them of what they do best."

When I come back from a relaxation timeout, I am reminded of what I do best. I have lost, for the most part, the tension, the feeling of straining, of being in over my head. I have regained, if only temporarily, the rhythm of my game.

That rhythm is different for each one of us. It is, however, always similar in principle. I am, as you are, like a reciprocating motor. Deep in my chest, I feel the pulsation of my heart, alternately filling and emptying. And this same systole and diastole occur in all my other activities.

There is work and play, effort and rest, times when I store energy and other times when I discharge it. The good life is a product of· this balance, this alternation that enables me to accept and make the most out of the inevitable tensions and stresses I meet.

It is interesting that stress expert Hans Selye sees no need for these relaxation techniques. We would be better occupied, he states, in taking a different attitude toward the events in our life. Attitude determines whether we perceive an experience as pleasant or unpleasant. It is in adopting the right attitude, he says, that we can convert a negative stress into a positive one.

His criticism is true to an extent. The effect of a period of relaxation is brief. When I come back, nothing has been radically changed, any more than it would be if I had taken a nap. I might have been given time to remember my game plan, but I haven't discovered anything new about myself or the game.

So Selye is right. There may be a place for sitting still and making my mind a blank. But what I need more is some positive method of relaxation—one that is associated with play and movement, with creation and contemplation. So for me the supreme relaxation technique is, again, running.

Selye himself swims or bikes in the morning, then swims and lifts weights at night. These are periods of time where he is, it seems to me, employing his own relaxation techniques, which are quite similar to mine.

What we should remember is that, in dealing with stress, good intentions are not enough. In the final analysis, we need the tools, we need the skill, we need the techniques. We have come to a time when a person who cannot play is illiterate, a person who cannot relax is a barbarian, and a person who cannot meditate has not yet learned to live.

—HOW TO FEEL GREAT 24 HOURS A DAY, 1983

What Dr. Sheehan Means to Me

BY ANDREW SHEEHAN

"LIFE," HE SAID, "IS an experiment of one."

My father's own experiment took him through uncharted territory. Today we runners blend into the landscape so seamlessly we go virtually unnoticed, but when he took to the streets in the early '50s, he was a curiosity and worse—a laughing stock in our home town. "Why does your father run around in his underwear?," our classmates would taunt.

But he forged on undaunted, blazing his own trail. In his own experiment, running was his laboratory, and several days a week, he would test his ideas over a 10-mile route. Running, he found, was an inexhaustible wellspring of creativity, challenge and change, and he ran his way into a new life, finding it full of continual exploration. He escaped his predestined and sedentary existence and discovered, like William James, that "the strenuous life tastes best."

"Performance artist" is a label that comes to mind. His life seemed to be a kind of performance—played out in public. His workouts, racing, and talks were all on public view, and whatever he learned, he put down on page for all to read. His journey would cover tens of thousands of miles, but it also an inner journey. He chronicled all the emotional and spiritual changes. And if on that road the siren song of fame would at times lead him astray, he was saved by his own self-honesty.

A critic of misguided modern medicine and complacent America, his self-appraisals could be the most brutal—as his writing attests. He would take his full measure in the mirror, and he would not flinch. In the end, it humbled him, and it sweetened him, and it allowed him to find his most important discovery: the love of friends and family.

10/Dealing with Our *Lesser Angels*

he wise men have spoken of this. For every hundred men who can handle adversity, they concluded, there is but one who can handle success. Flying home, I knew I was not that one.

RUNNING & BEING, 1978

"THERE IS ONE PHENOMENON in daily living so degrading, so shocking, so miserable," wrote English novelist Arnold Bennett, "that I hesitate to mention it." He was alluding to losing one's temper. "This constitutes," said Bennett, "the most curious and humiliating spectacle that life offers."

Often that's an accurate description. The devil has broken his chains, civilization recedes a thousand years, and it's all because someone touched a tender point.

But oddly enough, getting angry is occasionally the right thing to do. There is a time not to be in a temper, but there is also a time to be in a temper. "Anger," said Greek philosopher Aristotle, "is a weapon for virtue and valor." At one time it was needed for survival. And frankly, I think it still is. It's just that now the threats to survival are more likely to be psychological than physical—verbal assaults instead of saber-toothed tiger attacks.

My youngest son put it this way when we were discussing anger at the dinner table recently: "You should only lose your temper when you are violated."

The rest of the family was silenced by the strength of that word violated. Until he spoke, we had been talking about ways to manage rage, not justify it. Temper, in our view, was just another of man's weaknesses. "To seek to extinguish anger utterly is but a boast of Stoics," said 13th-century English philosopher Roger Bacon. The best most of us can aspire to, then, is to minimize the damage, diminish the number of casualties and the consequences of our episodes of anger.

"Internalize it," another son (the new doctor) advised. "I like people who internalize their anger. I want no part of those people who rant and rave. I avoid them then and later."

But a third son disagreed. "Externalize it," he advised, "or things just get worse. If you internalize, you become the victim: You get ulcers, hypertension, or a heart attack as a reaction to unexpressed anger. Let it all come out," he said, "and you will be saved."

But it was not until my youngest son made his observation that we could see temper in the right perspective. He repeated St. Paul's message to the Ephesians: "Be angry, but sin not. Let not the sun go down on your wrath." There are times, in other words, when righteous rage is the right response. Temper may be unsightly and a cloud on human intercourse, but there are occasions when a white-hot rage is the only weapon that will preserve us.

When? As my youngest put it—when we are violated, when we have been made less than human by others or even by ourselves. "Anger," wrote sociologist Ernest Becker, "is a reaction, a way of reasserting ourselves, a setting things in balance again and preventing a person's body from being flooded by the environment."

Temper, then, becomes life enhancing.

"Some people," stated Becker, "never learn that their organism has a right to take up space without shrinking, to assert itself without feeling guilt, to emit odors and digestive noise without shame, to scream in affront and pain when they are attacked."

The truth of the matter: There can be no last angry man. When there is, the world will have given up. Great deeds need hot blood, and great lives require great emotion. The fire down below, that smoldering source of energy, is what lifts us over obstacles, and keeps us moving when further motion seems impossible.

—PERSONAL BEST, 1989

◆

WHEN I GET MY Irish up, few things are safe. I've torn telephones out of the wall, smashed china, and, on one occasion when our third son would not get up for school, I threw a chair through a window. When I lose my temper, I am an anarchist: Anything that suggests order and stability is in danger.

Writer Arnold Bennett described this dreadful spectacle well.

"Temper," he wrote, "is an insurrection, a boiling over, a sweeping storm. Dignity, common sense, justice are shriveled up."

At such times, it is best to exhaust the storm with some vigorous but essentially harmless action. Sanity can easily be restored if only you have an alternative way to work off your wrath.

My father, who was subject to similar explosions of Irish ire, would dissipate his anger with a bar of soap. He would burst from his office in the basement of our house, displaying all the storm flags of an Irishman in a righteous rage, and ascend to his room. Once there, he would proceed to throw a large bar of soap against the wall for five minutes or so. Composure restored, he would then discard the soap, descend the stairs, and resume his office routine.

He had an Irish temper and so do I—I inherited it from him. I realize, of course, that it's not fashionable nowadays to think so ethnically. Of current writers, only Michael Novak seems to take one's country of national origin seriously. And temper is certainly universal: Irish or Polish, black or white, Scandinavian or South American, you are certain to have a temper. The sun never sets on anger in some form, including the Irish variety.

Yet we common folk know that anger is a cultural trait, a feeling flavored by locale: Each one of us is a survivor of generations of people exposed to a specific experience, each one of us formed from the unique stresses of a special geographic and political and social environment. In my case, that special place was Ireland.

My body is made up of the cells that enabled people to endure through centuries of what the Irish called the Troubles: war, famine, and general all-around hard time. I am the reaction, the final product, and I include among the necessary qualities that helped my ancestors survive my uniquely Irish temper—a temper distinct to the people of Ireland and the human experiment that occurred on that island.

I have inherited a Celtic approach to living and the temper that goes with it—a special kind of anger best compared with the steam held in by a pressure cooker. The history of the Irish is a story of frustration, of anger concealed. They inhabited an island that made them insular, had a church that made them parochial, and a foreign rule that led to a consuming inner rage. Their only freedom was of the mind.

But only those with great gifts rebelled. The rest of us managed in different ways—with humor, with stealth, with madness. And all the while, boiling away inside was a temper whose volcanic possibilities were rarely revealed. The Irish temper erupts only when the barriers of self-restraint and the acceptance of frustrations are finally breached. It is therefore an awesome display and, when abetted by alcohol, little short of terrifying. Consider: In New York of the 1880s when the Irish were working off their rage, the police would simply cordon off the Irish section and let them go at it.

The secret of the Irish temper (and remember, this is an Irishman speaking)? It is the only time, save being drunk or joking, when we can tell the truth.

—PERSONAL BEST, 1989

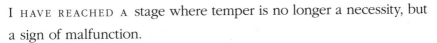

I HAVE REACHED A stage where temper is no longer a necessity, but a sign of malfunction.

Arnold Bennett, a follower of the Stoics, saw it in that way, too: Temper, he said, was a sure indication that one's human machine had gone awry. One must get the machine back on the track, stop conferring blame, accept the universe, realize that the only thing you can control is your own brain.

But should temper intervene—and Bennett, being a realist, knew that it would—then he took a different tack. Here he was pure English: "See yourself as a fool, behaving like a grown-up baby. Say to yourself, 'I am a dunce.'" It was his contention that reason would not prevail in such instances. Use instead, Bennett advised, the horror of looking ridiculous.

Given the fact that you wish to control your temper, there are better ways to do it.

"Hesitation," said Seneca, "is the best cure for anger." That ancient advice still holds. American thinker William James also ascribed to it. "Refuse to express a passion," he said, "and it dies. Count to 10 before venting your anger, and its occasion seems ridiculous."

James also believed that to be calm, we should act calm. "If we wish to conquer undesirable emotional tendencies in ourselves, we must assiduously—and in the first instance, cold-bloodedly—go through the outward movement of those dispositions which we prefer to cultivate."

Easier said than done, though—and unfortunately, when we do get angry, it is sometimes the weak and even the innocent who pay. My father, who was a doctor, said it was not the patient who got him mad who felt the wrath. It was his next patient.

Once, when that happened to me, the next patient was an elderly Russian lady I had taken care of for years. When she sat down and began to recite her usual litany of complaints, I interrupted her and shouted, "Why do you come here? I have not helped you and never will. You have the same complaints as the first day I saw you."

She looked at me and then said, "Where is my Dr. Sheehan? You are not my Dr. Sheehan. Where is my Dr. Sheehan?" She was, of course, seeing her real Dr. Sheehan—and seeing my ancestors as well.

—*PERSONAL BEST,* 1989

———————◆———————

THINGS THAT HAPPEN IN my life are never due to well-laid plans. My days fall into place at the very last minute, and if I do undertake a long-range project, it rarely survives the first rush of enthusiasm. In short order, I return to my immediate tasks, perfectly willing to let tomorrow take care of itself.

And, usually, it does. This 24 hours just naturally leads to the next. A journal or a book or a lecture just gradually evolves. But there is never a blueprint. I seize the day, and when tomorrow dawns, it is today but better.

Paradoxically, by living without a future, I assure it. Not that this is appropriate for everyone: If making a living was my main purpose, I could be in big trouble. A business or professional career requires foresight. There are guidebooks and maps and well-charted highways that lead to success. Detours are taken at your own peril, and every move has import in the months and years ahead.

Not so when one follows the dictates of the present. The future requires no thought, there is no specific road to follow. I am without precedent, a unique individual whose future has to be different from everyone else who ever lived. I live in a labyrinth in which each detour is a learning experience. And though I live entirely in that present, every move does have import for the months and years ahead.

The reason is simple: My day is my life, and this present moment is forever. At this very moment, to make the point, I sit at my typewriter in the newsroom, oblivious to all other possibilities. The feeling: This is where I would be, this is what I would be doing. Writing this essay isn't competing with anything else for my attention. The newspaper's large working area filled with people gradually recedes from my consciousness, and I await the words and sentences that come through my fingers on the machine.

What comes, comes. At times there is nothing but silence. The probings of my mind bring no response. The self has nothing to say. But when you live without schedules or plans, it is of no matter. Whatever does come must always be followed by more.

I create my life the same way, just as I would a play or a novel or this book: I do today what can be done today. Each day I fill the allotted pages, and each day I use my entire being in this ongoing drama. I am always in medias res—completely engaged in the creative struggle of the moment. The future is hidden and must remain so: Looking ahead means less attention for the moment—for now.

So, you see, it is not my future that determines my present, it is my present that determines my future. What I do today and the way I do it assures me of the same quality of life down the road. When the future comes, no matter what it contains, I will be ready.

The question for me then is not whether to live in the present but how. Here the Stoic philosopher Epictetus had the best rule. "Let what appears best," he wrote, "be to you an inviolable law." In modern speak, that means trust your instincts.

—*PERSONAL BEST,* 1989

EVERY WEEK I GO through the medical journals at the hospital library, reading case histories and looking for material for my column. And not long ago, I discovered a very interesting case history with some quite usable material in an article in the *American Journal of Psychiatry* entitled "Overview: Narcissistic Personality Disorder."

The interesting thing—the case was me, the material my life.

I had not seen myself described as accurately since reading William Sheldon's portrayal of the ectomorph in his Constitutional Psychology.

Drs. Salman Akhtar and J. Anderson Thomson had me right in their sights when they squeezed their scholarly triggers—they hit me simultaneously in the heart and the head and the gut.

They wrote as if firsthand about my failures in functioning. They understood my difficulties with self-image and interpersonal relationships. They were familiar with my troubles in social adaptation, and my deficiencies in ethics and ideals. They knew all about my inadequacy in love and sexuality, and were even cognizant of my problems in cognition—the inner tangles of my innermost thoughts.

Nothing that is wrong with me escaped them. Here were my sins and errors, my weaknesses and transgressions—there, the great gaping holes in my personality through which my life is leaking. Where most people saw only one or more of these deficits, these authorities had cataloged them all, lumping them under the single indictment, "a concentration of psychological interest upon the self."

I cannot deny any item in their litany. I might, it is true, admit to only minor tendencies in one area or another. But on the whole it is an all too accurate picture of the person I am—and God help me, will continue to be.

The narcissistic personality, the person in love with himself, is not a new psychiatric concept. It has been around as long as there were people. The Greeks discussed the condition millennia ago in the story of Narcissus. Later, Freud gave me official standing. The first detailed scientific description of my personality suggested three characteristics: condescending superiority, intense preoccupation with my self-respect, and a marked lack of empathy for others.

I am all of that and more. I admit to a self-knowledge brought on by the same qualities that are my undoing—thinking for thinking's sake and a preference for concepts over facts. I spend my time either thinking or writing about myself and my experiences. Eventually, the essential defects in my basic personality had to become evident. Blaming who I am and how I act on running and writing and my show-business life does not get to the heart or mind of the matter—a fundamental flaw in my personality structure.

Drs. Akhtar and Thomson nonetheless found some experts with a few good things to say about the narcissistic personality. Sigmund Freud wrote in 1931, "The subject's main interest is directed to self-preservation; he is independent and not open to intimidation. His ego has a large amount of aggressiveness at its disposal which also manifests itself in readiness for activity. In his erotic life, loving is preferred to being loved. People belonging to this type impress others as being 'personalities.' They are especially suited to act as support for others, to take on the role of leaders, and give fresh stimulus to cultural development, or to change the established state of affairs."

Mostly, however, the narcissistic personality has gotten a bad press, and rightfully so. What good can be said of an individual who can't love, lacks empathy, is chronically bored, and manipulates others?

Well, you might say, no one is perfect. But some people are closer to perfect than others. A Socialist author saw little good in the narcissistic personality and even less to hope for. The typical narcissistic, he wrote, "wants to be known as a winner, has little capacity for personal intimacy and social commitment, feels little loyalty and lacks conviction." And, he warned, "Once his youth and vigor, and even the thrill of winning are lost, he becomes goalless, and finds himself starkly alone." Since the loss of youth, vigor, and the thrill of winning seems inevitable, those on the outside see no hope. Apparently, that is what one critic meant when he wrote of Emerson and "the impenetrable agonies of his loneliness." But nevertheless—as Emerson might have said—within the agonies and the loneliness are brief but splendid periods of joy. There are moments when even the narcissistic personality becomes fully functioning. At those times, I am filled with all those qualities I usually lack, and become for that instant a normal, healthy, loving, and playful human being.

And frankly, narcissism just isn't as bad as popular mythology would have it. "Narcissus is not a victim of vanity," wrote Dag Hammarskjold, "but someone who responds to his unworthiness with defiance." Any thoroughgoing disciple of psychologist Alfred Adler would know that is true. A major inferiority complex is at the root of this preoccupation with the self.

Hammarskjold put it all in perspective. Narcissists are simply responding to the human condition, he told us. We are born, he said, for success. But in life, the truth appears to be the opposite: We fail and meet failure upon failure along the way. And like it or not, we will go the way of the grasshopper. Given that, how can we feel anything but this fundamental unworthiness?

I see my preoccupation with myself as humility, not vanity. I do not deny my faults. I accept them.

And admitting that one has a narcissistic personality is not the end of the world. There are some very positive implications. I can see in myself all the negative qualities psychiatrists attribute to those with this disorder, but I see also that I'm not to blame: These faults come from low self-esteem.

How best is one to deal with this situation? I read conflicting advice, but most experts feel something must be done to reduce this overwhelming concern with self. But my medical experience tells me that this is going in exactly the wrong direction. The way to lessen the impact of a fault is to develop a strength. And, frankly, knowing who I am, with my own strengths and weaknesses, is the beginning of wisdom. My personal opinion: If I am fated to play life's game as a narcissist, I'd better be the best narcissist I can be.

The main thing is not to quit on myself. There are always critics— and none more insistent than the one inside. I know that full well. It is imperative to see the good me in the mirror, too. I must see strengths, not weaknesses.

What I have lost, or indeed never had, is an understanding of other people's feelings. The word is empathy. What I have in its place is endless self-doubt. If there are successes in my life, they are little more than temporary bivouacs. The fight against failure resumes again in the morning.

But meanwhile, wrapped up in my own concerns, I fail in my response to other people. I neither communicate nor receive communication. The world spins and I stand still, lost in thought. I take to the roads and become pure body. I sit at the typewriter and become pure mind. The day goes by and I discover I have not eaten. No wonder, then, this isolation that I feel: If one does not even break bread, what need is there for a companion? I am a rebel as solitary as Thoreau, a revolutionary whose cause is my own life.

Still, that may be the way to salvation—not the conformity sought by psychologists, but simply remaining original. What the narcissist needs is not less self-love but more: I have to reach the point of knowing that everything that lives is holy, including himself.

And only when I love myself can I love my neighbor.

—*PERSONAL BEST,* 1989

———————◆———————

MY FRIEND TOM OSLER, who is a 50-miler and teaches math at a state college, says that depressions are part of life. The runner, he says, must expect them, even welcome them. They are just as normal, just as inevitable and just as necessary as the happy times.

And now in the depths of my semiannual, or is it quarterly, depression, I am inclined to agree. Periodically, no matter how I try to avoid it, I run myself into this growing inner discontent. Every 6 months or so, I develop this feeling that every task is too difficult to do and not worth the effort anyway.

My running suffers most. In fact, it is the first indication that things are amiss. I no longer look forward to my daily run. And should I ignore this lack of zest and run anyway, I tire easily and don't enjoy it. But the running and this loss of enjoyment are only part of it. My emotions, my moods, my concentrations, my attention span, my attitude toward myself and others are all affected. Instead of battling anoxia and lactic acid and muscles depleted of sugar, I am in hand-to-hand combat with dejection and dependency, with rejection and self-pity, with guilt and loneliness. I am truly in the dark night of the soul.

In the real night, I awaken repeatedly for no apparent reason. And in the morning I am not refreshed or ready for the new day. I would like to pull the covers over my head and wait for this terrible state to pass over.

Is all this something inevitable, as Osler states? Or is it simply because I have run myself into some temporary physical state? And could I not, with a little prudence, avoid all these unnecessary sufferings?

I think not. Such periods are inescapable. Ecclesiastes was right. There is a time for everything. A time for running. A time not to run.

Human nature frowns on prudence. It demands that we maximize ourselves. That whatever we do, we do it with all our might. And, predictably, this means periodic exhaustion, periodic failure, periodic depression, and, as happily, periodic reevaluation.

I am now in those days of Ecclesiastes. "The fine hammered steel of woe," Melville called this book. I believe it. Now words cannot describe the weariness of things, and days give me no pleasure. And now it does seem as it did to him that "all effort and achievement come from man's envy of man."

The peculiarity, as Ecclesiastes noted, is that these depressions occur not when things are going badly, but when they are going well. Not in times of failure, but in times of triumph. These depressions are not proceeded by tragedy, but by celebration. Not by the worst race I have run, but by the best.

Less than 2 weeks ago, I ran a taxing and courageous and outlandishly fast 10-miler in Central Park. I ran to my limits, met the challenges of several runners who might normally have beaten me, and then ran the last 5 miles faster than the first, never giving an inch to those trying to catch me. It was an hour and 4 minutes and 15 seconds of being as good a runner as I could be.

Later, as I sprawled on a chair in the parish hall of the Church of the Heavenly Rest, watching my fellow runners fill up on coffee and doughnuts, I felt warm and tired and satisfied. I turned to a friend next to me and said, "George, right now I could pull the sword out of the stone."

Today, if I said that, it would be presumptuous. I have lost what Yeats called "radical innocence." But I know there is and there always will be a time of running. A time when running is enough. When it is enough to race the same races, run the same roads. Enough to live out the cycle upon cycle of the running year. And thereby to fulfill myself in the many ways I do when running is the focal point of my life.

But there is also a time of not running. Time to see that the good can be the enemy of the best. That it is not merely the trivial that clutters up my life, but the important as well. I have, as Anne Lindbergh wrote, a surfeit of treasures. And it is time for me to answer the question of Ecclesiastes, "What is best of men to do during their few days of life under the sun?"

If it were not for the depression, I would have thought that unanswerable question answered. But now I know that running is not enough. The answer "Sheehan's my name, running's my game" is not enough. There are more ways to understand life, it now appears, than running. Or business or politics or the arts or the sciences, for that matter.

I am reminded that Bernard De Voto once said to Robert Frost, "You're a good poet, Robert, but you're a bad man." Perhaps he was and perhaps he wasn't. To me, it seems that could be almost anyone's epitaph, including my own. And my periodic depressions make me realize that life may well be a game, but God judges the player, not the performance.

Not the race, but the runner.

—PERSONAL BEST, 1978

◆

THE FLIGHT HOME WAS depressing. The weekend in Crowley, Louisiana, had been a peak experience. Had been, in fact, a climax of my life as a runner and as a writer, and perhaps as a person. I had worn the number "1" in the National AAU Championship Marathon and finished in the top third of the field.

Before the race, runner after runner had come and shook my hand, saying, "Dr. Sheehan, I loved your book and just want you to know it." One said he had given 18 copies as Christmas presents. All weekend they sought me out to tell me how much I helped them. Later, at the awards dinner, I was given a plaque. I was, the inscription said, the outstanding distance runner of the year. A similar plaque the previous year had said the same thing about Frank Shorter. I was being classed with the immortals. And then, as a final gesture of esteem, I was permitted to talk.

The talk was more than a talk. It was a love affair. I spoke to each face in turn. And saw in each reflection of my feeling for them. I told them of the beauties of our bodies, and how we needed play. I told them we were all to be heroes in some way and if we were heroic enough we would see God.

And when I finished I was in tears, and so were they. And then we all stood and applauded who we were and what we had done and the feeling that was in that great room. And now I was flying away from all that. Flying toward what?

Where was I to go from here? What was there to reach for that would surpass where I had been? Where would I get the size and strength and presence to be more than I was that day?

Life, I saw again, was a problem that will never be solved. At no time is this more evident than when we are close to the solution. No time more evident than when we succeed. When we have come far, but not far enough.

The wise men have spoken of this. For every hundred men who can handle adversity, they concluded, there is but one who can handle success. Flying home, I knew I was not that one. My elation had disappeared. I was fearful of the future. I had exhausted my potential and could see nothing ahead but repeating what I had already done. Doing the few things I did well over and over again for the rest of my life.

The man next to me was a runner who had completed his first marathon. "What do I do now?" he asked, echoing the thought in my mind. His answer would be my answer.

What do I do now? More of the same, only better. Run another and learn that much more about myself and the world and Who made me. Run another and another. Bathe myself in pain and fatigue. Reach for energies I have yet to use. Run another and another and another. Make my truth out of that experience, out of what happens.

What do I do now? No matter what I have done, there is still more to do. No matter how well it has been done, it can still be done better. No matter how fast the race, it can still be run faster.

Everything I do must be aimed at that, aimed at being a

masterpiece. The things I write, the races I run, each day I live. There can be no other way.

I thought then of the ancient Egyptians, who believed there was a judgment after death and the initial step was to weigh the heart. It seems so true. The heart is the measure of our energy, our courage, our intuition, our love. It is the measure of our days, of what we have done, of who we are.

Was I ready, then, to have my heart weighed? Was this as far as I would go? Was I ready to rest, to obey the commandments and await my reward?

The plane was bringing me back to earth. Without thinking, I took my pulse. A slow, steady 48, and only a day after a marathon. And I knew then, as every runner knows, my heart is capable of anything. All it asks is the time to do it.

When I have run my best marathon and written my best piece and done my best deed of love for myself and my neighbor, I know the cry will still come from my heart: "There is more, there is more. I Who have made you know." What else is a heart for, then, but to be uneasy, to ask for what seems impossible and never be satisfied? So my heart will be restless until it finds its final rest.

Then they can weigh it.

—*RUNNING & BEING*, 1978

What Dr. Sheehan Means to Me

BY JOE HENDERSON, FORMER EDITOR-IN-CHIEF OF *RUNNER'S WORLD*

IF YOU'VE RUN LESS than 20 years, you can't be expected to know the name George Sheehan. If you started running before 1993, we can assume that you'll never forget him.

I never will. George was the best friend I've ever had in this sport. He was my confidant, mentor, and model for the writing and speaking roles that we both played, and was almost my second father.

We were teammates. He was the essayist and I the editor, from his first *Runner's World* appearance in 1970 until he finished his last book 23 years later. I had the honor of seeing his columns before any reader of the magazine did, and to hear the private stories behind these public gems.

The most dramatic of those stories began in 1986, when George stood at the top of his many games. His books had made bestseller lists, and his columns were the best-read feature of the magazine.

He also was one of the best-known speakers on the running, fitness, and sports medicine circuits. He was one of the country's best runners for his age, 67 at the time.

Then came the type of medical exam that he'd ordered for his own patients hundreds of times. Back came the chilling report on himself that he'd delivered to others: "We have found a growth . . ."

He had cancer of the prostate, and the disease already had spread into his bones—beyond the reach of surgery. His first reaction to this diagnosis was to surrender. "I planned my will and turned down speaking engagements," he wrote. "I wasn't sure I'd be around in 3 months to fulfill them."

He also stopped writing and dropped out of racing. But he soon realized that waiting to die was no way to live his remaining time.

"There is nothing more certain than the defeat of a man who gives up— and, I might add, the victory of one who will not," he wrote at the time. "I know that Robert Frost was right. I have promises to keep, and miles to go before I sleep."

George resumed his full menu of activities. While fighting the disease to a standstill for the next 6 years, he delivered hundreds more speeches, ran scores more races, wrote dozens more columns, and published two more books.

More importantly, he patched up his personal life. He ended a long separation from his wife, Mary Jane, and eased the resulting strains with their 12 children.

By his own admission he became less self-absorbed. He was quicker to say his thank-yous and I-love-yous.

"I am still under sentence," he said, "but I have been given a stay of execution. Time to set things right and achieve what I was sent here to do."

That time stretched many more years than his doctors expected. They were good, happy, productive years before his disease finally took its inevitable course.

Even after the cancer went (in his words) "into fast forward" in 1992, forcing him to quit running and then speaking, he kept writing. His journal-style essays became a frontline report on his final battle.

"There is a healthy way to be ill," Dr. George Sheehan had long advised his patients, readers and listeners. His final book, completed in his final week of life, tells how well he took his own advice. As long as his writing is read, a part of George Sheehan lives on.

11/*Cancer*

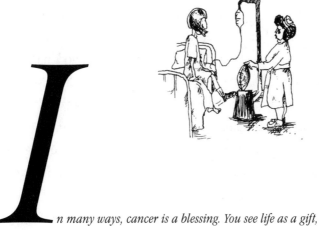

n many ways, cancer is a blessing. You see life as a gift,
and every day becomes precious—and that's a lesson you never forget.

GOING THE DISTANCE, 1995

IN 1 HOUR I will know whether the nodule in my prostate is benign or malignant. In another 60 minutes, the urologist who did the biopsy will be calling on the phone with the result. In a very brief time my future will be decided.

This drama began only a week ago. I was in Dallas to give a talk at a fitness festival. The day before, I went over to challenge Dr. Ken Cooper's treadmill at the Cooper Institute for Aerobic Research. I had set a record for my age group the year before and someone had come along and broken it. I was of a mind to get it back. I did, and by a large margin. Afterward, as I lay on the table recovering, I felt as if I were joining the immortals: Despite my age, I had performed in the

99th percentile of the 70,000 treadmill tests done at Cooper Institute for Aerobic Research.

But then Dr. Cooper told me he was going to do a physical examination of me. Before I could protest, I was stripped down in his examining room and subjected to everything ordinary people go through when they go to a doctor. And that was when he discovered the suspicious area in my prostate. The news was paralyzing: I had just joined the immortals when suddenly I was made aware of my mortality.

It hardly seemed possible that only a week ago I had been fretting and worrying about the normal vicissitudes of life. My running, for one: My times had deteriorated over the past year. I was running a minute slower than usual in 5-mile races—running 6:20 miles instead of 6:10s. I had rarely thought of my aging before, but now I was becoming preoccupied with it. I had finally reached a point where no amount of training made me improve.

The worst part was that aging as a runner meant aging as a person. I live in social circles that are one and two generations younger than I am. I had never felt that difference to any great extent, and neither had they. But lately, I'd become resigned to being no longer a contemporary in body or even in mind. I had become a bore, and I'd found that I was even boring myself.

My writing was proof. Many times before, I had thought that I was written out. This time it was really true. When I took on a new subject I almost uniformly found that I had done it before, and better. I started writing years ago with the pledge—for years, easily kept—never to repeat myself. The phrases would leap onto the typewritten page. Now, none appeared that did not land with a thud and then lie there lifeless. I could no longer come up with a sentence that made me laugh or cry.

But all these defeats I had also known in the past. One loses love at 50. One ages at 55. One has writer's block at 60. The cycles come and go. One finds another love. One recaptures one's youth. One writes an absolute bestseller as age continues.

I know all this and fret still. I look for causes of rhythms that are as natural and fundamental as the seasons—and just as unchangeable. I should make up my mind not to complain about those rhythms but to enjoy them. The best of all know the worst of times—and then use those experiences when the bright, beautiful, and productive days return.

The big question: How should one live one's life? Basque philosopher Miguel de Unamuno y Jugo had this answer: "Our greatest endeavor must be to make ourselves irreplaceable—to make the fact that each one of us is unique and irreplaceable, that no one can fill the gap when we die, a practical truth."

In the past week, I learned that I have done that. If not always as well as I could, I still have made that fact a practical truth—I will be irreplaceable, I will leave a gap. Each day, family and friends have affirmed my importance to them.

But I also learned the corollary of that truth. There are people in my life who are irreplaceable. No one can fill the gap when they are gone. And I know now who they are. When you are between the sword and the stone, you know whom you want standing beside you. When time becomes short, those who are essential to your life become obvious.

That is what I will take away from this experience, even before I hear the result of the biopsy. My future has been decided: Whether this nodule turns out to be benign or malignant, my life has been unalterably changed. The lesson: I've made every day count. But what I have not done is make every person count.

—*RUNNER'S WORLD* MAGAZINE, 1987

I HAVE MADE MAJOR mistakes in my lifetime, but none equal to this one. I gave no thought to being checked for cancer. I knew better. I had virtually eliminated the possibility of coronary disease. A combination of heredity and running had shorn me of coronary risk factors. Even in early adulthood, I was marked as least likely to have a heart attack.

Adding to the security was my avoidance of the preventable causes of death. The athletic life had made me a nonsmoker and no more than a moderate drinker. My driving, while not impeccable, was guided by a defensive philosophy that kept me safe on the roads. When I took health-hazard appraisals I scored high except for one very important item—an annual checkup.

Like most Americans I had gone years and years without being examined by a physician. I recall once at an American Medical Association convention they set up a section where physicians could get a physical examination and have the routine laboratory work done. They snared hundreds in this net, many who had not been seen by a fellow doctor since their stint in the service or when taking out insurance.

Actually, what needs to be done in a physical exam requires very little time. Since there are no symptoms (or the person would have already sought help), the history takes only a few minutes. The laboratory work takes only minutes more. This leaves time so that even a 10-minute visit is adequate for a physical examination. And here we should be searched for those silent but life-threatening malignancies. When risk factors for heart disease are absent, the examination should concentrate on breast, prostate, and colon abnormalities. Any suspicious skin findings or abnormal lymph glands should be noted.

The evidence for prevention is not as clear in cancer as it is in coronary disease. With cancer our main aim is early detection. Daily I meet people long after an early cancer was detected and removed from their bodies. There are now medical miracles occurring with later and later detection, but nothing surpasses finding a malignancy early and dealing with it before there has been a chance for it to spread.

I know all this now. And you do, too. Being a physician I am very much aware of this need for early discovery. The education of the public has paralleled that of the medical community. Most people have learned that cancer is curable if it is caught soon enough.

However, most people take the view that it will not happen to them.

I am one of them.

—*GOING THE DISTANCE,* 1995

———◆———

WHEN I LEARNED I had inoperable cancer of the prostate—inoperable because it had spread to the bones—I went through a familiar sequence: panic, then denial, and finally depression. I lay awake nights thinking of this alien eating up my body. I stopped scheduling talks. I began to live with death.

But in time I realized that this was not the end. If one is lucky—and I was lucky—prostatic cancer is testosterone-dependent. Remove this male hormone from the body and the tumor stops growing—even regresses. In time, cancer cells that do not need the hormone for growth will take over. But that can be far down the road—several years, perhaps, or maybe even a decade.

I was one of the lucky ones. Offered the choice of castration, female hormones, or a daily injection of hypothalamic hormone GhRH, I chose the last—and it worked. In fact, it was almost miraculous. The pain disappeared, the bone scan improved, and serial tests for prostatic specific antigen—proteins the body manufactures in response to prostate cancer—showed only a negligible amount of cancer tissue in my body. Still I remain apprehensive. If there is one guarantee on any form of castration, it is that the cancer will eventually break through. The enemy within will win the war.

I also had to worry about the other life-limiting conditions that come with my age. Some, perhaps with more immediate consequences. "People with prostate cancer," said my son, the endocrinologist, "usually die of something else."

There is good reason for people with prostatic cancer to die of another disease. Their average age is 67 years old. And the average 67-year-old is unfit, and carrying around all sorts of other risk factors for heart disease and stroke—cigarettes, for example, or too much weight. Many have already incurred life-threatening disease. So considerable numbers succumb to heart attacks, strokes, and pulmonary diseases.

But I remembered something basketball player–turned-politician Bill Bradley said about his attitude when training for basketball: "I might lose because I wasn't tall enough, I might lose because I wasn't fast enough. But I wasn't going to lose because I wasn't ready." I decided then and there: I might die of prostate cancer, but I was certainly not going to die of anything else.

I chose the Bradley approach: Become an athlete, develop all the functions my body possesses, and let the cancer look for help elsewhere. So I went about the business of making myself the best body possible. I wasn't going to die because I wasn't ready, and what I could control, I would control.

I also chose to ignore most of the modern medical community—those doctors who allow elders like myself to have higher cholesterols, more body fat, and high blood pressure.

At what they consider my advanced age, health-care professionals ease up on restrictions—especially for cancer patients. They justify it on a lost-cause basis; why worry when the patient's going to die anyway? Enjoy what's left of life is the attitude.

"I prepare my patients for death," one oncologist told me. As if I would enjoy it more and be better prepared if I suddenly discarded my athletic life—stopped running, gained 15 pounds, drank myself into oblivion every night, and took up smoking cigarettes. Is that the way my life should end?

I admit, there is some temptation toward complete self-indulgence. But true self-indulgence is the reverse. The athletic life is the good life. Becoming the best you can be makes you feel the best you can feel. And from that renewed body comes a renewed attitude that would satisfy the most ardent proponent of mind over matter—important when you're battling an opponent like cancer.

My daily injections have not given me a reprieve: My cancer has not been cured. In other cases, radiation or surgery or chemotherapy may eradicate the tumor, in which case the person is returned to the land of the living. But I am still under sentence. I have been given a stay of execution. Time to set things right—I was about to say, get things right, which is part of it, too—and achieve what I was sent here to do.

In many ways, cancer is a blessing. You see life as a gift, and every day becomes precious—and that's a lesson you never forget.

Paul Tsongas, for example, quit the U.S. Senate when he found he had cancer. He has now apparently been cured of it. But Tsongas said he prefers not to think of being cured.

"The problem with the notion of cure is that I don't want to go back to the assumption of immortality," he said. "I think I am better served by being aware of life's fragility than going back to the assumption that we are all going to live forever."

Most of us do assume exactly that, however—that we're going to live forever. I know I did. Like writer William Saroyan, I knew that everyone must die but an exception would be made in my case. Death may have been a fact of life, but not in my life. It simply did not concern me.

Except on Ash Wednesday, and while attending funerals, I have never thought much on death. Now, however, every day is Ash Wednesday. I am constantly reminded that I am dust and unto dust I will inevitably return.

Death will not take me unawares. I expect now to be cut down in my prime, doing well at what I do best. Cancer has put urgency into my life. I, still unworthy, am about to return to my Creator. And I am learning something critically important about the human condition: No one, no matter his age, should ever retire from life.

We must be forever enlarging our lives, not diminishing them. "Sin is closing the circle," wrote a contemporary theologian. Once we exclude anything or anybody we cease to grow. We join forces with sin and age and death.

Emerson made this the theme of one of his greatest essays, "Circles." He invited us to see that only by ever enlarging our circles of life and endeavor do we progress toward the perfection that always seems beyond our reach.

When we cease to do that, we age—and we age irrespective of

our years. Conversely, we grow younger as we aspire to be more and more.

All around him, Emerson saw forms of old age—rest, conservatism, inertia. "We grizzle every day and I see no need of it." He urged us to live as when we were filled with zeal, fired with enthusiasm, always going beyond what we have already thought or done.

Now that death has entered the picture, I am no longer in danger of grizzling. Death makes the everyday magical, the ordinary unique, and the commonplace one-of-a-kind. And all this is done without introducing anxiety. Once I accept death, I center on the present. I concentrate on this new day, this—in Emerson's words—"everlasting miracle" I am presented with each dawn.

Living has now become a matter of life and death. The imperative? Meaning. To have a death worth dying, you must have a life worth living. And that can only be done by giving meaning to our lives.

According to another thinker, the real cause of our anxieties and depression, our inability to be happy and feel joy, is a life that lacks meaning.

Each day for me is now a separate life. I arise, take my morning swim, and prepare for battle. The cancer is always at the gates. "I feel like Israel," said Tsongas. "I have to win every war."

There is no sense now in faking anything. When I was in the Navy I did that. I always carried papers so it would appear that I was working on something. Now I truly am, and that something is me. Because I now have cancer and can see death plain; I have begun to live. And when the big sleep comes, I'll sleep—but not a minute before.

—GOING THE DISTANCE, 1995

AT ONE OF OUR post-race parties, one runner had to leave early. In the past few years he had been faced with caring for his sick parents.

Our current medical care has been able to postpone dying. Americans are living longer than ever. What it has not done is prolong successful living. As we near our last years we are now threatened with the prospect of being one of the living dead.

If I polled the 50 or more runners chatting out on the deck or inside watching the Olympics on why they ran, I would get a variety of answers. People run for physical, mental, psychological, and social reasons. But almost universally they plan to run for the rest of their lives. It is that sentiment that interested Wilfred Graham, a professor of religion at Michigan State University. In questioning 20 female runners he found this secondary but universal motivation expressed in one way or another: "I'm going to run until I can't put one foot in front of another and then I'll be dead. No geriatrics ward for me."

"Running is a scientifically approved way of extending life," writes Graham. "Runners, however, do not so much want to gain an extension as they want to insure mobility until death comes." Runners' seeming preoccupation with youth and their defiance of age is actually their dread of what Graham calls terminal helplessness.

That, it seems, is the deeper meaning of "I'll run until I drop." Death, as it does for every age, will come to the runner. It is beyond our control. What is possible, however, is what is technically called "compression of morbidity." This means limiting the disability and dependence of our final years to a minimum. The ideal would be to emulate the wonderful one-horse shay that lasted for a hundred years and dissolved into dust in a single instant.

Graham firmly believes that many converts to running have done so to guarantee that their bodies will not slowly decay in a convalescent home. "Hidden somewhere in the pursuit of regular exercise is the notion that if one keeps moving, one will never be caught in the wires and tubes and sterile unprivacy that the aged suffer today."

I heard one story of a man in his late sixties whose family decided to put him in a nursing home. When he heard that he said, "I came to the realization that my lifestyle must be completely wrong." He completely reversed his way of living, followed nature's rules, and remained independent.

A nursing home is probably not in the consciousness of my partying runner friends who have just finished a 5mile race. Nevertheless, a little probing can bring it to light. After all, many if not most of these runners began running in their mid-thirties, a time when the body provides subtle but definite dues that you are on the down slope of life. With a life expectancy of 72, 36 becomes middle age and instinctively people know it.

My own aim is to live out the biblical span and more, with as little "down time" as possible—to be a competitor in life, right up to my final days. The athletic life protects me as long as possible. I dread to join the thousands who, as Graham points out, "languish in homes for the aged, their minds and spirits exhausted but their bodies helpless to die."

I looked around at the lean, fit, vital people of all ages who filled our house, and remembered my thoughts jogging to the starting line earlier that day. "This is a great day to run. This is a good day to die."

—GOING THE DISTANCE, 1995

"YOU ONLY LIVE ONCE," said the humorist Fred Allen, "but if you do it right, once is enough." The import of this aphorism undoubtedly varies with our age. In our ascendant years we know just how to go about living life successfully. At 45 we are torn between trying to remedy the mess we have made or going back and starting over. I can attest to two truths: It is still possible to do it right, and no, I would not want to go through it again.

Life is a long, hard struggle. But it is also a positive-sum game. Everybody can win. The lives of other people, relatives, friends, public figures may serve as inspiration or warnings but do not add or detract from our performance.

The successful life in many ways is difficult to define.

Satisfaction is internal. Establishing behavioral criteria for success is difficult. The profiles we use frequently miss the mark. Success in marriage, a good health record, ability to enjoy a vacation, and doing better than one's parents may well identify successful people. Still, many who have failed in all those categories may feel good about doing it their way.

Doing things right means doing things right for us. At my age this emerges as a primary rule in life. From my porch I look at the passing throng on the boardwalk and note the development of character with age. The young are homogenous, but each of the elderly stands out. They are no longer members of the herd.

To some degree we differ from everyone else in the world. Whatever the general rule, it has to be applied individually. We function in fundamentally different ways in areas as diverse as religion, art, and physical activity. Our careers are, or should be, vocation—a call heard only by our own ears.

How varied we are is only too evident. Consider the religious life, and count the different ways in which that life can be led. If science be preferred, how many the forms of expression. We have only to read *The Varieties of Religious Experience* by William James and *The Varieties of Human Values* by Charles Morris to see the enormously different ways in which we find peace and happiness on one hand and virtue and strength on the other.

Fortunately, we set forth on this journey equipped for success. The powers we need are available to all. The *arete* or excellence sought by the Greeks is possible for anyone. The Sermon on the Mount is writ large on every heart. Even the bad experiences are universal and corrective. Distrust, guilt, isolation, and despair can bring us to know and practice their opposites and get us back on track.

Although good fortune may be needed for happiness, it appears that what is essential to the good life is always available. Thornton Wilder pointed this out in writing about *Our Town:* "I have tried to find a value above price for the smallest events in our daily life."

That daily life is the setting and stage for our own drama. We come to know that we fail or succeed according to how we handle the ordinary, commonplace events going on around us. It is in apparently trivial events that we most clearly show who we are. Not mortal sins but venial sins alter lives. And they reveal the lukewarm, the would-be respectable trimmers.

Allen was right. Make this one life you have a work of art. Live with class and you'll go out in style.

—GOING THE DISTANCE, 1995

"LIFE IS A TERMINAL illness," writes Samuel Beckett. When my prostate cancer spread into my bones this process went on "fast forward." I was forced to deal with the stages of death and dying.

The first is denial. When I heard the cancer diagnosis, I had a feeling of disbelief. This can't be happening to me. It was difficult to believe that yesterday was a normal day and now I was dealing with a fatal disease.

Next, for me, was fear. A fear, I might say, close to panic. I had a week of sleepless nights until I realized that, for now anyway, I felt the same as last month.

What usually follows is anger. Dr. Edward Creagan, an oncologist at the Mayo Clinic who has written on this problem, says that the anger may be directed at oneself, a spouse, a physician, or the system. I must admit I spent no time in this stage. Being a runner, I accepted no excuses. This was the luck of the draw.

After that comes bargaining. We recognize this from adolescence, when we make a pact with a "higher power." We promise to do better, return to the righteous life, or contribute to the community in exchange for a reprieve.

Next comes depression. When it becomes evident that the treatments are not effective—and those waiting to be tried not much better—depression ensues. Patients tend to give up. They become withdrawn and lose energy. They have no enthusiasm for their daily tasks.

During these stages I spent most of my time searching for a cure. There were newsletters and support groups that had information on various programs around the country. I spoke with or visited experts at the most prestigious institutions. I learned that every now and then they had an exceptional result—but these exceptional results were truly exceptions.

Meanwhile, I was being taught how to deal with the inevitable. I was gradually coming into the final stage, acceptance. Dr. Creagan describes this as a complete reversal of attitude. The attempts to find a magic cure or reprieve from the disease decrease. Patients become less focused on their illness, tests, and treatment. They go back to living each day to the fullest.

Dr. Creagan tells the story of a prominent member of his community. This man was obsessed with finding a cure for his terminal cancer and had investigated treatment options throughout the world. When he finally accepted the reality of his situation, his conversations centered on his golf game and his family instead of some new treatment.

Acceptance, as difficult as it is for the patient, may be even more difficult for the family. The cancer victim, having won this peace, has to deal with loving relatives who are still engaged in the search for a cure.

I recall something my sister said to me when she was getting chemotherapy for her fatal cancer. "I wouldn't take this, George, except I want the family to be sure I did everything."

For the cancer patient, "doing everything" is reaching acceptance, or what Friedrich Nietzsche called *amor fati*—the love of our fate, whatever that turns out to be.

—GOING THE DISTANCE, 1995

"SHEEHAN, PAY ATTENTION!" HOW often I heard that admonition in school. The order that I put my daydreams aside and join in the lesson being taught. The teacher demanding my presence, asking that I be not merely "here," but actively engaged in the subject at hand.

But there I sat, my eyes glazed, my ears unhearing, all senses on hold. No longer aware of what was going on around me or indeed even where I was. My imagination was at the controls as I journeyed into my inner space.

The teacher's task is to circumvent this escape. Teaching, William James once said, is the insertion of a creative mind between a fact and a pupil. Nothing can be accomplished without undivided attention from both parties to this undertaking.

Both in life and in school we must pay attention. Daydreams come true only when preceded by the serious mental effort that learning requires. Yet what I did as a student I have continued through my adult life. I am off in a world of my own making.

At times I am pulled up short. Some inexcusable ignorance, some error in judgment, an instance of pure cowardice, a neglected friendship, the acceptance of indolence, and suddenly I hear that inner voice: "Sheehan, pay attention!"

I realize, then, that I have stopped learning. I am no longer present. I am preoccupied with the inconsequential. I miss the significant. I am daydreaming while life is trying to teach me how to live. I would learn from experience but I fail to notice I have had an experience. I am absent when the day's events spell out insights on the human condition.

It is no excuse to say I am a philosopher; a philosophy does not develop a priori, it comes into being a posteriori—after the event. We shape ourselves and our philosophies through observing and understanding the occurrences of the day. If philosophy is, as someone has said, "disguised autobiography," we must live it to write it.

"The world's a stage," said Shakespeare. And more than that. It is the school where life, the great teacher, goes over the lesson for today. Yet we sit there, or at least I do, and look out the window thinking of other worlds.

"Sheehan, pay attention!" If only this Japanese miracle on my wrist would intone that phrase on the hour. It would bring me back to the living, back to using my five senses, back to extracting the "how" and especially the "why" of what is happening around me. Teaching myself, because now I am both student and teacher, that the world is filled with miraculous things and none more miraculous than we humans who populate it.

Now, more than ever, I want to know. Know how the world works. But even more I want to know why. Why I am here. Why I must die. I can make this search in several ways. I can retire into myself and think about it. Or I can go day by day seeing the world as my school-room and paying very strict attention.

—GOING THE DISTANCE, 1995

WHEN HERBERT HOWE WAS preparing for his doctorate at Harvard, he learned he had cancer. Radiation and chemotherapy were begun. That was his physician's reaction, the scientific one. Howe's reaction was the intuitive one. He became an athlete. With an 80 percent chance he would be dead in 5 years, he committed the greater part of each day to sports.

"I swam an hour a day," he reports, "furiously punched the heavy bag and ran consistent 6-minute miles over a 12-mile course." Eventually, he took up skateboarding, hang-gliding, and scuba diving. Shortly after the chemotherapy ended, he completed the world's longest 1-day canoe race. When he finished the 72 miles, he collapsed and spent 3 hours in the emergency room.

Why all this? Why, faced with pain in the future, seek more pain now? Why, faced with death, take the chance of hastening it? Why push on and struggle when he could take the time to enjoy life? Howe sees no incompatibility between pain and joy. For him, they coexist. "I had to believe that my body was not decaying," he writes. "I had to believe I was winning."

Then, he quotes Michael Novak on winning as "a form of thumbing your nose, for the moment, at the cancers and diseases that, in the end, strike us all down."

To keep from decaying, to be a winner, the athlete must accept pain—not only accept it but look for it, live with it, learn not to fear it.

Herbert Howe decided to do more and more, to work harder and harder no matter how much it hurt. He then found that perseverance and pride became synonymous. Significantly, he notes, "I gained new confidence." Confidence and, of course, faith and trust grew out of the new man. He had reached a point where his experiment and experience had earned him self-certainty, self-trust, self-reliance.

Howe plunged on. He had come to see his chemotherapy and his doctoral dissertation as two marathon events. Since, he says, pride lasts longer than pain, he pushed on harder than ever before. He was supported and sustained in this by the discipline and absorption of his athletics. He was made whole by the fact that he had gone out to meet pain and grasped it, and having defeated his self-doubts about his physical condition he was ready to face the uncertainty that lay ahead.

Herbert Howe had discovered the athlete's secret, a secret they all share and cannot really express. For one thing, pain is always personal. One's pain cannot be felt by another. No matter how earnest the desire to communicate it, the effort falls short. We can almost, but not quite, understand the total reaction of the protesting body, the undecided will, the questioning reason, the hopeful and courageous heart.

Because it is personal, private, and secret, pain is a subject that has baffled theologians, frustrated philosophers, sent psychiatrists to other psychiatrists, and caused thinkers to wonder how much the mind can explain. Somewhere inside of pain and suffering is the mystery of existence.

Most of us can see the biological necessity of pain. It protects us, keeps us out of harm's way. Pain is nature's early-warning system. Very few of us, however, can imagine pain as a logical necessity. Josiah Royce, almost as much a theologian as a philosopher, wrote of pain that way. Through our suffering, he declared, God suffers. God must suffer to be whole and just, and so must we.

Royce's theory is unique, as far as I can see. It is much more common for people to see evil and pain as the expressions of a bad body, due to Original Sin. There are others who see pain simply as a bad joke.

For the athlete, pain is neither of these. His life is good, and to live it well is to suffer well. He recognizes his pain as necessary.

"Live in the uncomfortable zone," a man once advised me, "and when you die you will have no regrets."

For one thing, you will have lived, tried everything, discovered your limits. And there is always the chance that you will do what Herbert Howe did: combine pain with joy, and discover that you and your life have no limits.

RUNNER'S WORLD MAGAZINE, FEBRUARY 1979

What Dr. Sheehan Means to Me

BY DR. KENNETH COOPER, MD, MPH

I REMEMBER CONDUCTING A preventive medical examination on George on December 2, 1983. (It was the first time he had been evaluated at the Cooper Clinic and his first examination of any kind in over 25 years.) Since he had run more than 60 marathons at the time of his exam, with a personal record of 3:01:10 (the Marine Corps Marathon, at age 62), I expected his treadmill performance to be outstanding. It was, ranking in the top 2 percent for men over 60.

A complete examination was not performed at that time, only laboratory studies, a resting electrocardiogram, and the previously mentioned stress electrocardiogram; all were normal. I encouraged George to return for a full preventive examination, and that was performed November 30, 1984. On the treadmill his performance was a minute and a half longer than in 1983, placing him in the top 1 percent for all men tested at the Cooper Clinic at that time. This included many men who were much younger.

The disturbing finding was that his prostate was three times its normal size, with a hard nodule in the left lobe. Based on that discovery, I encouraged him to consult a urologist, which he did shortly thereafter. George was very pleased with the results, as they came back negative.

Approximately a year later, he and I both were speaking at a sports medicine event in Colorado, and while having dinner with him that night I asked if he had had the prostate biopsied. He said no, and I told him that on many occasions patients of mine with prostate cancer had a normal first biopsy. In early 1986 he went for a biopsy and it came back abnormal; by then he had metastatic prostate cancer.

After the diagnosis, George and I continued to communicate on a regular basis. In December 1989 one of his columns documented his evaluation at the Cooper Clinic and the discovery of his cancer. At that time, he was doing quite well.

In a letter I wrote on January 8, 1990, I thanked him for sending a copy of one of his columns. He was quite pleased that he had been cancer-free for 4 years.

But that October, it was discovered the cancer had returned, and he was placed on hormones since he was no longer a candidate for any type of surgical procedure. In the October issue of *Runner's World*, he wrote an article titled "Resuming the Fight" about what he was doing to try to stop the progressive disease. Also at that time, I congratulated him on his 1500-meter national championship; even though he had recurrence and metastasis of his prostate cancer, he was still running regularly.

In January 1993 he was told that his cancer was refractory to hormone therapy and that he would have to rely upon radiation to control the pain. He was still ambulatory but could no longer run.

The last letter I received from George was dated October 2, 1990. At that time, he wrote:

"I do so appreciate your letter and the kindness and consideration that comes through in every sentence. I'll never forget, and constantly remind others, that you were the one who found my cancer—and urged the second biopsy when the first was negative.

"As for myself, if I am depressed, it is only when I find the creative powers on hold. My mission now is to deal with cancer, its therapy, and all the implications, and tell others what it is like. To the writer, as one playwright said, 'Every tragedy is a treasure.'"

12 / Final *Revelations*

*I*n the past I defined myself as a runner and did not realize what that fully
meant. I was the runner deep in thought on the ocean road. I was suffering in the race.
Now I am the runner sharing my life with other runners. I have come full circle.
I have become, in the words of Blake describing age, "a child grown wise."

PERSONAL BEST, 1989

AS I TOOK MY early-morning swim one day, I noticed a runner
watching me from the boardwalk. Later, as I was toweling off on the
porch, he approached and introduced himself as reader of my column. Then he asked, "What is the most important thing in your life?"

If I were asked that question at seven o'clock in the evening, it
would draw a philosophic reply, like "What is 'important'?" Or: "What
do you mean by 'life?'" The sort of evasions that come after another
day of living with myself and others, leaving me full of doubt.

But at 7:00 in the morning, my answer was simple and direct as the newly risen day. Without hesitation, my head and heart responded, "My family."

It was the absolutely certain reply of a 70-something male who has entered the seventh stage in Erik Erikson's eightstage life cycle. I have attained what Erikson terms generativity—concern about the welfare of the generations to come, particularly my family.

Of the virtues and values I had to acquire in life, generativity was the most difficult to attain. According to Erikson, this is a rule of human nature. I doubt it. For males, perhaps this is true.

But for women, generativity is a force from the arrival of their firstborn.

When our children were born, I was primarily concerned with my self-development. My wife and family were part of that self only peripherally. They were in intimate association with me, I was responsible for their growth and development. But they were nevertheless external to the self I was making.

In my pursuit of excellence, in my profession, and later in my associations, I devoted a minimum amount of time and attention to my family. At times, I wanted to be free from all the hassle of family life.

A lot of married men develop this desire to escape and pursue some idyllic life with another person. A very good family practitioner once told me, "If all the men in this town who wanted to leave their homes did so, there would be very few families with fathers."

And even when families remain intact, that life may be difficult. "The proper word for family is 'strife,'" writes Ortega y Gasset. The family is kept intact by knowing what can be said and what can't. At times, it's like walking on eggshells. This tension and its more overt manifestations have led to the concept of dysfunctional families. My own belief is that all families malfunction at one time or other. An assembly of egos in all stages of development can hardly be expected to operate friction-free.

My solution was to more or less detach myself from the group. In that position, I was not a positive influence, but at least I wasn't a negative force. I am a loner, a person interested in ideas rather than people. I liked to have people around me, but I preferred to read a book while they were there.

The antithesis of generavity is self-absorption. I was heavily involved in creativity and productivity. But I was more and more self-absorbed. The attraction of any action was what I would personally derive from it. My motivation was my own needs and satisfaction.

I was late in coming to generativity, which is no less than the virtue of caring. Its theological counterpart is charity. It is going beyond the self. One theologian described sin as "closing the ring of concern." I had closed it around myself. I now include many people inside the ring and am learning to open that ring more and more.

Growth and the attainment of a new plateau did not come simply because I was in my late sixties. In truth, it should have occurred decades back. Reaching a certain stage in the life cycle does not come automatically.

I came to this love for my family and others through a familiar life-giving force, adversity. Cancer, its attendant pain, and an awareness of my isolation brought me back to a patient, loving wife and our sons and daughters.

In giving me cancer, fortune had smiled on me. Pain was a key to opening up a new and larger life. The interests of my past are still present, but now finally seen in perspective.

That's why I was able to answer without hesitation when a stranger asked me to put my present life into one word: "Family."

Guilt or shame might have altered my conduct, but only temporarily.

I lived the life of the runner-writer with little need for the input of the many lives that impinged on mine.

Now I remain a writer—but no longer a runner. My world has shrunk. I need the support, the laughter, the love that these offspring bring to the family table.

And now I can use what is probably an overused expression, "quality time." What it contains are the relationships, not present before, but now being born between us. They give me moments of happiness, moments that come with the "letting go" I could never achieve in the past.

There should be no regrets on either side. Whatever way time was spent—with the family or not, with the parents or not—it was a natural outcome of the making of a self. It was a part of a much larger project I was carrying on. "Follow your bliss," says Joseph Campbell. *Amor fati* (love of fate), says Nietzsche. Carl Rogers has told us this making of the self is done by recognizing the not-self. When Campbell writes of life as a labyrinth, he is telling us of the necessity of following false leads in order to make a successful attempt.

— *RUNNER'S WORLD* MAGAZINE, APRIL 1992

◆

"THE BOY WHO RODE on slightly before him sat a horse not only as if he'd been born to it which he was but as if were he begot by malice or mischance into some queer land where horses never were he would have found them anyway. Would have known that there was something missing for the world to be right or he right in it and would have set forth to wander wherever it was needed for as long as it took until he came upon one and he would have known that that was what he sought and it would have been."

The boy riding ahead is John Grady Cole, the young hero of Cormac McCarthy's remarkable novel *All the Pretty Horses*. The man riding behind is his father, who will die of cancer before the story is finished.

He dies without regrets. His son has found what all of us seek— the absolute certainty of what he was born to be. He is a horseman on a journey that becomes a heroic quest. John Grady, who is as resourceful as Huckleberry Finn and as pure as Billy Budd, tells one lie and thereby unleashes evil and brutality and eventually comes to redemption.

Every parent wants this experience for his or her offspring. Free, of course, of encounters with violence and brutality, but still a trip to discover the self and the other world that somehow influences ours. It matters not what the consuming passion is, save that it must be a passion, some all-absorbing, self-renewing compulsion.

"I must always be at work," said the great Rodin. So it is with anyone who has heard the call within. "Thurber! You're writing again!" James Thurber's wife would admonish him at dinner parties. The same total involvement is expressed in the first line of Norman Maclean's *A River Runs Through It:* "In our family there was no clear line between religion and fly fishing."

This struggle for self-discovery is universal. Life, as Ortega put it, is a desperate struggle to become in fact what you are in design. Knowing your design is the chanciest part. Struggles, no matter how desperate, come easier when you are certain of the goal.

And looking around at my children, now adults doing their thing, I realized that somehow, sometime, somewhere they had gotten the message. Each had found what the horse was to John Grady. Each was doing his or her own thing.

I could see them riding ahead of me—the doctor, the artist, the horse trainer, the teacher, and whatever else they had become. And I knew if they had been born where those possibilities did not exist they would have searched until they found them and would know that was what they sought and it would have been.

—*GOING THE DISTANCE*, 1995

———————◆———————

THIS SPRING, AFTER 40 years of marriage, I began wearing a wedding ring. It was an announcement that I had finally achieved what Erik Erikson stated was the fifth stage of an individual's eight-stage life cycle, "intimacy."

George Vaillant, a psychiatrist who has studied the subject of male psychological health for over 30 years, gives great importance to attaining intimacy. Vaillant believes that intimacy is a phenomenon that marks the point at which a child becomes an adult.

Vaillant has pointed out that the evolution from one stage to another is neither chronological nor automatic. If a person misses a stage, that person (in Vaillant's subject, the male) must go back and repeat it.

Beyond "intimacy," which Vaillant defines as living successfully with a non-family member for 10 years or more, there are more virtues a person must achieve. Identity, caring, in Erikson's term "generativity," and finally, wisdom. Each one of these stages represents, as does intimacy, a crisis. It is possible to fail them individually or serially and to have to repeat them as well.

We must, therefore, succeed in each one of Erikson's eight stages. In that way we evolve in a progression that begins with the raw material of temperament, grows into a distinctive personality, and finally achieves character. That assures our destiny.

Vaillant's studies have emphasized certain characteristics that portend a good end result. Competence in adolescence is more important than IQ. A good relationship with parents is helpful when we reach our fifties. Our feelings toward our siblings become decisive to happiness in our sixties.

We have to succeed in every stage. And this success is measured against what is possible and potential in us. It is not a competition against others. But this concept points out the danger of negatives in weighing our strengths and weaknesses. The challenges we accept or that others propose to us must be possible.

The most difficult progression surely has to be from child to adult. The qualities needed for intimacy are not prominent in a child. Patience, discipline, dedication, compassion, selflessness are hard-won virtues. They do not come easily or automatically. And some of us are very slow learners.

Our society, of course, reflects failures at every one of Erikson's stages and Vaillant's as well. Few of us have no need for courses in remedial living. We have to make up for deficiencies in the evolutionary pattern of our lives.

My marriage satisfied Vaillant's definition of success in intimacy; but despite that I came to recognize that I had never made the transition from child to adult. In my writings I had extolled being childlike, which is something to be desired. It is quite another matter, however, to be childish.

By rights my marriage should have foundered long ago, but my wife made up for both of us. She is a definition of why relationships work. Others marry or have relationships who are not that fortunate. Still children, they are frequently living with a person who is more child than adult as well.

After 49 years I passed through another life crisis to become the adult husband I was meant to be.

—GOING THE DISTANCE, 1995

———◆———

As I neared the 2-mile mark of a 5-mile race in Ocean County Park, New Jersey, last spring, I was running dead last, 107th in a field of 107.

At that point, a park ranger, who was working as a course monitor, called out to me. "How are you doing?" he asked.

"The best I can," I panted.

For me, doing the best I can is routine, but being last is an unusual experience.

Once, when I ran in a national cross-country championship in my 40s, I was lapped by the entire field. But not since then had I held the position that defines the end of a race.

There was no question that I was last. I turned around several times to be certain. Surrounded by silence, I felt as if I were alone on a training run in the woods.

Then came the final proof. I could hear just behind me the vehicle that brings up the rear. Most races have one to pick up anyone who might need help getting back to the finish line. And now, for the first time in my life, this vehicle was shadowing me. About 200 yards ahead, my friend Jason was holding his steady pace. Beyond him I could intermittently see a small group of stragglers winding through the tree-lined streets. Each of us wrestled with our private struggle, trying to maintain the level of exertion a 5-mile race demands.

Not only did I have to work hard, but I had to fight off temptation as well. This was a two-loop course, and as I neared the halfway point, dropping out seemed like a wonderful alternative. We all know what this feels like. On loop courses, where the opportunity presents itself every lap to pack it in, we can't help but have at least a transient impulse to call it quits.

But just as in wartime, where there are cowards but no cowardice, in races there are quitters but no one ever quits. Within a few strides the thought passed, and I knew if I started into the second loop it wouldn't come again.

It never did. I was last and probably would finish last, but it didn't matter. If you asked me why, I wouldn't be able to put it into words, nor would, I suspect, any runner or coach or sports psychologist.

But the philosopher William Barrett has. In his book *The Illusion of Technique*, Barrett writes that the runner who's lapped by the entire field but nevertheless tortures himself to keep going is "more admirable than the victor we crown." And of the last-place finisher in the Boston Marathon he writes, "There simply cannot be a question of his quitting. An image of the man of faith."

Faith and belief and prayer—these subjects dominate Barrett's writing. And for him, the ritual—in this instance, the race—provides a discipline and gives our lives meaning. The effort and concentration we bring to racing confirms the faith we are not certain of in other moments.

I had a mile to go. Jason was beginning to come back to me. Both of us in this hour were finding our meaning in apparently meaningless suffering. Both of us sending a wordless prayer to a higher power. Both believing that what we were doing made the best statement of who we are.

In the last 20 yards, still trying to do my very best, I finally caught Jason and sprinted by him. Beyond the finish line, where I lay gasping on the ground, Jason came by to congratulate me. Then I heard someone say, "The best race of the day was for last place." He didn't know the half of it.

—*RUNNER'S WORLD* MAGAZINE, AUGUST 1992

———◆———

TO MANY PEOPLE GROWING old seems like the endgame in chess: life winding down in a series of small moves with lesser pieces. As I age I have discovered this is not true. I am not an elderly king stripped of my powers, reduced to a ragtail army of pawns. My life is not a defensive struggle of restricted options. Growing old is a game of verve and imagination and excitement.

The aging game is chess at its best. The opening gambit may have been made long ago. The responses long since set in motion. Some pieces have indeed been lost. But the board is still filled with opportunity. The outcome is not now a matter of strength, although that still remains, but of faith and courage, hope and wisdom.

The aging game is a sport for which childhood and youth and maturity are no more than a preparation. Its scope comes as a surprise.

It expands my life at a time when I expected it to diminish. It demands an excellence that no longer seemed necessary. It asks me to surpass what I did at the peak of my powers. Age will not accept second best.

In the aging game I must be all I ever was and am yet to be. What has gone before is no more than a learning period. A breaking in. Life, someone has said, is boot camp. If it is, age is the combat for which I was trained. Now I must take this person I have become and make each new day special. I must make good on the promise of every dawn I am privileged to see.

Life goes from a minor to a major key. The game builds to a climax. Every move assumes importance. One feels like a virtuoso. The gifts we have been given, the powers that empower us, the marvels that make us marvelous are evident as never before. The truth is that we have lost nothing. The problem is not that I am less than I was when I was young, it is that I am not more. It is past time to become my own person. That is why the aging game begins with the awareness of one's need to grow and expand in every sphere of one's existence.

One also learns that honesty is the only policy. As I age I find less and less need to dissemble. I have little difficulty looking truth in the eye and admitting it. Lies and deception are time-consuming, and time becomes essential.

Time is what shapes the aging game. The clock and the calendar force me to make a move. Age does not permit the dallying with options that characterize youth. A labyrinth might be sport to the young. It brings panic to the old. My goal must be clear. The project outlined. The requirements understood. I must decide—if not this way, then there is no other way.

Fortunately, I find this commitment no problem. I accept the game and the goals I have developed in those formative years. I enjoy the self I have become. I no longer desire to be what I am not. My dissatisfaction is only in my failure to accomplish what is dearly attainable.

Such revelations frequently come late in life. They may arrive after decades of going in the wrong direction. I have a letter from a 74-year-old woman who had just run the Honolulu Marathon. "I have felt great ambivalence because by nature I seem to be a selfish person involved in understanding myself," she writes. "I picked social work as a career and was never really happy with it. I was much more interested in a variety of creative contemplative activities: dance, print making, poetry, all things hard to make a living at. Now I am retired and my own person. It is a new and wonderful life."

This woman is a master at the aging game, in part because she brings to it the enthusiasm and zest and urgency that had been bottled up during those long years of social work. She is finally a united self.

I continue to strive for that state. On the other side of my chessboard of life is a self with different interests. I look at this mirror image of me and see opposite tendencies. My alter ego sits there attempting to destroy my game, to block the forays of my knights, the hammering of my rooks, the sweeps of my bishops. This contented self wants to play the sacrifice game. This lesser "me" is playing for a draw, letting the clock run down and looking to the postgame comforts, rest and relaxation, and retirement.

There are, you can see, two ways to play the aging game.

—*GOING THE DISTANCE*, 1995

BACK AT HOME ON the Jersey shore, I went for a 40-minute run with my daughter. The next day I joined a dozen or more runners for the Saturday morning run—a fixture in our town for the past 15 years. This was followed by breakfast at a pancake place and an hour of laughter before we broke up and headed for home.

I mention these runs because they are completely out of character with the runner I once was. For me running was two experiences: solitary training runs and all-out competition. If I was not antisocial, I was asocial. I went to a place, waited for my award, and went home.

Cancer has its rewards, and one of them has been finding other values in my running. My therapy has put me far back in the race. When I come to the finish line there are few runners behind me. Competition, and the trophies that go with it, no longer attracts me. For the first time the most important thing about running has become my fellow runners.

When I run now I am a nonstop talker. It is as if I spent the last 6 months in Antarctica alone, like Admiral Byrd—and I can't wait to find out what's going on in the rest of the world. And this is not a monologue, but a conversation.

Let me say first that contemplating death has a salutary effect on a person. I have been called a curmudgeon in some circles but not recently. I have been overwhelmed by how nice people are—and of necessity I am nice in return.

I was always a loner. My family recognized that. "My father likes to have people around when he's reading," one of our daughters remarked. And for years that was the limit of my sociability.

As the cancer grew nearer to the gates I realized this was not enough. A friend told me of his 2-week family vacation in a rented house in Hawaii.

It sounded nice to me, so 2 years ago we spent a week in a large Georgian house in Ireland. Last year we did the same in a spacious house on Long Island.

Although these get-togethers were seemingly unrestricted, they actually were circumscribed. Abby, one of the grandchildren, told her mother, "This isn't a family party, it's a sibling party." And so it was. You had to be of college age to make the roster.

These get-togethers show us at our best, which is what all clans are best at—the relating and shaping of myths. That's why it is so necessary in the late, late stages of life to fashion the myths by which, in our family at least, you will be immortal. A skill we can always call upon.

Those families to whom these concerns present no problem are fortunate. Here, paradoxically, my lifestyle proved to be a vaccine. Being myself allowed them to be themselves. They don't need to be taken care of, for one thing. And in that expression I include the global needs of all of us.

Like anyone else they need support, but not in excessive or unusual amounts. Family, education, friends, religion (whatever their version), no gainsaying that. They are, furthermore, all doing their thing and doing it well. No need to worry about having enough time to attain their goals. For them the cliché is true: The travel is more satisfactory than getting there.

Sin, as we must be constantly reminded, is "closing the circle." Our appointed task is to admit everyone—the family and beyond, if possible—to that circle. We do have to take care of people, to like them and to love them. A formidable task.

Edward de Bono, the Cambridge University professor, has reduced this obligation to "respect." Something every one of us is capable of. Love is an emotion; it is, in a sense, a skill and not always available to us. Respect, however, simply requires effort and hence is forever a possibility.

It is Saturday morning, and a little to the north of us at Lake Takanassee they are having a 5-mile race. Ordinarily nothing short of an injury would have kept me from being there. But I'm on my way south toward Spring Lake to join a group that meets for a leisurely run on the boardwalk every Saturday morning at eight o'clock. I have added another dimension to my running life. I have become a social runner.

I still compete, of course, and on a regular basis—but the social self is growing. There was a time I rarely ran with anyone else. I wanted to be alone with my thoughts when I was out on the road. Without a companion who might interrupt my stream of consciousness, I could follow any idea at any pace.

In my middle years running was an escape from people. And in that solitude, my writing was born. But where there were once too many people in my life, now there are too few. There was a time when I would have told anyone who asked to run with me that I had already run, when that was not true. Now I look forward to running with people. I need people to talk to. I need people to listen to. I need people to be with.

I went through a transition period when the person who ran with me was little more than an audience. After one run a friend told me, "That was a great conversation you had." He had let me pour out my ideas without interruption during our hour on the road.

Now I have real conversations. I have revived what had become a dying art in my life. I actually listen to what people have to say instead of simply waiting until they stop so I can talk.

On the pleasant Saturday runs, there are no monologues. The ideas bounce from person to person. Topics surface and are gone. Paces vary. Places change. I run next to someone for a while, and then someone else takes his place.

A prayer we say at the beginning of our run makes us instant kin. We join hands in a little ceremony that had its origin years back when this coming together first started. Then we jog off, sharing feelings and thoughts, successes and failures, our joys and our woes. And at a deeper level we share the competent rhythms of our bodies. This innermost nonverbal communication makes everything else we share possible. Our efforts bind us together.

Later, most of us go to a pancake restaurant that is a mile or so back from the ocean and share again in food and laughter. This is what the Dairy Queen was to my Little League sons, the part we will remember best when we get older: who was there and what they said and what we ate. This is the time for guilt-free pancakes and waffles with all the toppings. We have paid for this enjoyment with our sweaty hour on the boards.

In the past I defined myself as a runner and did not realize what that fully meant. I was the runner deep in thought on the ocean road. I was suffering in the race. Now I am the runner sharing my life with other runners. I have come full circle. I have become, in the words of Blake describing age, "a child grown wise."

If not grown wise, I have at least come to understand how important friends are. I knew that well when I was a child. Social animals, children rarely do things alone. They find their friends are at the hub of a frictionless existence. That may be idealizing the childhood experience, but it comes close to what happened as I entered the final stage of my life. People have again become important.

For years I looked at this Saturday gathering with wonder. Why would anyone waste time on a leisurely jog on the boardwalk when there were races available? Why would anyone subject himself to an hour of banter when there were great ideas to be discovered alone?

Now I know that while competition and solitude are both sources of happiness, there is yet another source of happiness to be found in running—a return to the companionship of youth and childhood. I now have comrades. I am a member of a gang.

What has happened to me proves the truth of English writer Hilaire Belloc's words:

From first beginnings out to undiscovered ends, nothing worth the winning, save laughter and the love of friends.

—PERSONAL BEST, 1989

Afterword

BY ANN SHEEHAN

WHEN I THINK OF MY FATHER, I picture him in his signature blue walking up the back stairs of our house into the kitchen with four books and a yellow legal pad under his arm. He never read one book at a time; there was too much to learn. My father was blessed with an amazing mind, and he loved to use it. The books under his arm were for learning, and the yellow pad was for sharing his knowledge and experience with others. He did this through his writing, his lectures, and his conversations.

When Dad was diagnosed with cancer in his late sixties, he turned his attention to learning all he could about cancer and its treatments. As was his way, he searched tirelessly for knowledge and understanding. He read the medical journals, studied the cancer research, and spoke to the medical specialists.

At the same time he began to address the challenge of living with cancer, and to answer the question, "What is my aim in the time I have left?" As always, for inspiration and guidance he turned to the great writers and philosophers, but now he added a new group: his fellow cancer patients, others who were facing this experience with him. His writing changed to reflect the changes in his life. His final project was his book about his cancer. He wrote of the experience of being diagnosed with inoperable prostate cancer, the years of living with it, and ultimately facing his own death. In the introduction to the book, he explains his purpose:

"Anything worthwhile must come from my own experience. This book is what dying actually means to the person undergoing it. This book is also a communion with others experiencing dying. And it is an evaluation of my life, some estimate of my success in being the self I was meant to be."

Dad was not in denial—he took on the challenge of re-examining his life, now that his time was limited. He began to look at his relationships. He writes:

"When you are between the sword and the stone, you know who you want standing beside you. When time is short, it becomes obvious who the essential people are."

Dad wanted to spend more time with family and friends. A friend had told him of a 2-week vacation he had taken with his family in Hawaii. Dad liked the sound of this, and when my sister Mary Jane and her husband, Rick, invited our family to join them for a week in

Ireland, Dad was on board. He saw this as a wonderful opportunity to be together and encouraged his sons and daughters to come along. We all loved being away together, and this would be the first of four family vacations held during Dad's last years.

The idea of a family vacation was actually very new to us. Because we were such a large family—12 children and my parents—we rarely traveled together, and we had never taken a family vacation. We grew up near the ocean in New Jersey, so our vacations were our summers at the beach. Dad had a lot of good ideas, and taking these family vacations was definitely one of them. Looking back, I think he was inviting us to come together and play. To leave our homes and responsibilities behind, and to join together in the play of running, swimming, sailing, storytelling, laughing, and crying.

In his final book, Dad writes of the importance of these family reunions for him:

> "The pressure of losing my battle to cancer has made these reunions essential to the evolution of my new self. Without the urgency to get it right my life would have followed its usual solitary course. Now I am living a new life, spending more time with a loving and appreciative family."

I remember most clearly the last two vacations, which took place in 1993, the summer before Dad died. Both were near the ocean: one on New York's Long Island, and one in Rehoboth Beach, Delaware. Dad had imparted a love of the ocean to all of us, so it was wonderful to spend the time together there. Before those final reunions, Dad had told us that his cancer had gone into "fast forward" and he was facing his final months, and we wanted to be with him.

During our time on Long Island, although his body was weakening, his mind was as alive as ever. He continued to write his book and was facing the big questions: "After I die, what?" leading him back to "Before I die, what?" Searching for answers, he began to explore different religions. He became very interested in the Quakers and discussed with us his desire to attend a Quaker meeting to see what it was all about. We thought this was terrific and so like Dad, still searching for meaning and truth.

As much as he was able, he joined the activities of the day—a sail on Peconic Bay, a swim, and a barbecue at the beach. I remember the night of the barbecue, he was sitting on the boardwalk, looking out at the ocean, and he told us, with such sadness in his eyes, "I don't want to go."

Later that same summer, while I was visiting in New Jersey, Dad asked me, "Do you think the family would want to do another vacation?" "Of course," I said, and so we did. That last reunion, in Rehoboth Beach, was in a house right on the beach. Here, much weaker now, Dad could sit and see the ocean from the porch. We would come in from the beach to visit with him throughout the day. He loved the conversation, the stories, the laughter. He wrote, "I need the support, the laughter, the love that the family brings to the table."

While in Rehoboth, Dad wanted to take a swim in the ocean. With my brothers holding him, two on each side, he went bravely into the surf of his beloved ocean for what would be his final swim.

Once more, on this last reunion, Dad also showed us the vitality of his mind. He was very excited about a new author he had discovered. He told us all about Edward Hall, an anthropologist. He was busily reading not just one but all of his books, and had become fascinated with the field of anthropology. When he returned to New

Jersey after the trip, he signed up for an anthropology course at the local community college, 2 months before he died.

That was my Dad: always engaged in the excitement of learning, seeking new ideas, knowledge, truth and meaning. I will always miss my lively conversations with him. I miss his engaging lectures—he was such a gifted speaker—but I am so grateful that he shared himself with all of us in his writing. His columns and books will continue to inspire us and will remind us that, in the words of philosopher Miguel de Unamuno, he has made himself irreplaceable.

Acknowledgments

*I*F WE WERE TO acknowledge every person who has been a source of strength and comfort to us these many years, the litany would be book-length. In light of that, the Sheehan Family would like to name just a few and trust that the rest of you know who you are. While many of our dad's closest friends and fellow pioneers like Fred Lebow and Jim Fixx have left us, Joe Henderson, George Hirsch, Kenneth Cooper and Walter Bortz remain forever young. So too, Jeff Galloway, Joan Benoit Samuelson, Amby Burfoot and Tim McLoone still carry the message. Elliott Denman, Phil Hinck and the rest of the striders on the Shore A.C. are in line for special mention for keeping the tradition going at Takanasee Lake and the George Sheehan Classic every summer. And, we would be remiss if we did not extend our deepest gratitude to dear relatives and friends Joan and Dick Sexton and Eleanor McCabe.

This book would not have been possible without our partners at

Runner's World and is the brainchild of Editor-in-Chief David Willey, who had the idea and was unwavering in his commitment to bring our dad's work to a new audience. John Atwood provided needed insight and encouragement, and Rodale Executive Editor Mark Weinstein shepherded the project from its inception to fruition with amazing patience and calm. We are fortunate to have had our agent David Larabell's sage advice and steady hand guide us through the intricacies of the publishing world. Each of the running luminaries who contributed their remarkable remembrances to this book did so without hesitation. We thank them all.

We also thank all of you runner-readers who have embraced our dad's words and philosophies and have put them to the test during training runs on your local streets. The stunning and continued growth of running in America and throughout the world is a testament to the fact that this was no passing fad. Like our dad, you've found that running with take you places you never dreamed of going.

About the Author

Dr. George Sheehan was a respected cardiologist, accomplished runner, bestselling author of eight books, and popular lecturer on the importance of exercise and sport. One of the pioneers of the fitness boom of the late '70s, he was viewed by many as the "guru" of runners, but his audience eventually encompassed all athletes. His contributions to the fields of health and fitness have been widely recognized. As medical editor of *Runner's World* magazine and a member of the Presidential Council for Physical Fitness, Sheehan traveled the world to teach the benefits of the "athletic life." He was named posthumously as the first recipient of the George Sheehan Media Award, presented at the inaugural ceremony of the National Distance Running Hall of Fame. He died in 1993 at the age of 74, after a 7-year battle with prostate cancer.

Andrew Sheehan, one of the sons of the late Dr. George Sheehan, is an investigative journalist for the CBS television affiliate in Pittsburgh and the author of *Chasing the Hawk: Looking for My Father, Finding Myself,* a memoir of his experiences with his father.

Index

A

Acceptance stage of dying, 265
Adams, Sarah, 19
Addiction, 63, 189, 210, 220–21
Adversity, managing, 231, 247, 275
Aerobic capacity and fitness, 75, 193
Aerobics, 8, 62–63
Aerobics (Cooper), 62
Aftermath as part of athletic experience,
    157, 199
Age and aging
    Boston Marathon and, 173–76
    chess game analogy and, 282–83
    fitness and, 3
    longevity and, 6–8
    performance and, 134, 173–76
    racing and, 133–36
    "rebirth" and, 23
    running and, 133–36
    true, in "rebirth," 23
Age-group racing, 134–36, 139
Age-rated performance, 134
Aggressive individual, 27–28
Aging game, 282–84
Air stirrups, 118
Akhtar, Salman, 239–40
Alameda Seven rules for good health, 7–8
Alcohol, 80–81, 218–19

Allen, Bill, 64
Allen, Fred, 262
All the Pretty Horses (McCarthy), 277
Amiel, Henri Frédéric, 44
Amor fati (love of our fate), 265, 276
Anger
    Aristotle's view of, 232
    Bennett's view of, 231, 233–34
    body's reaction to, 222–23
    culture and, 234–35
    exercise in diffusing, 222
    externalizing, 232
    hesitation as cure for, 236
    internalizing, 232
    justified, 232–33
    managing, 222, 235–36
    Seneca's cure for, 236
    stage of dying, 264
Anticipation before running, 109–11
Anxiety, managing, 222
Appetites, 222
Aquinas, Thomas, 65
Arch supports, 117
Aristotle, 232
Artists, 47, 190
Asceticism, 153, 164
Athletic experience, 157–58, 199–202
Attitude, importance of, 228, 256

Autumn, racing during, 143–45
Avocation, 195

B

Bacon, Francis, 67, 189
Bacon, Roger, 232
Bannister, Roger, 87, 112, 191
Bare Minimum program, 84–85
Bare Minimum Track Club, 84
Bargaining stage of dying, 264
Barrett, William, 281
Bassler, Thomas, 66–67
Battle of Monmouth 5-mile race, 127–28
Becker, Ernest, 233
Beckett, Samuel, 264
Belloc, Hilaire, 289
Belly-breathing, 71
Bennett, Arnold, 42–44, 46, 231, 233–36
Benson, Herbert, 225, 227
Berdyaev, Nikolai, 48
Berkshires Masters Ten-Kilometer run,
        121–22
Bessel, Joe, 135
Best, doing, 131
*Biological Rhythms of Psychiatry and
        Medicine* (Brown, Bertram S.), 47
Blake, William, 22, 29, 34, 201, 273
Body
    anger and reaction of, 222–23
    James's view of, 207
    listening to, xix–xx, 3, 9, 45–46, 48,
        56–57, 72, 82, 101, 158
    mind's connection to, 12, 17, 28, 219,
        225–26
    religion and, 28
    science of, 79–80
    soul's connection to, 3, 197, 225–26
    stress and, 111
    stress on, from running, 98
    temporary insulation of, 107
    transformation and, 3
    "warranty" on, 70-year, 6
    weighing, 70
Bohannon, R.L., 61–62
Borg, G. A., 116
Boston Marathon
    age and, 173–76
    course, 167–70
    faith and, 181

first miles of, 167–68
1976, 120, 181–84
1980, 173
Odyssey analogy of, 165–66
qualifying times for, 173–76
Sheehan's first, 149–50
the wall and, 176–79
Bowel movements and running, 71
Bowerman, Bill, 67, 114
Bradley, Bill, 200, 256
Brant, John, xi
Breakfast, eating good, 80
Breathing exercises, 71, 75
Breslow's rules, 80–81
Brown, Bertram S., 47
Brown, Jerry, 53
Burfoot, Amby, 58, 146–47

C

Campbell, Joseph, 276
Cancer diagnosis
    adapting to, xx, 255–59
    as blessing, 251, 257, 285
    cancer patients and, fellow, 292
    Cooper and, 270–71
    death and, dealing with, 258–59
    family support and, 275–76
    first reaction to, 249–50
    healthy way of dealing with, 250
    learning about cancer and, 291
    living with, 292
    neglect in preventing, 256–57
    self-indulgence and, temptation
        toward, 257
    waiting for, 251–53
Cannon, Walter, 15, 113
Carpenter, Edmund, 1
Carroll, Noel, 116
Celtic approach to life, 235
Cesar Rodney half-marathon
        (Wilmington, Delaware), 133
Challenge, seeking, 191, 204, 207
Change, 52–53, 63
Cheating, 137
Chesterton, Gilbert Keith, 65
Christian Brothers Academy, xviii
Circadian cycles, 44
Clocks, 47, 128, 137, 139
Cloney, Will, 173–74

Clothing, running, 71, 106–7
Coaching, 103–5
Cold packs, 119
Cold. *See* Cold-weather running
Colds and running, 72
Cold-weather running, 106–8
Coleridge, Samuel, 101
Community, sense of, 32, 65, 216
Competition, 32, 147, 289. *See also*
    Marathon; Racing
Compression of morbidity concept,
    260–61
Computers, 56
Comrades Marathon, 104–5
Consumer, 34
Contemplation, 65
Contest, 180, 188
Contest as part of athletic experience
    (*agon*), 157, 199, 201–2
Controlling days and life
    play, 39–42
    present, being in, 49–50
    prioritizing, 51–54
    rhythms, creating, 46–48
    self-actualization, 44–46
    technology, managing, 54–57
    time management, 42–44
Conversation, art of, 65
Cooper, Kenneth, 8, 62, 64, 193, 195,
    251–52, 270–71
Cosmic consciousness, 226
Costill, David, 112–13, 152
Creagan, Edward, 264–65
Creativity
    Maslow and, 36
    peak in, 33–35
    perspective of, 36
    play and, 35–37
    of running, 3
    subconscious and, 126–27
Critics, 126, 242
Cureton, Thomas, 67

D

Daily life, 42–44, 263
"Daily miracle," 42–44
Dana Farber Cancer Institute, 199, 202
Dancers, 217
Date (calendar), 55

Death
    cancer diagnosis and, 258–59
    facing, 292
    medical care and, current, 260
    stages of dying and, 264–65
De Bono, Edward, 286–87
Declaration of Independence, 197
Dehydration, 101–2
Denial stage of dying, 264
Depression
    mild, 58
    stage of dying, 264
    as weakness, personal, 243–46
Desires versus needs, 195
De Unamuno y Jugo, Miguel, 253, 295
De Voto, Bernard, 245
Dickey, James, 49, 154
Diet and running, 70
DiMaggio, Joe, 36
Disease
    exercise in preventing, 61–64, 67, 79
    heart, 67
    illness versus, 74
    lung, 73–76
    muscles and, well-trained, 29
Distance and training, 93–95. *See also*
    Marathon
Dogs and running, 72
Dos versus don'ts, 219
Drinking. *See* Alcohol; Water intake
Drives versus desires, 195
Dr. Scholl's 610s arch supports, 117
Dr. Scholl's Flexors arch supports,
    117
Duration of exercise, 115–16
"Dynamogenic agent," 151

E

Ecclesiastes, 244–45
Effort
    of champions, 198–99
    James's view of, 89, 151, 197
    life demands of, 28–29
    performance versus, 131
Egyptians, ancient, 248
Elizabethan drama, 139
Emerson, Ralph Waldo, 12, 150, 173–75,
    185, 187, 190, 196, 241, 258–59
Emotions, 222–24. *See also specific type*

Endurance, 165–67
Energy, 10–12, 14, 150
Enthusiasm, 11–13
Ephesians, 232
Epictetus, 201–2, 214, 238
Equality of people, 197, 199
Equilibrium, upsetting, 140–41
Erikson, Erik, 274, 278–79
Excellence, pursuing, 191, 274
Exercise. *See also specific type*
  addiction of, 63
  aerobic capacity and, 75
  in anger management, 222
  in anxiety management, 222
  breathing, 71, 75
  daily, 70, 81
  dangers of strenuous, exaggerated,
    65–66
  in disease prevention, 61–64, 67, 79
  duration of, 115–16
  energy for, 10–12
  frequency of, 116–17
  health benefits of, 61–64, 66–68, 76,
    193–94
  intensity of, 116
  large muscles and, 115
  medical technology versus, 76
  misguided modern medicine and
    dangers of exercise, exaggerated,
      65–66
    lung disease and exercise, 73–76
    running as exercise, 61–64
  mode of, 115
  motivation for, 28–29, 194
  physiology, 75
  as play, 24–29
  programs, typical, 68
  regular, 70, 81
  in running injury prevention,
    98–100
  "second wind" and, 72
  selecting individual, 63–64, 115
  spiritual benefits of, 193–94
  stamina and, 115
  strengthening, 99–100
  stretching, 98–99
Experiential biology, 56–57
Exploration and running, 33
Externalizing anger, 232

F

Failure-to-thrive syndrome, 86–87
Faith, 181, 281
"Faithful fighters" analogy, 171–73
Family, importance of, 275–76, 289, 293
Fartlek, 110
Faulkner, William, 205
Fear stage of dying, 264
Feet
  running injury prevention and, 117–18
  socks and, 107–8
  stress on, from running, 98
Fidrych, Mark, 214–15
Fight-or-flight response, 15, 27
Finish line
  as element of sport, 128
  marathon, 181–84
  uphill, 133
Fitness
  aerobic, 75, 193
  aging and, 3
  earning, 78
  equation, 71
  existence and, enlarging, 3, 220
  factors, 115–17
  formulas, general, 93–94, 115–17
  in hospitals, lack of, 77–79
  monitoring programs, 10
  movement, 194
  play in promoting, 68–69
Fixx, Jim, 209–10
Flight-or-fight response, 15, 27
Fluid intake, 70, 100–102
Form, running, 71
Foster, Brendan, 91
Foucault, Michel, 200
Frequency of exercise, 116–17
Freud, Sigmund, 240
Friends, importance of, 289
Frost, Robert, 52, 159, 201, 245, 250
Fuller, Bucky, 63
Function follows structure concept, 15–17
Fun of running, 9–10, 109–11, 150

G

Galen, 67
Galloway, Jeff, 58
Gandhi's rule, 5
General Adaptation Syndrome, 73

Generativity, 275
Genesis Diary, A (Nouwen), 210
Gibson, William, 225–26
Giegengack, Robert "Gieg," 38
Glanville, Brian, 63
Glasgow, Ellen, 134
Gloves, 107
Glycogen replacement, 116
Goals, training, 103–4
Gordon, David Cole, 30
Gordon, Whitney, 32
Graham, Wilfred, 260–61
Greek drama, 139
Greeks, ancient, 9, 17, 34, 167, 188, 240, 263
Gross national product (GNP) analogy of
    aerobics, 62
Gruber, Adolph, 168

H

Hall, Edward, 294
Hammarskjold, Dag, 241
Happiness, 163, 220, 263, 289
"Happy Warrior" (Wordsworth), 123
Hardin, Doug, 221
Hats, 107
Health. *See also* Medical issues
    aerobics and, 62
    Alameda Seven rules for good, 7–8
    behavior and, 6–8
    Breslow's seven rules for good, 80–81
    exercise and, 61–64, 67–68, 76, 193–94
    responsibility for, personal, 9
    sleep and, 81
    transformation and, 6–8
Health Insurance Plan of New York
    Study, 66
Heart disease, 67
Heart rate, monitoring, 10
Heat. *See* Hot-weather running
Heel counter supports, 118
Heel lifts, 73, 118
Hegel, Georg, 124
Hemingway, Ernest, 126
Henderson, Joe, xv, 58, 249–50
Herd mentality, 13–14
Herndon, James, 68
Heroism
    Hoagland's novel on, 191
    of individual, 192

Lipsyte's article on, 191–92
marathon and, 151, 153–57, 191
need for, 125
Ortega's definition of, 192–93
play and, 205
potential for, 41, 143
running and, 223–24
Hesitation as cure for anger, 236
Hills, 131–33
Hoagland, Edward, 191–92
Holistic approach, 74–75
Honesty, 283
Honolulu Marathon, 284
Hooten, Earnest, 17
Hospital physiology departments, 77–79
Hot packs, 119
Hot-weather running, 94, 102, 120, 181–84
Howe, Herbert, 267–69
Huizinga, Johan, 136–38
Humor, 111–12, 209
Huxley, Aldous, 4
Hydration, 70, 100–102

I

"If" (Kipling), 123
Illness versus disease, 74
Illusion of Technique, The (Barrett), 281
Imagination, 21–23
Immortality, 215–17, 258
Innersoles, 118–19
Insulation, temporary body, 107
Integration of conscious and unconscious,
    219
Intensity
    exercise, 116
    training, 83–85, 94, 96, 105
Internalizing anger, 232
Interval training, 85, 87–90, 95
Intimacy, 278–80
Irenaeus, xix

J

James-Lange theory of emotions,
    222–23
James, William, 25–26, 89, 110, 125, 151,
    153, 162–65, 171, 194–97, 203,
    205–6, 216, 218, 230, 236, 263, 266
"Japanese Watch Syndrome," 55
Jipcho, Ben, 135

Jogging programs, 61–62. *See also* Running
John of the Cross, St., 214
Johnson, Ralph, 12
Joyce, James, 165
Justified anger, 232–33

K

Kazantzakis, 49
Kennedy, Bobby, 62
Kipling, Rudyard, 123
Knee strap, 118
Knowledge of self, 17–18, 42, 45, 240
Kuscsik, Nina, 120

L

Land, Edwin, 220–21
Law of diminishing returns and mileage, 114
Learning, 24, 266, 294–95
Leonard, George, 217
Levin, David, 212–13
Life. *See also* Controlling days and life
  aging game and, 282–84
  Beckett's view of, 264
  Celtic approach to, 235
  change and, 52–53
  cycle (Erikson's stages of), 274, 278–79
  daily, 42–44, 263
  effort demanded by, 28–29
  family and, importance of, 275–76, 289, 293
  humor and, 112
  important things in, identifying, 273–74
  James's view of, 163
  making self irreplaceable and, 253, 295
  marathon analogy to, 159, 166
  nostalgia and, 48–49
  play and, 23–27, 29
  as problem not to be solved, 247
  "rebirth" and, 1–3, 23
  rhythms, creating, 44, 46–48
  with risk, 189, 204
  without risk, 189, 204
  running in extending, 260
  struggle of, 262, 277
  successful, 262
  as terminal illness, 264
  tomorrow in, fleetingness of, 39, 50
Life expectancy, 61

Lindbergh, Anne, 245
Lipsyte, Robert "Bob," 146, 188, 191–92
Listening to body, xix–xx, 3, 9, 45–46, 48, 56–57, 72, 82, 101, 158
Logical mind, 209, 224
Loneliness, 31–33, 241
Longevity, 6–8, 61
Long johns, cotton, 106
Love, 287
Lung disease and exercise, 73–76

M

MacLean, Norman, 277
MacMitchell, Leslie, xvii
Maharishi Mahesh Yogi, 225–26
Manhattan College xvii
Manhattan Prep School, 38
Marathon. *See also* Racing; *specific name*
  aftermath of, 157
  age and, 173–76
  as athletic experience, 157–58
  challenge of, 155
  as contest (*agon*), 157
  emotion of finishing, 181–84
  endurance and, 165–67
  "faithful fighters" analogy and, 171–73
  finish line, 181–84
  heroism and, 151, 153–57, 191
  James and, 162–65
  last six miles of, 149, 151–53, 176
  life analogy and, 159, 166
  memories, 179–80
  motivation for, 159–62, 184–87
  parts of, 157–58, 157–59
  preparation for, 157–58
  success and, 159
  3-hour barrier and, 154–55
  training for, 154, 158, 170–71
  the wall and, 149, 151–53, 176–79
Marcus Aurelius, 44, 67, 213–14, 224
Marine Corps Marathon (Washington, DC), 154–57, 173, 175
Marine Corps Marathon (Washington, DC) dinner, 208
Maslow, Abraham, 9, 24, 27, 36, 44–46, 56–57, 203, 213–14
Matisse chapel (Vence, France), 22
Matisse, Henri, 22

May, Rollo, 33
Mazer, Bill, xix
McCarthy, Cormac, 277
Medical issues. *See also* Health
   Breslow's seven rules, 80–81
   healthy running rules, 69–73
   holistic approach, 74–75
   hospital physiology departments,
      77–79
   misguided modern medicine
      dangers of exercise, exaggerated,
         64–69
      lung disease and exercise, 73–76
      running as exercise, 61–64
   running injuries, 58–61
   Sheehan (George) as brutal critic of,
      59, 230
Meditation, 216
Melville, Herman, 244
Mental health, 204–5
Mental pressure, 204–5
Mental training, 111–12
Mid-life crisis, 2
Mileage
   exercise health benefits and, 67
   law of diminishing returns and, 114
   running injuries and, 95, 117
   time versus, 93–95
   training and, 112–14
Mile barriers, breaking, 128
Mind
   body's connection to, 12, 17, 28, 219,
      225–26
   logical, 209, 224
   soul's connection to, 3, 197, 225–26
Minutes-per-mile statistic, 86–87
Mittens, 107
Monastery life, 210–12
Moore, Kenny, xv
Moran, Gabriel, 24
Morgan, William, 116
Morris, Charles, 263
Motivation
   defining, 195
   for exercise, 28–29, 194
   for marathon, 159–62, 184–87
   for running, xiv, 5, 189–91, 194
Mountain climber's rule, 132
Muncie (Indiana) study, 32

Muscles
   disease and well-trained, 79
   glycogen replacement in, 116
   imbalances of, 98–100
   large, 115
Musée Matisse (France), 22
Mystical experiences, 214–16. *See also*
      Spiritual issues
Mystics, 216

N

Narcissism, 239–43, 275
National AAU Championship Marathon
      and aftermath, 246–48
National Jogging Association, 61
Natural Mind, The (Weil), 219
Needs, 195
Negative injunctions, 219
New Age movement, 194
New York City Marathon (1981), 170–73,
      184–87
New Yorker article on running, 64–65
Nichols, Rod, 135
Nietzsche, Friedrich, 34, 264, 276
Nostalgia, 48–49
Nouwen, Henri, 210–12
Novak, Michael, 234, 268

O

Ocean County Park 5-mile race (New
      Jersey), 280–82
Odyssey (Homer), 165–66
Odyssey, The (Kazantzakis), 49
Olympic Games, 9, 199
Opponents, real, 200
Ortega y Gasset, José, 5, 28–29, 154,
      192–93, 274, 277
Orthotics, 73, 118
Osler, Tom, 243–44
Our Town (Wilder), 263
Overdressing for running, avoiding,
      106–7
Overtraining, avoiding, 91–93

P

Pace
   comfortable, 71, 83, 96–97, 116, 190–91
   individual, 67
   racing and, 130–33

Pace *(cont.)*
    talk test and, 67, 71, 116
    training and, 96–97
Packs, hot and cold, 119
Pain
    listening to body and, 158
    necessity of, biological, 269
    in play, 25
    racing and, 124, 126, 143
Pascal, Blaise, 214
Passion, 12–13
Peaceful feeling after racing, 121–24
Peak performance, 213
Pepsi Challenge (10K), 136–38
Perceived Exertion, 116
Perfection, seeking, 225
Performance
    age and aging and, 134, 173–76
    age-rated, 134
    effort versus, 131
    improvement, cyclical nature of, 87
    intensity of training and, 83–85, 105
    peak, 213
Physical education versus play, 30–31, 68
Physical energy, 10–11
Physical work capacity, 79. *See also*
    Aerobic capacity and fitness
Physiology departments in hospitals, 77–79
Physiology, exercise, 75
Picasso, Pablo, 22
Pindar, 166
Planning, lack of, 237–38
"Plateau" experiences in running, 213
Plato, 18, 24–25, 91, 199
Play
    advocating, 41–42
    as answer to people's existence, 23–27,
      217
    in controlling days and life, 39–42
    creativity and, 35–37
    exercise as, 24–29
    fartlek, 110
    fitness and, promoting, 68–69
    heroism and, 205
    imagination and, 21–23
    learning and, 24
    life and, 23–27, 29
    as oasis of sanity, 64
    open-endedness of, 129

    pain in, 25
    physical education versus, 30–31, 68
    pleasure in, 25
    pluses of, 30
    religion and, 24, 205
    running as, 9–10, 128–29, 190
    self-discovery and, 29–30
    sport and, 69, 128–29
Pleasure in play, 25
Poets, 49
Pollack, Michael, 93
Positive injunctions, 219
Preparation, 129–30, 157–58
Present, being in, 49–50, 133, 237–38
Price, Jonathan, 217
Prioritizing, 51–54
Psychics and psychic phenomena, 194
Pulmonary-function tests, 75
Pulse, taking, 69–70

R

Racing. *See also* Marathon; *specific name*
    age and, 133–36
    age-group, 134–36, 139
    in autumn, 143–45
    best and, doing, 131
    cheating and, 137
    clocks and, 128, 137, 139
    as contest, 180
    drama in, 139–43
    as education, 86
    hills and, 131–33
    in hot weather, 94
    minutes-per-mile statistic and, 86–87
    pace and, 130–33
    pain and, 124, 126, 143
    peaceful feeling after, 121–24
    physiological preparation for, 130
    as a play, dramatic, 136–38
    post-surgery, 16–17
    preparation for, 129–30
    psychological preparation for, 130
    against self, 147
    as sport, 128–29
    struggle in, 198
    success and, 126–27
    training and, 86–87
    truth and, 121, 125–27, 147
    values evoked from, 147

"Radical innocence," 245
Rank, Otto, 89
Reality, finding one's own, 2–3
"Rebirth," 1–3, 23
Relaxation, 122
Relaxation response, 226–28
Relaxation Response, The (Benson), 227
Religion
  body and, 28
  play and, 24, 205
  running as, 209–12
  worry and, remedy for, 205
Respect, 287
Rest, 92
Rewards and sacrifice, 51–54
Rhythms of life, 44, 46–48, 93, 228
Riger, Robert, 33
River Runs Through It, A (MacLean), 277
Road Runners Club, 144
Rodin, 277
Rogers, Carl, 276
Royce, Josiah, 269
Run-despite-injury-or-illness attitude, 104
Runner's high, 212–15
Runner's rule, 132
Running. *See also* Marathon; Racing;
    Training
  addiction to, 189, 221
  for aerobic fitness, 193
  age and, 133–36
  anticipation before, 109–11
  boom, xviii–xix
  bowel movements and, 71
  clothing for, 71, 106–8
  coaching and, 103–5
  colds and, 72
  in cold weather, 106–8
  creativity of, 3
  critics of, 64–66
  diet and, 70
  dogs and, 72
  economically, 71
  exploration and, 33
  in extending life, 260
  fartlek, 110
  feet and, stress on, 98
  form, 71
  fun of, 9–10, 109–11, 150
  health benefits of, 66–67

heroism and, 223–24
in hot weather, 94, 102, 120, 181–84
insider's perspective of, 4–5
involvement in, total, 64–65
as lifetime activity, 105
listening to body and, 158
loneliness and, 31–33
low cost of, 117
misguided modern medicine and, 61–64
motivation for, xiv, 5, 189–91, 194
as mystical experience, 214–16
New Yorker article on, 64–65
outsider's perspective of, 4
overdressing for, avoiding, 106–7
physique and, 15–17, 188
"plateau" experiences in, 213
as play, 9–10, 128–29, 190
as process and product, 186–87
as religion, 209–12
rules for healthy, 69–73
runner's high and, 212–15
sharing experience of, 273, 285, 287–90
shoes, 71, 73, 117–19
simplicity of, 5
sleep and, 72
solitude and, 31–33, 145
spiritual benefits of, 193–94
"staleness," 91–93, 104
stress on body from, 98
in stress management, 202–4
as thinking person's sport, 158
"third wind" and, 113
time for, 245
time for not, 245
in traffic, 72
transformation and, 3–5, 202–4
values found by, xiv, 65, 285
whole person and, becoming, 189–91,
    196, 203
wind direction and, 108
Running injuries
  mileage and, 95, 117
  misguided modern medicine and,
    58–61
  preventing, 98–100, 117–19
  Sheehan's (George) experiences with, 60
  Sheehan's rules for treating, 117
  substitute activities with, 72
  training and, 73, 104

S

Sacrifice and rewards, 51–54
Sacrogard belt, 119
Salazar, Alberto, 82
Saltin, Bengt, 75
Sand weights, 119
Santayana, George, 125, 140, 161,
    200–202, 210, 216
Satisfaction, 262
Scientists, 40, 47
Scoring, 128
Scottish Games at Grandfather Mountain,
    179–80
Scott, Robert, 12
Season in Heaven, A (Gibson), 225
"Second wind," 72, 110, 113
Sedentary lifestyle, 34, 207
Self-absorption, 239–43, 275
Self-actualization, 9, 24, 44–46
Self-discovery, xviii–xix, 29–30, 158–59,
    277
Self-indulgence, 257
Self-knowledge, 17–18, 42, 45, 240
Self-mastery, 200
Self-rule, 200
Self-study, 18
Self-treatment of running injuries, 117–19
Selye, Hans, 45, 73, 228–29
Seneca (Roman statesman), 236
Shainberg, Lawrence, 25
Shakespeare, William, 267
Sheed, Wilfred, 23
Sheehan, Andrew "Andy", xii–xiii, 230
Sheehan, Anne, 291–95
Sheehan, George
    books and, love of reading, 291
    books published by, overview, xiii
    childhood, xvii–xviii, xxi
    collection of writings selected, xii–xiv
    college years, xvii
    efforts of, xix
    family and, importance of, 275–76,
        289, 293
    goals of, xix
    Hawaii family vacation, 286, 292–93
    influence on
        Adams, Sarah, 19
        Brant, John, xi
        Burfoot, Amby, 146–47

Cooper, Kenneth, 270–71
        Galloway, Jeff, 58
        Henderson, Joe, 249–50
        Kuscsik, Nina, 120
        Lipsyte, Robert, 188
        Salazar, Alberto, 82
        Sheehan, Andrew, 230
        Sheehan, Anne, 291–95
        Sheehan III, George, 208
        Shorter, Frank, 38
        Willey, David, ix–xv
    inspiration of, continuing, xiv–xv
    learning and, lifelong, xxi, 295
    legacy of, xix–xxi
    Long Island (New York) family
        vacation, 293–94
    middle-age years, xviii–xix
    as "performance artist," 230
    Quakers and, interest in, 294
    "rebirth" of, 1–3
    Rehoboth Beach (Delaware) family
        vacation, 293–94
    running boom and, xviii–xix
    running injuries of, 60
    women runners and, xix
Sheehan III, George, 208
Sheehan, Michael, xii, xvii–xxi
Sheehan, Tim, xii, xvii–xxi
Sheldon, William, 239
Shock absorbers for shoes, 118
Shoes, running, 71, 73, 117–19
Shorter, Frank, 25–26, 38, 246
Sillitoe, Alan, 31
Simplicity of running, 5
Sin, 286. *See also* Weaknesses of
    individual
Ski masks, 107
Skin protection, 108
Slater, Philip, 31
Sleep
    early rising and, 44
    health and, 81
    need for, 53
    running and, 72
    training and, 72
Smoking, avoiding, 80
Snacking, avoiding, 80
Socializing individual, 27
Socks, 107–8

Socrates, 9, 18, 48
Solitary individual, 27
Solitude, 31–33, 145, 216, 287, 289
Soul-body-mind connection, 3, 197, 225–26
Spenco arch supports, 117
Spenco innersoles, 118–19
Spirit, 12–13
Spiritual energy, 11–12
Spiritual issues
   immortality, 215–17
   meditation, 216
   mystical experiences, 214–16
   runner's high, 212–15
   running as religion, 209–12
Sport
   elements of, 128
   play and, 69, 128–29
   racing as, 128–29
   soul-body-mind connection and, 225–26
   team games, 180
"Staleness," running, 91–93, 104
Stamina, 115
Steiner, Richard, 67
Stevenson, Robert Louis, 43
Stickball, 21
Strengthening exercise, 99–100
Stress
   attitude and, importance of, 228
   body and, 111
   General Adaptation Syndrome and, 73
   James's view of, 206–7
   psychological, 111
   relaxation response in managing, 226–28
   of running on body, 98
   running in managing, 202–4
   tools for managing, 229
   of training, 73
Stretching exercises, 98–99
Subconscious, 126–27
Subjective biology, 56–57
Success
   becoming oneself, 42, 193
   managing, 231, 247
   marathon and, 159
   meaning of, varied, 262
   racing and, 126–27
Summer weather. See Hot-weather running
Surgical felt, 119
Suzuki, D.T., 48

T

Taking things easy, 198, 202
Taking things hard, 198
Talk test, 67, 71, 116
"Talk of the Town" column of *New Yorker,* 64–65
Teaching, 266
Team games, 180. *See also* Sport
Technology
   exercise versus medical technology, 76
   managing, 54–57
   pros and cons of, 56
   sedentary lifestyle and, 207
Temper. *See* Anger
Tennyson, Alfred, 167
"Third wind," 113
Thomson, J. Anderson, 239–40
Thoreau, Henry David, 13, 26, 31
3-hour barrier and marathon, 154–55
Thurber, James, 277
Tiberius, 9, 18
Time
   in aging game, 283
   managing, 42–44
   mileage versus, 93–95
   training and, 94–95
Tincture of benzoin, 118
TM, 225–27
Tobacco, avoiding, 80
Tomorrow, fleetingness of, 39, 50
Traffic, running in, 72
Tragedy as treasure, 271
Training
   Bare Minimum program, 84–85
   coaching and, 103–5
   in cold weather, 106–8
   distance and, 93–95
   excessive, 91–93
   fitness factors and, 115–17
   frequency of, 84–85
   fun of running and, 109–10
   goals, 103–4
   high-intensity, 84–85
   hills and, 132
   humor and, 111–12
   hydration and, 100–102
   intensity of, 83–85, 94, 96, 105
   intensity over time formula, 94
   interval, 85, 87–90, 95

Training *(cont.)*
  for marathon, 154, 158, 170–71
  mental, 111–12
  mileage and, 112–14
  muscle imbalances and, 98–100
  pace and, 96–97
  as part of athletic experience, 199
  performance and intensity of, 83–85,
      105
  racing and, 86–87
  rest and, 92
  rhythms of life and, 93
  running injuries and, 73, 104
      preventing, 98–100, 117–19
  Sheehan's personal, 83–84
  sleep and, 72
  "staleness" and, 91–93
  stress of, 73
  "third wind" and, 113
  time and, 94–95
  time versus mileage and, 93–95
Training as part of athletic experience
      (askesis), 157–58, 199–201
Transcendental Meditation (TM),
      225–27
Transformation, personal
  athletic experience and, 201
  body and, 3
  energy and, 10–12
  function follows structure concept and,
      15–17
  health and, 6–8
  herd mentality and, 13–14
  listening to body and, 3, 9
  "rebirth" and, 1–3
  running and, 3–5, 202–4
  self-knowledge and, 17–18
  sharing running life, 273, 285,
      287–89
Truth and racing, 121, 125–27, 147
Tsongas, Paul, 258
Turtleneck shirts, cotton, 106
24-hour daily activities, 42–44

U
Undergarments, running, 106
Uniqueness of individual, 13

V
Vaillant, George, 278–79
Varieties of Human Values, The (Morris),
      263
Varieties of Religious Experience, The
      (James), 194–95, 263
Vaseline, 108
"Vermont Alternative," 64
Virtue, 263
Vocation, 195

W
the wall, 149, 151–53, 176–79
Watches, 54–55, 108
Water intake, 70, 100–102
Waters, Pete, xvii
Weaknesses, personal. *See also* Anger
      depression, 243–46
      narcissism, 239–43
      planning, lack of, 237–38
Weighing body, 70
Weight maintenance, 80
Weights, sand, 119
Weil, Andrew, 219
Weiner, Norbert, 48
Wheeling (West Virginia) race, 132
White Rock Marathon, 171
Whole person, becoming, 189–91, 196, 203
"Why Do I Run?" (Sheehan, George), xii
Wilder, Thornton, 41, 263
Willey, David, ix–xv
Will and willpower, 12–13, 52, 89, 106, 197
Wind direction, 108
Winter weather. *See* Cold-weather running
Withdrawing individual, 27
Wonder, 21–23, 41
Wordsworth, William, 123
Wyeth, Andrew, 36–37

Y
Yeats, William Butler, 144, 245
Young, becoming, 22–23
Youth, unspent, 173–76

Z
Zonas tape, 118